CYBERPHOBIA

CYBERPHOBIA

Identity, Trust, Security and the Internet

EDWARD LUCAS

BLOOMSBURY

NEW YORK · LONDON · OXFORD · NEW DELHI · SYDNEY

Bloomsbury USA
An imprint of Bloomsbury Publishing Plc

1385 Broadway	50 Bedford Square
New York	London
NY 10018	WC1B 3DP
USA	UK

www.bloomsbury.com

BLOOMSBURY and the Diana logo are trademarks of Bloomsbury Publishing Plc

First published in Great Britain 2015
First U.S. edition 2015

ISBN: HB: 978-1-63286-225-9
ePub: 978-1-63286-226-6

Library of Congress Cataloging-in-Publication Data
Lucas, Edward, 1962–
Cyberphobia : identity, trust, security and the Internet / Edward Lucas. —First U.S. edition.
pages cm
Includes bibliographical references and index.
ISBN 978-1-63286-225-9 (HB)–ISBN 978-1-63286-226-6 (ePub)
1. Computer crimes. 2. Computer security. 3. Internet. I. Title.
HV8079.C65L83 2015
364.16'8—dc23
2015015882

2 4 6 8 10 9 7 5 3 1

Typeset by Newgen Knowledge Works (P) Ltd., Chennai, India
Printed and bound in the U.S.A. by Thomson-Shore Inc., Dexter, Michigan

To find out more about our authors and books visit www.bloomsbury.com.
Here you will find extracts, author interviews, details of forthcoming events,
and the option to sign up for our newsletters.

Bloomsbury books may be purchased for business or promotional use. For information on bulk
purchases please contact Macmillan Corporate and Premium Sales Department at specialmarkets@
macmillan.com.

To Sarah Lucas
Aunt, Godmother and Friend

CONTENTS

GLOSSARY

Air-gapped: keeping a computer or network physically isolated from any outside system. Harder than it seems in the era of miniaturisation, as any nearby electronic device can try to connect to the supposedly air-gapped computer.

APT: advanced persistent threat – the kind of targeted and sophisticated cyber-attack launched by a nation-state's intelligence agency against its opponents or rivals.

Attack surface: the points at which a malefactor can gain access to a target, for example if its computer or network is connected to the internet.

Bitcoin: a kind of crypto-currency or digital money, based on solving ever-more complicated sums, which can be used to make untraceable payments over the internet.

Botnet: a remotely controlled network of computers, whose owners are unaware anything is amiss.

Browser: the program used on most computers to visit websites on the internet.

Captcha: a simple test to tell humans and machines apart involving retyping a selection of distorted letters. Easy for people, hard for computers.

Chips: the microprocessors which are at the heart of
                    any electronic device. If you imagine the data
                    flowing like trains over a railway network, the
                    microprocessors are the junctions.

Cloud: a big network of computers run by someone
                    else – useful for storage, until something goes
                    wrong.

Cryptography: the branch of mathematics dealing with
                    encryption. This typically involves the unique
                    properties of prime numbers. Multiplying
                    them is easy – but the reverse process is
                    hard.

Cyber: a prefix used to indicate a loose connection with
                    computers and networks, as in cyber-warfare,
                    cyber-guru, cyber-hype, cyber-nonsense.

Data: the information stored and processed by
                    computers and networks. If the computer is
                    the railway, the data are the trains that run on
                    it.

DDoS attack: swamping a computer – such as a server which
                    runs a website – so that legitimate users cannot
                    get through to it.

Download: data or a program copied on to a computer
                    from a network.

Drive-by attack: a way of infecting computers through the
                    browsing habits of their users.

Floppy disks: old-fashioned portable storage devices – a
                    'floppy' disk of electromagnetic material in a
                    plastic casing.

Hard disks: the way most computers store memory, on a
                    rapidly rotating disk inside a rigid casing.

HTTPS: Hypertext Transfer Protocol Secure – a way for a
                    computer to communicate securely with a website.
                    Usually indicated by the presence of a padlock
                    next to the address.

Hardware: the chips, devices and circuitry which constitute
                    a computer. Roughly equivalent to the tracks,
                    stations and points in a railway system.

Heartbleed: an error in the software which allows secure SSL
                    connections to be set up.

IP address: the label which provides an address, a name and a
                    route for any computer or device connecting with
                    the internet.

Key-logger: malware which records every keystroke made
                    on the infected computer. Useful for stealing
                    passwords.

Links: the directions to a page on the internet, such as
                    http://www.edwardlucas.com/contact. These can
                    be shortened using a link shortener, such as t.co or
                    is.gd, so they become shorter and more memora-
                    ble, like this: is.gd/elucas

Malware: programs used in attacks on computers and
                    networks.

Malvertising: advertisements designed to infect a visiting
                    computers with malware.

Open-source: software usually written and maintained by volun-
                    teers, with limited or no copyright.

P2P: Peer-to-peer – a decentralised arrangement where
                    users, not a central body, store data, take risk or
                    provide processing power. Used to evade copyright
                    restrictions in sharing files, in Skype messaging
                    and in finance (Zopa, Lending Club, Bondora).

Patch:	a repair to a flawed program (or hardware) which users can download in order to protect themselves from attack. Can be installed and downloaded automatically.
Phishing:	sending e-mails with links or attachments which will infect the victim's computer if opened.
Secure Socket Layer (SSL):	a widely used way for computers to communicate securely by creating, in effect, an encrypted tunnel between them.
Shellshock:	a mistake in the Bash shell – a widely used piece of open-source software which allows outsiders to give instructions to a computer's operating system.
Ransomware:	malware which locks files on a computer unless a ransom is paid.
Remote desktop software:	legitimately used by technicians fixing problems on a client's computer, this is a boon for thieves. It allows one computer user to see what is happening on the screen of another, and to take control of the machine.
Rogueware:	malware masquerading as legitimate software.
Root-kit:	stealthy malware which conceals its existence from anti-virus and other programs that might detect it.

Rubber hose attack: using physical force to extract password information.

Scareware: malware (q.v.) which pretends to be security software.

Server: a computer which runs a database, website or other resource and responds to requests from clients.

Social engineering: the use of human skills such as flattery, appeals for help, impersonation and intimidation to gain access to a computer or network.

Software: the sets of rules which govern how a computer works. Has the same relationship to hardware as a railway timetable does to the trains and track.

SQL attack: a way of infecting a computer through a website which it manages.

Terabyte: Storage on computers is measured in bytes. A byte is eight 'bits' of information – in effect 1s or 0s. A kilobyte is a thousand bytes, a megabyte a million, a gigabyte an (American) billion and a terabyte a trillion. It would take 50,000 trees to make enough paper to print out one terabyte. The same amount of data would fit on 150 DVDs.

Tor: a browser and network which conceal the identity of the user by bouncing the information around many different computers. Often used for those seeking anonymity from government agencies.

Two–factor authentication: a system which requires the user
                              not just to type in a password, but
                              also to provide some other informa-
                              tion, such as a code sent to a mobile
                              phone, or generated by some other
                              device.

USB stick: a small storage device – sometimes
                              called 'thumb' or 'pen' drive – which
                              can be used to move data or software
                              between computers.

Watering hole attack: planting malware on a website which
                              will infect a certain category of visi-
                              tors (see Drive-by attack).

Zero-day: a flaw in software or hardware which
                              is not publicly known, and for which
                              therefore no patch has been made
                              available.

PREFACE

Charlie Chaplin's film *The Great Dictator*, completed in 1940, attracted the ire of Hitler's Germany for its portrayal of the Nazi leader's buffoonish and brutal personality cult.* It was banned in all German-controlled countries in wartime Europe (though the dictator himself obtained a copy, watched it twice, and cried).[1] Imagine that the Third Reich's intelligence service had been tasked with retaliation against the Charlie Chaplin studio, and United Artists, which distributed the film. Hitler's spies could have burgled the offices where the prints of the film were kept. They could have disrupted operations – perhaps by simple criminal damage – arson at the studio – or by arranging for a pro-Nazi mob to mill about outside (the United States was not then at war). All these would have been highly risky and probably futile. They would have given little if any thought to electronic communications. They might have briefly jammed the telephone switchboard, or sent spoof telegrams. But these would have been trivial annoyances – more like practical jokes than acts of warfare.

Contrast that limited range of options with the anonymous and highly effective attack on Sony Pictures Entertainment, the company which made *The Interview*, a crude comedy film about the assassination of Kim Jong-Un, the North Korean dictator. Not only was this attack at the time one of most devastating breaches

* Charlie Chaplin said later he would not have made a comic film had he known of the mass murder of Jews under Nazi rule.

of a computer network ever publicised, it was also unclear who had perpetrated it, how they had done so and even what their real motive was.

As became clear over the Thanksgiving weekend in 2014, the attackers had used 'malware' – secretly installed computer programs designed to do harm – to wipe data from the company's computers. E-mail simply stopped working. The company was paralysed. This was carried out with extraordinary thoroughness, across a range of networks. It suggests that the attackers knew their way around the company and had been scouting for many months before the attack. Wiping data was purely destructive – the electronic equivalent of a major fire in a company's most important building. But that was not the most damaging part of the attack. What was much worse was the quantity and quality of data stolen – believed to be 100 terabytes in total.

Assessing that was difficult, because so many computers had been wiped. But it became clear that at least five unreleased films had been taken and released on the internet. The attackers had also copied and published personal information of 47,000 current and former employees, contractors and freelancers (including celebrities), and a large number of e-mails. All of these were damaging. The lost films directly hit profit margins: studios go to great lengths to prevent unauthorised copies of their productions leaking out before the launch, or being made after it. The employee information is legally protected. Employees can sue a company that does not keep their personal data properly secured. Some lawsuits had already started in late 2014.

But perhaps worst of all was the publication of messages which those writing them had thought would be private. In particular, the e-mails contained excruciatingly embarrassing exchanges between senior executives. Writing to the company's chairman, Amy Pascal, a senior producer, Scott Rubin, described the Hollywood star Angelina Jolie, one of Sony's most important actors, as 'seriously out of her mind' and as a 'minimally talented spoiled brat'. Another e-mail from a scriptwriter dismissed a famous Irish-German actor in these terms: 'I don't know who Michael Fassbender is and the rest of the world isn't going to care.' Perhaps the worst was an exchange – racially insensitive at best – mocking President Barack Obama, with the implication that he was interested only in films featuring black people.

Details of the attack on Sony have dribbled out slowly. It has not ruined the company. Nor did it prevent the release of *The Interview*. After an embarrassing flip-flop in which Sony seemed to have given in to threats of violent retaliation against any cinemas which showed the film, the company released the North Korean comedy to online viewers and to a limited number of independent picture houses at Christmas 2014. It has made at least $18 million, against a production budget of $44 million.

But what is known (and perhaps more importantly what is not known) about the episode exemplifies the main themes of this book: the importance of computers and networks to modern life, and their unseen and unrecognised vulnerabilities.

The internet – the network of networks which links most of the computers on the planet – has become not just the central nervous system of modern life, but also its greatest vulnerability. The rate of change is startling. If the Soviet Union during the Cold War had tried to attack Hollywood for the many anti-Soviet films made there, it would have had the same rather limited options as the Nazis had against Charlie Chaplin: physical intrusions, sabotage and political pressure.

It was not until 1989, when the Soviet empire was crumbling, that Tim Berners-Lee invented the World Wide Web – the way computer users browse the internet. Designed to help scientists at CERN, a particle physics laboratory, it was, in effect, a way of label-ling data on a network so that many people in different locations could view the files they needed. The idea that it could be used for destructive purposes, or that it could become a multi-trillion dollar industry, was not even on the most distant horizon.

It was not until the mid-1990s that anything resembling the modern internet took shape, and another five years before companies began to use it as a serious business tool. In 1995 just sixteen million people – most of them computer enthusiasts – used the internet. That was 0.4 per cent of the then world population. Though perhaps they should have done, few gave much thought to security. The internet had grown up as a way of connecting academic networks. Its main purpose was to enable researchers to collaborate. They did not store sensitive private information on their computers, or use them for banking or shopping. Ten years later, the figure was over one billion, or 15.7 per cent. Now it is over three billion, approaching half the world's population. In rich countries, use of the internet is close to universal – 88 per cent of Americans are online.[2]

The importance of the internet lies not just in the numbers who use it. It is the most important messaging system in the world. In 2015 the number of e-mails sent every day passed 200 billion.[3] That means that two days' worth of e-mails outnumber the world's total postal traffic for a whole year.[4] Few of the 2.5 billion people who send e-mails understand how they reach their destination, but – wrongly – they expect them to arrive reliably and privately. Perhaps even more mistakenly, they assume that an e-mail they receive comes from its purported sender.

Computers have also become the way the world stores its data. A single computer drive the size of a thumb can contain more data than 528 million typewritten pages, or roughly the amount of data thought to be contained in a human brain.[5] Film studios used to store their works on plastic coated with silver salts. Stealing them would have involved carrying bulky reels of film out of a closely guarded storage facility, watched by human eyes and with doors that could be opened only with a physical key. Now these films, like most other valuable intellectual property, are stored on electronic media, controlled by computers. With the right password (and sometimes without it) the data can be copied, deleted and moved, invisibly and silently.

It is not just intellectual property that is stored on computers. We keep all the day-to-day details of life there. Among the data stolen in just one file from Sony Pictures Entertainment were:

> 3000 or more Social Security numbers, names, contact details, contact phone numbers, dates of birth, email addresses, employment benefits, workers compensation details, retirement and termination plans, employees' previous work history, executive salaries, medical plans, dental plans, genders, employee IDs, sales reports, copies of passport information and receipts for travel.[6]

Some of the information a company stores on its computers is trivial – does it matter where Sony Pictures Entertainment buys its paperclips? But all too often the networks which contain important data – private or valuable – are hooked up, wittingly or by accident, to less important ones.

In short, the internet has become the stage of modern life. It is already where we exchange messages, relax, store memories, find information, make friends and do business. It will become still more important in the years ahead, as it moves from being a means of connecting people to one that connects things. That will mean that machines in our homes – for example, our electricity meter, thermostat, fridge and oven – will work together to use electricity economically. In industrial processes, machines will connect to each other without human intervention. Supermarket tills already alert warehouses to changes in demand, ordering more goods and booking the transport capacity needed. Many billions of devices and machines will be online – far outnumbering the human beings on the network.

At an individual level, increasing our dependence on technology makes sense. The marginal benefits are clear: increased convenience, dependability, flexibility and security. The cost of not using computers and networks when your rivals and partners are doing so is severe. A company that forswears e-mail may lose orders. Someone who refuses to carry a mobile phone may miss important messages. Life is unforgiving. Time moves on. Stay up to date – you may not get a second chance.

But at a collective level, those individual decisions create a problem. If everyone depends on a technology, it had better be dependable. In the case of the internet this quality is questionable. It was designed for flexibility and openness, not security and reliability.

The founders of the internet were academics who took users' identities on trust. When only research cooperation was at stake, this was reasonable. But the lack of secure identification is now hampering the development of e-commerce and the provision of public services online. In day-to-day life, from banking to dating, if you don't know who you are dealing with, you are vulnerable to fraud or deceit, or will have to submit to cumbersome procedures such as scanning and uploading documents to prove who you are.

The internet has some advantages over the real world. It is not (thanks to the way it has been upgraded) running out of addresses, the way that some big cities run out of phone numbers. Unlike the transport system, the internet is not affected by bad weather. Indeed, thanks to the way it is designed the internet is inherently resilient. Unlike the telephone system, the internet does not connect people directly. Instead the information is chopped up into tiny 'packets' of data, which make their way to their destination by whatever means is most convenient. If one route is congested or blocked, they take another. The packets are then reassembled at the other end – re-creating the original e-mail, picture, document or whatever.

The much greater vulnerabilities are intricacy and confusion. Computers and networks are too complicated. When we use them, we do not know reliably what we are doing or whom we are dealing with. This creates a paradise for attackers of all kinds. These can be spies, soldiers, hooligans, pranksters, criminals or commercial rivals – or a mixture of all of the above. Attribution is the single most difficult issue in securing our networks and computers because it makes it hard to know how to retaliate. The culprits in the attack on Sony may have been the North Korean regime, which was offended by the denigration of a leader it portrays as a demigod. But it could also have been hackers from other countries, paid for by the regime in Pyongyang. Or it could have been activists who dislike Sony's stance on digital copyright issues. Or, some security experts say, a disgruntled employee.[7] The messages posted online by the purported attackers gloating about their exploits were vague, but a linguistic analysis of the stilted and error-strewn English suggested that the person or people writing them might have had Russian as a first language. The FBI claimed that North Korea was responsible, though without releasing any conclusive proof. Twice during the Christmas period, North Korea's internet and mobile phone system collapsed for some hours: no big deal in what is probably the least-wired country in the world, but still a striking coincidence. Was that the promised American retaliation? Or perhaps something else? Could the same tools be used against another country? As so often in the world of computers and networks, the answer was unclear.

The confusion and complexity of life online outstrips the ability of our bodies and minds to cope. Our sense of security in the wider world outside our homes and workplaces is instinctive. We know that some neighbourhoods are safer than others, that some times of day require special precautions. We may avoid conspicuous behaviour in some circumstances, such as when we travel. Shopping in a bazaar on holiday in a poor country we will browse, negotiate and pay differently from the way we would behave when visiting an upmarket boutique in a rich-world city. We negotiate trust quickly, judging strangers on their appearance, behaviour and tone of voice, and using introductions and connections to establish obligation and privileges. A heavily built, scruffy and somewhat drunk young man on my doorstep in the small hours is a threat – until my sons remind me that they are expecting guests.

Like many generations before us, our security in real life depends on locks and keys, and we have gained a pretty good idea about their strengths and weaknesses. We would not lock our house with a child's padlock. And we would not use an elaborate anti-burglar system to secure our garden shed. When sharing keys with others, we instinctively balance risk and convenience: a teenager may get one key to the house, but not a complete set. Inside our homes, we may have a safe or strongbox for valuables and documents. We also know that locks alone are not enough: our homes and offices may be fitted with burglar alarms, motion detectors and even CCTV. We back these up with humans: a receptionist at work, a concierge in an apartment block. In a really bad neighbourhood, even the strongest lock is no guarantee of security. And in the safest parts of the countryside, people do not bother to lock their doors, and may even leave their keys in the car for convenience.

We are dimly grateful that the people who design, manufacture, install and maintain locks have great expertise. But few of us have the least interest in the details. You do not need to be a locksmith to use a key, any more than you need to be a car mechanic to drive a car, or a doctor to stay healthy. Modern life has given us many capabilities which we need neither knowledge nor dexterity to master fully. We know, by experience and instinct, their strengths, and their limitations.

In short, evolution and education have given us a huge range of skills to balance risk, security and convenience. We are programmed to trust and help others – primitive man could not survive solo – while at the same time engaging in a constant series of observations and actions, mostly unconscious. Our eyes, ears and noses tell when we are safe or in danger, what to do, where and when.

Once we venture online, all that vanishes. Our real-world senses are constrained: all we have to go on are the words and images on a screen, plus tinny sounds coming from a small loudspeaker. It is a simulacrum of the real world, but a deceptive one. We may feel confident in our familiar routines – shopping, browsing, Skyping, e-mailing – but in truth we are helpless, unprepared and vulnerable to thieves, manipulators and enemies. We cannot see the people we are dealing with; we cannot judge their tone of voice, body language or facial expressions. We cannot smell them or touch them. We cannot place them in the history and geography of our lives. Nor do we understand what we are trying to protect. Locks and keys are an only partially useful analogy. Data is not like physical property: its value depends on context. A list of names and addresses means nothing on its own. Once it is labelled as a directory of confidential police informants the lives of everyone it mentions is in danger. But we have to deal with this world – and using technology which most of us do not understand.

Moreover, the protection we have taken for granted when dealing with institutions in the real world is often absent when we go online. If we lose our keys, we risk our house being burgled. But if we lose our passport, we do not expect a thief who finds it to be able to loot every part of our lives. If a bank, for example, is fooled by someone who looks, dresses and speaks like a customer, forges his signature and withdraws some money using a stolen passport, it is still the bank, not the victim of the theft, who must pay up. All the injured party needs to do is to show that he did not actually visit the bank and make the transaction.

But the internet has changed that. Electronic security shifts the responsibility for spotting and preventing fraud from the business to the customer. If your password and login are used to steal your money, then the bank will argue that you are to blame for not safe-guarding them. It may well be that the details of your bank card were stolen by a doctored ATM, fitted with clever devices which steal the card number and PIN. Maybe your login and password for online banking were copied because of something a thief has installed on your computer. But in either case the onus will be on you, not the bank, to prove that you are not at fault. Computers have shifted the burden of proof against the individual, in a way of which we are still only dimly aware.

Cyber-security used to be a niche problem: complicated, boring and of marginal significance. Now it is of mainstream importance, but still hard to understand. This book tries to explain the issues around the security of our computers and the networks which connect them. Just as you do not need to be a medical doctor to have an opinion on health care, or an automobile engineer to have a view on road congestion, you do not need professional qualifica-tions in computer science to understand what matters in the safety of your computer and others which connect to it.

Like medicine, law, politics and other walks of life colonised by professionals, this subject abounds with acronyms, technical terms and strange uses of language. Is your company hiring a 'pen tester' who uses 'social engineering' in order to assess your 'attack surface'? Sounds baffling. But what you are actually doing is hiring a professional confidence trickster to see if your security is as good as you think it is. If a 'white hat hacker' is attacking your 'silos', then another trickster, who uses purely electronic means, is seeing if different kinds of information are kept sensibly separate.

This book is called *Cyberphobia* because so many people are so put off by needlessly complicated technical language that they fail to realise the importance of the issues at stake. Many books about this subject explain in great technical detail how to build and defend a supposedly secure network of computers. These are rather like technical manuals for locksmiths: interesting to the specialist, but useless for the layman.

The central message of this book is that our dependence on computers is growing faster than our ability to forestall attackers. Criminals, hooligans, activists and hostile foreign powers are constantly attacking individuals, businesses, organisations and governments. They are winning and we are losing. Unless our thinking and behaviour change, we will become less safe, less free, less healthy and less happy. Most of all we need to understand that cyber-security is not a technical issue, any more than road safety is about engineering. This book is about how we need to rethink our behaviour – as individuals, organisations and societies – in dealing with the threats we face online. But above all, this is a book about humans, not about machines.

Introduction

We are staking our future on a resource that we have not yet learned to protect.

George Tenet, director of the
Central Intelligence Agency, in 1998

Modern life depends on the trusting exchange of electronic data. But the computers, networks and systems that we use to do this were not designed with safety and reliability in mind. Much of the time they work amazingly well, but behind the machines' shiny casings and the glitzy graphics of the software is a ramshackle mess of improvisation and recycling. Modern life, in effect, is dependent on a patchwork of compromises made in the past decades at a time when nobody involved could have realised the consequences of their decisions.

As consumers, we are partly to blame. We want computers and software to be easy to use, cheap and flexible. We want them to work with anything new that we like, but also to be 'backwards compatible' – to work with much older programs and machines. We want our computers and networks to be tailored to our needs, but we are unwilling to spend much time learning new tricks and ways of working. The result of all this is compromises, all of which come at a price. One is reliability. Meeting our expectations most of the time means that the systems fail some of the time. The other is complexity. Computer chips, and the programs which tell them what to do, are now so complicated that no one person can understand them.

Yet the fundamental principles are simple. Anyone who has ever made a railway journey can understand them. The computer is like a railway. Without instructions, it sits still. It is a machine, but without the ability to run on its own. What brings it to life is software – a set of rules, written in code that machines can understand. When the power comes on, switch on this light. Then connect to a keyboard and a monitor. Then start up this storage device, and follow the instructions you receive. Even the most complicated tasks can be broken down into simple instructions. The genius of software writers is to analyse a real-life problem and then to solve it with instructions that a machine can understand and implement.

Software and hardware are in principle interchangeable. Software can be written into a chip when it is made, so that few further instructions are necessary – a good example is the chip in a child's toy. Pull the string and a small computer inside will play a nursery rhyme. Simple hardware can be made to do a lot of exotic things with the right instructions and inputs of data. The earliest programmable digital computer was Colossus, built by British technicians at Bletchley Park during the Second World War to help crack German codes. It needed to be programmed by hand, with technicians using switches, plugs and cables. Later, software was loaded on to a computer by punched paper tape, and later from electromagnetic media (readers of my generation may remember loading computer games on to a primitive computer from cassette tapes). Next came 'floppy disks', then CDs, and now, in most cases, downloads from the internet. Software has become hugely more complicated, as we will see. But in essence, it is simple.

A railway timetable is a kind of software program. It explains in precise detail who has to do what, where and when. Signals change colour, trains stop and start, points switch back and forth. If the network is the hardware and the timetable the software, the third element in a railway system is the trains themselves. Getting them and their contents from A to B is the point of the whole exercise. On a computer, the equivalent of the trains is data. Imagine, for example, that you take a picture on an electronic camera and transfer it to your computer. That is a trainload of data – an enormous series of 1s and 0s which determine every dot of colour captured by the camera, now to be rendered on the screen or reproduced on a printer. Depending on your computer's capabilities, the software installed on it and the instructions you give it, that picture can be sent to a friend, posted on the internet, or cropped and tweaked to look better. But a lot of things have to go right for that to happen seamlessly. The picture may be in a format that your computer software cannot read. Or it may be stored on a memory card which your computer cannot deal with. The quantity of data may be too big for a small computer – for example a phone – to deal with. The data may be 'corrupted' – meaning that a tiny error in the hardware or the software has affected the information. That is the equivalent of the wrong railway truck ending up in the wrong train: an error that can be trivial or catastrophic depending on the circumstances.

Most such errors never come to public attention. Computer users are inured to mysterious problems which seem to come and go without rhyme or reason. Most of the time you simply restart your machine and hope that the problem does not return. But some of the errors are so fundamental that they do make headlines. A startling example of this came in September 2014 with news of a mistake, perhaps the worst bug in the history of computing, which was discovered in a crucial part of the ubiquitous UNIX operating system. Most computer users have probably never heard of UNIX,

but it is the basis of most big electronic systems. Unlike the software sold by Microsoft and Apple, it does not have a single owner.
It is, broadly speaking, available free of charge, and maintained and
developed by volunteers.

'Bash', as it is known, is a crucial bit of code which connects
computers running UNIX software to the outside world. For example, it allows users to give their computers instructions, or for the
computers that connect with websites to receive them. Bash was
first written in 1989. But it contained a flaw, which, in theory, could
allow an outsider to deliver a bogus instruction to a computer. The
so-called 'Shellshock' bug was not the result of attackers' cleverness
or users' carelessness. It was simply because of an innocent mistake
in the software. Millions of users were at risk as a result.[1] An outsider,
using Shellshock, can take over another person's computer, give
himself all kinds of privileges, steal and corrupt data, and so forth.

On computers that are run by humans, remedying this flaw is
fairly straightforward. But millions of other devices run UNIX-
based software, too, such as routers – the small blinking boxes
which run home and office wi-fi networks – as well as internet-
enabled thermostats, industrial machines and other devices. And
these computers (which is what they are) are for the most part
designed to operate autonomously. Updating their software is a
fiddly task, for which their owners may not have the time or the
aptitude. As a result, many of the devices vulnerable to Shellshock
may never be patched, and are therefore wide open to outside
attack, and will remain so for many years to come.

We were warned about this. As noted at the start of this chapter,
George Tenet, director of the CIA, said in 1998: 'We are staking
our future on a resource that we have not yet learned to protect.'[2]
His words were not heeded. Since then we have become far more
dependent on computers, and the gap between attackers' prowess
and defenders' abilities has become bigger, not smaller.

When Mr Tenet made those remarks, most attacks on the internet were perpetrated by pranksters, driven by curiosity or ego. The amounts of money involved were usually trivial. Kevin Mitnick, who became America's best-known hacker (and following a stint in jail is now a reputable consultant on computer security), began by working out ways to cheat the Los Angeles public transport system. He bought his own ticket punch, so that he could use discarded transfer tickets. He was bored, clever, plausible and fascinated by rules and the loopholes in them. His greatest skills were not technical expertise, but trickery – what is now called 'social engineering'. He was an enthusiastic amateur conjurer, giving him an insight into the gap between perception and reality, and how to exploit it. He was an adept practitioner of what was then called 'phone phreaking' – using tricks such as whistles and clicks to fool the phone system into allowing free phone calls. Mr Mitnick's simplest means of breaking into computer networks was by phoning control centres and pretending to be a technician on a field trip. With a bit of friendly chit-chat, and some convincing seeming details, he was able to persuade bored, careless and unmotivated employees to give him the passwords and logins he needed. But his goal was neither mayhem nor riches. Most of the time, he was simply enjoying the thrill of having successfully breached the system. Sometimes the booty was the ability to make free telephone calls. Sometimes he would simply amuse himself by reprogramming the network so that a friend's number would be mistakenly categorised as a public coin-operated phone. The baffled subscriber would try to make a call – and receive an automated message telling him to deposit a coin first.

Now these attacks have become weapons of politics and statecraft, as well as a huge and lucrative criminal business. Activists use attacks on computers as part of their campaigns – against the secretive Scientology cult, for example, or to punish companies whose policies displease them. The attack on Sony was described by one security expert as the company being 'nuked from inside'.[3] As I show in Chapter 5, the Chinese government has launched a colossal campaign of state-sponsored theft of intellectual property from Western businesses.[4] Russia steals state secrets from its geopolitical competitors. Both these countries, and others, contract these attacks out to private groups and individuals, just as in previous times governments might have hired mercenaries and freebooters.

At the heart of all this is the biggest way in which the online world differs from real life. We have no easy, dependable way of proving who we are; conversely, it is hard for us to know who we are really dealing with. Our single weakest point is our electronic identities: the messy, unreliable, easy-to-forget mixture of logins, passwords, security questions and other means we use to control and authenticate everything we do online. Only a few years ago, these were a small part of our lives. Now the balance has shifted. In modern life, if something goes wrong with your electronic identity, your real life suffers, too. Solutions to this problem exist – but they will require radical changes in the way we use our computers.

Our online identity may feel as secure as a locked door, but it is wide open for an attacker. You may not have heard of 'noods', but if you are female and famous you are prey to people who steal, collect and exchange these 'nudes'. In late 2014 it emerged that pictures of celebrities such as *The Hunger Games* star Jennifer Lawrence, the model Kate Upton and dozens of others had been stolen from computers managed by Apple, and were being traded in an illegal online marketplace. This somewhat chilling (and anonymous) post on an online message board gives some of the details.

> There wasn't just one hack
> There isn't just one leaker
> There's been a small underground nood-trading ring that's existed for years

Why wasn't it revealed earlier? The only way to join the ring is by buying in with original pics ('wins', as they call them) you've acquired by yourself

Also these guys are greedy fuckers. If you were the only person in the world in possession of jlaw [Jennifer Lawrence] nudes, would you really give them out? For free??

These guys conduct individual attacks on celebs through (I presume) a mix of social engineering and (esp for more high-profile targets) straight-up hacking

They trade with each other to expand their collections

Circle hardly ever widens to include more people – very few people find out about this ring, and fewer still have noods to buy in with . . .

Except for self-style 'rich kid' . . . it appears he bought a few sample pix and blew the lid on this whole operation by sharing them with outsiders for the first time

Spotting their chance, and realising that existence of the nood collections was revealed, a couple of other guys from the circle came out of the woodwork offering up some of their collection for donations

It is easy to dismiss such people as creeps and perverts, but for their victims it is no laughing matter. Even the most energetic and expensive legal response cannot scrub the stolen photos from the internet. As fast as you persuade or order one site to take them down, another puts them up. You can never be sure that they will not appear again – someone, somewhere, has them on his computer, and publishing them takes just a couple of mouse-clicks.

One of the first lessons of the computer age was that machines can break down. So users like to make copies of their data, and store them in different locations. But avoiding one kind of problem has created another. The celebrity victims of the attack outlined above did not store their precious photos on just one computer or phone, because together with safety they also wanted convenience. Uploading material to the 'cloud' (a big network of computers run by someone else, such as Google or Apple) means that you can get hold of it wherever you are, whenever you want.

The convenience is a genuine advantage. But the feeling of safety was illusory. It was all too easy for outsiders to get hold of these photos because Apple – one of the biggest computer companies in the world – had made it astonishingly easy to break into its users' accounts.

Apple denies this. It says that it was 'outraged' to learn of the theft, which it blamed on a 'very targeted attack' on usernames, passwords and security questions. None of the cases, it said, resulted 'from any breach in any of Apple's systems'. That is true. The hackers did not use clever hacking techniques to break into Apple's computer networks. Instead they exploited a series of flaws in the company's security procedures. The first step is to guess the victim's e-mail address. That is not too hard, given that you can have, in effect, as many tries as you want. You can try to register an Apple account with any e-mail you like: if the e-mail is already in use, then you have got your first bit of information. For example, were the great Humphrey Bogart still alive, you might try to register an Apple account in the name of humphrey.bogart@gmail.com or some other easily obtainable variant such as humphrey.bogart@me.com, humphrey.bogart@yahoo.com etc. When you find an e-mail that works (i.e. one that Apple says is already in use as a user ID), you have, in effect, identified the lock you probably need to open. Now all you need is the key.

To find that, you now try to log in as Humphrey Bogart, using the e-mail which Apple has told you is in use, and say that you have 'forgotten' the password. Apple then offers you two options. One is to send a message to your e-mail address, containing a link.

Click on that and you can reset your password. Even that is not particularly secure, because an attacker (as we will see later) may get control of your e-mail account. But the other is even easier. Unless you have enabled some extra security precautions, Apple will reset a password online to anyone who can provide your date of birth (easily ascertained for celebrities) and give answers to some rather feeble security questions (such as names of family members). Anyone with a Wikipedia or Facebook entry has given those away already. A bit of detective work on the internet can also easily find them out from other sources. Once the attacker has reset the password, he can log in – and gain access to the victim's photographs and other private data.[5]

Punishing those who enjoy sneering and jeering at other people's private lives – and private parts – is all but impossible. If someone copies your keys and then enters your house and steals pictures from your bedroom, the police can look for fingerprints, witnesses, even DNA. But attacks on your bedroom via the internet, especially using copies of your own logins and passwords, leave far fewer traces, if any.

Identities guard a lot more than just our private lives. In real life you would be unlikely to lose your keys, passport, driving licence, passport and wallet all at once, and even if you did a thief would not be able to make use of all them instantly. Your electronic identity combines all the features of the physical possessions which govern access to your life. And it is far more easily compromised and can be far more speedily used. The consequences are correspondingly more damaging. Data are easily copied, and the copies last for ever: once we entrust them to someone, we do not know for certain how many more copies will be made, or where they will end up. Misused, the data can endanger our welfare – by allowing others to impersonate us. Or they can put other people at risk, even those we have never had any dealings with.

At first sight this is hard to grasp. Our thinking about security relates our own carelessness to our own misfortunes. If we fail to lock our car, it may be stolen – but other vehicles are not affected. If we lose our keys, our home is at risk, and also the security of people who live with us. But it does not affect our neighbours. Stolen data and credentials, however, are potentially much more damaging than a lost set of keys. This is because of the way our identities online are different from our real-world ones. The contents of someone's handbag (make-up, purse, documents, keys, photos, and so forth) do not help me impersonate the owner to her neighbours and colleagues. These people will recognise that my voice, face, gender, mannerisms and so forth do not match the physical token of the key or passport. But if I steal my victim's online credentials – her login and password – I can pretend to be her quite convincingly. That means I can gain access to her work computer (and snoop, steal property or cause damage there). I can send e-mails, purport-edly from her, to friends and colleagues, with attachments or links which, if they open, will expose them to harm. I can even use her e-mail to send dangerous messages to total strangers. If she has an impressive sounding e-mail address, they may click on the links and open the attachments they contain.

You do not have to be rich or famous to suffer this kind of attack. Naoki Hiroshima, a software developer based in Palo Alto, California, was attacked because he had a short, snappy Twitter 'handle' (username).* As the use of Twitter has exploded, to more than 250 million active users at the time of writing; most of the

---

* Twitter is a 'micro-blogging' service in which users can send, read and exchange short messages of 140 characters. The shorter the name or 'handle' you use, the more room you have for the rest of the message. Memorable names are also desirable because other users will notice you more readily. Mine is the rather dull and long @edwardlucas

desirable short names have been used up. Mr Hiroshima had been lucky, signing up for '@N' – one of only twenty-six single-letter Twitter names. It was worth a lot of money – he had turned down an offer of $50,000.

The disappointed purchaser did not give up. He attacked. He seized control of Mr Hiroshima's websites, Facebook account and other parts of his online life and warned him that they would be destroyed – wiping out Mr Hiroshima's business, and sabotaging his personal life, unless he handed over his Twitter handle. Mr Hiroshima complied, regaining his life but losing his cherished '@N'.[6] Only after he wrote about the scandal did Twitter intervene and restore his property.

Online voyeurs, and people wanting to steal Twitter handles, are just a tiny part of a much bigger problem. Breaches are happening in colossal numbers. Even before the latest breach, in 2011 hackers gained access to the credentials of 100 million Sony customers who use its PlayStation and Online Entertainment networks.[7] In mid-2014 security experts reported that a gang called CyberVor ('vor' is Russian for 'thief') had stolen 1.2 billion unique credentials. If true, that would be the biggest (known) single crime, in terms of the number of people affected, in the history of the internet – and the world.[8]

The people attacking our computers and networks may be gangsters, pranksters, politically motivated 'hacktivists', or government agencies, or a combination of the four. They may be one person or several. The members of the group perpetrating the attack may change over time. Not all of them may know what the ultimate purpose is. Tracing the attackers through the payment is all but impossible, too. They do not ask for cash to be handed over, or for money to be sent via wire transfer. Instead they use what are known as digital currencies – a new breed of money which exists only on the internet. The best known of these is Bitcoin. These currencies have many disadvantages. They are not widely accepted. Their value fluctuates widely. They are based on complicated mathematics which may contain so far unknown flaws. But they have one big advantage: payments are all but untraceable. If you send someone a Bitcoin – which, for a technically savvy person, is as simple as sending an e-mail – nobody knows that you sent it, or that he has received it. As a result, finding out for certain who is behind an attack is far harder than in the real world – and bringing the perpetrators to justice even more difficult.

Most of the time the perpetrators of attacks are anonymous. But tracing them is only hard, not impossible. They have human weaknesses, including the desire to boast about their talents, decry their enemies and support their friends. This offers openings to investigators, both from government agencies and public-spirited outsiders. One such independent investigator is Brian Krebs, an American security researcher and author. He claims to have traced the person behind a website called Rescator, where stolen credit card details are on open sale. Rescator is a shockingly brazen example of the way in which crime on the internet is organised like a legitimate business – complete with online ordering, seasonal sales and rules about refunds. Card details are sorted by country, bank, provider and quality – so the full details, complete with address and security number, for a US-issued American Express card cost more than the plain credit card number from a less desirable account.

According to Mr Krebs, the figure behind Rescator is a young man called Andrey Hodirevski, based in Odessa, Ukraine, who is part of a Russian crime gang specialising in credentials theft – but with strong anti-Western political overtones, as his online manifesto, in a translation provided by Mr Krebs, shows.[9]

The movement of our Republic, the ideology of Lampeduza –
is the opposition to Western countries, primarily targeting the

restoration of the balance of forces in the world. After the collapse of the USSR, we have lost this fragile equilibrium face of the planet. We – the Senate and the top people of the Republic are not just fighting for survival and our place under the sun, we are driven by the idea! The idea, which is living in all of us – to return all that was stolen and taken from our friendly countries grain by grain! We are fighting for a good cause! Hot blood is flowing in us, in citizens, who want to change the situation in the world. We do not bend to other people's opinions and desires, and give an adequate response to the Western globalism. It is essential to be a fighter for justice!

Perhaps we would be living completely differently now, if there had not been the plan of Allen Dulles, and if America had not invested billions in the collapse of the USSR. We were deprived of a common homeland, but not deprived of unity, have found our borders, and are even closer to each other. We saw the obvious principles of capitalism, where man to a man is a wolf. Together, we can do a lot to bring back all the things that we have been deprived of because of America! We will be heard!

Citizens of Lampeduza – 'free painters' ready to create and live the idea for the good of the Motherland — let's first bend them over, and then insert deeper!!![10]

Uncovering the real identity of such a figure requires big efforts either from a government or from a talented researcher such as Mr Krebs. Most attackers do not need to fear exposure. This creates a moral universe of a kind that rarely exists in real life, where our moral instincts are bolstered by a calculation of risk and reward. We may be tempted to do wrong, but we are aware that we may be under scrutiny, and that if we are seen to do something wrong there will be consequences, ranging from social censure through to criminal prosecution.

Some 2,500 years ago, the Greek philosopher Plato theorised about the world which the internet has now created – one in which it would be possible to do wrong invisibly. He posited a magical token, which he called the Ring of Gyges, which would confer invisibility on the person who wore it. For those who believe that morality is only, or chiefly, a matter of risk and reward, the ring would therefore remove all constraints on immoral behaviour.

We are now able to test Plato's ideas in real life, and the results are depressing for those who believe that morality is instinctive. Under the cloak of anonymity which the internet bestows, people feel they can be rude, menacing or outright dishonest. The best example of this is 'trolling' – the posting of gratuitously offensive and irrelevant comments in social media or in response to articles published online. The motivation for this behaviour is a matter of debate – though academic studies suggest that the transience and anonymity which the internet officers unleash tendencies towards sadism, exhibitionism and heartlessness.[11]

It is not just that the costs of bad behaviour are low on the internet. The benefits are high. Attacks can be automated, and carried out hundreds or thousands of times. Even small hauls, in large quantities, make the attacks worthwhile because the internet is so pervasive. If you want to intrude on people's privacy, you no longer need to snoop through their windows: you raid their Apple account where they store their private photos. If you want to steal money, you do not need to rob a bank – you can rip people off over the internet. If you want to damage a rival's reputation, you can smear him without stepping away from your keyboard. Scale and distance used to disadvantage attackers of all kinds: now the internet has killed distance, so that a malcontent in Singapore can destroy the life of an opera singer in America whom he has never met. And the same trick can work again and again. If you can doctor the terminal in a shop to steal the details of one credit card, you can steal hundreds. If you can break into a database to collect the private details of one individual, you can steal everything else, too. In the pre-internet era, an individual's vulnerabilities consisted of his home – meaning access through its doors and windows – plus the telephone and postal services he used, and his physical presence outside the home, for example shopping, recreation or work. But for the malefactor (for example, a confidence trickster, or nosy parker) that 'attack surface', to use a technical term, offered limited scope and mostly required physical proximity. Now the same individual is likely to shop, bank, message and socialise through his computer. And the same flaws in his security will most likely be shared by millions of others.

Although I dislike the term 'cyber-crime' (or indeed anything with the prefix 'cyber', which serves to mystify and glamorise, not to explain) computers have indeed created a new category of criminal behaviour involving deception and scalability. In theory, it would be possible for a fraudster to make money by creating a bogus bank: renting a building, decking it out to look like a bank, putting accomplices behind the counter and defrauding customers who came in. But this would be cumbersome, risky and unlikely to work. A more profitable fraud in the past was to install a doctored Automated Teller Machine (ATM) in some public place. Victims put their cards in, then their Personal Identification Numbers (PINs) and then receive an error message. The details thus collected can be used to create fake cards which are then used to loot the victims' bank accounts. But that was cumbersome and costly, too. Doctoring a legitimate ATM is much easier. And stealing the money purely by computer, without stepping away from your keyboard or even setting foot in the victim's country, is easiest of all.

Attacks on our computers and networks are hard to understand, and the debate about what to do is plagued by vagueness as well as secrecy. Estimating the costs of any type of crime is hard: crime involving computers and networks is particularly hard to nail down. What is the cost of business foregone because of security worries? What price do you put on breaches of privacy? Much of the damage being done today may not become apparent for months or years. As Richard Danzig, an American expert, noted in a recent report, the data on the cost of internet crime are 'sparse, irregularly collected, drawn from changing populations, inconsistently labelled and aggregated, erratically shared and published, and most commonly analysed by parties with an economic interest in conclusions that are drawn'.[12]

Just as security firms like to exaggerate the cost of crime, victims tend to keep quiet about it. Not only do many fail to realise that they have been attacked but those who do find out tend to want to lick their wounds as privately as possible. It is bad for business to admit that you cannot keep your customers', suppliers' and employees' data safely. Your shareholders will not be impressed if you lose your company's intellectual property – design secrets and formulas – or if market-sensitive information leaks about mergers, acquisitions, product launches and the like. What bank would like to admit that its customers' data may have been tweaked by an outsider, or that its ATMs have been sabotaged? Barring strong legal sanctions to mandate openness – which currently do not exist – it is better to keep quiet. Even if you want to defend your company, it is hard to know what to do. As the Lex column in the *Financial Times* noted, 'the secrecy of the security industry works against them. Without information on attacks and breaches, it is nearly impossible to determine whose software is best.'[13]

Even with those provisos, the figures are startling. A recent report by McAfee, a security firm, put the cost of cyber-crime worldwide at more than $400 billion.[14] It counted the losses from pure fraud, typically against banks and financial institutions, as well as the cost of stolen intellectual property (such as designs) and the resulting effects on profits, investment and on future innovation. It also included the cost of preventive measures and the distorting effect of cyber-crime on economic activity – and employment (the report estimates that criminal attacks on computers cost 200,000 American jobs and 150,000 in Europe). Using similar methodology the British government (in a report produced by a computer-security company) reckoned in 2011 that crime on the internet cost the country £27 billion a year.[15]

Even allowing for hype, vagueness and self-interest, the striking point here is the proportions: McAfee estimates that the internet economy annually generates between $2 trillion and $3 trillion, of which criminals extract between 15 and 20 per cent. By contrast, the global aviation industry is about that size ($2.2 trillion in 2012). If criminals were looting $400 billion a year from hijacking planes, stealing baggage, fraudulently issuing tickets and scamming the supply of fuel and spare parts, that would be a scandal. Even if the figure was half or a quarter that, it would still be a huge amount of money flowing out of our pockets into the criminal economy.

The consultants' advice, gadgets and software are not always useless, but many are snake-oil remedies, bought in a panic in response to half-understood threats.

Sales talk for computer security products often includes mention of a 'digital Pearl Harbour' – a surprise cyber-attack by one country against another, dealing a devastating, instant defeat by destroying electric power networks, banking systems or some other element of modern life. The way to deal with this, supposedly, is to buy expensive gadgets and software, and hire a lot of consultants. Such threats cannot be ruled out, but they are by far not the most likely danger.

Confusion about the scope and origin of attacks has created a lucrative business opportunity for the merchants of hype and jargon. It is easier to portray the threat in dramatic (if unrealistic) terms rather than boring but relevant ones. It is a lot easier to sell an expensive, simple and useless product that the customer under-stands than a complicated cheap one that may actually work.

Amid the confusion, one statistic is more or less clear: the amount customers spent on cyber-security. That was $67 billion in 2013.[16] It is rising by 8 per cent a year and is expected to reach $80 billion in 2015. That is a hefty price to pay for the carelessness and greed which lie behind the woes of computer security. It is akin to the aviation industry spending nearly 10 per cent of its turnover on preventing planes being hijacked.

Both the bill and the less quantifiable damage we suffer come about because our thinking about safety on the internet is muddled and out of date. It is easy to think about security in terms of locks and keys. But analogies involving health, immune systems, infec-tion and disease are generally more helpful in understanding the problems we face with the security of our computers and networks. The crucial points are 1) that the immediate victim may have no idea that he has been infected, and 2) that the infection may be doing no particular damage to him, but great harm to other people. Similarly, if you take precautions you protect not only your own computer, but everybody else's, too. Just as vaccinating your children or completing a course of antibiotics helps make the rest of the population healthier, so keeping your computer clean, and shunning any involvement in criminal activity, helps make every-one else safer online, too.

I focus the book on the biggest direct threat for ordinary people. This is not the attention of nosy or hostile governments or pranks and stunts perpetrated by political activists. It is from online gang-sterdom, which has created a sophisticated market in criminal services, marketed and delivered over the internet. Those who steal our logins and passwords tend to be experts in doing that, rather than exploiting the information they have stolen. As in any other business, specialisation pays off. An expert car thief does not usually drive the vehicle he has stolen – he sells it to someone who has expertise in disposing of 'hot' cars. Similarly, stolen identities are a commodity, to be bought and sold in elaborate illegal markets. Even the humblest computer user is vulnerable. Good identities – fleshed out with details such as phone numbers, home addresses, banking credentials and the like, are worth more. They enable elaborate crimes. Flimsy identities – just an e-mail address, for example, are worth less. Simple credit card details may be worth $4 on the black market. Credentials for an online bank account with a balance between $75,000 and $150,000 cost around $300.[17] So many stolen identities are now available that the black-market price has plunged. But even a crumb of someone else's identity is worth something to somebody.* Some make no effort to conceal their trade. The Rescator site, run by the opinionated young man from Odessa, allows customers to fill their shopping basket with whatever they will find most useful. At the time of writing the account details for a European customer's American Express card cost $8.

Impersonation based on stolen credentials enables attackers to hijack computers, steal money and defraud other people. They can also be springboards for other, more sophisticated attacks. Many – probably most – victims will not know that they are at risk. Many of the sites from which the identities are stolen do not know they have been breached – if they find out at all, it is from a third party, usually the government.

Individuals are easy prey for criminals because the attacks on them can be automated and spread like an infection: once you

---

* The stolen records can be customer data (home address, credit card details etc.), or they could be the details that employees provide to their employers, or data held by governments on their citizens. They could simply be the usernames and passwords used to access a service such as e-mail, or a 'social networking' site such as Facebook or Twitter. All of these can be traded on the criminal black markets.

have got control of one victim's computer, you can use it to attack everyone they know. But targeted attacks – in which the victims are organisations, businesses and government departments, and the loot is money or information – are increasing, too. In 2013 two banks in the Middle East lost $45 million in a few hours – the biggest bank robbery in history, according to some commentators.[18] Criminals broke into the bank's computers, and changed the settings on a small number of pre-paid debit cards – the kind that people typically buy to take on holiday when they do not wish to use their own credit cards. The attackers simply removed the limits on those cards and sent details to criminal gangs in twenty-seven countries, who created hundreds of copies of the cards and simply walked from ATM to ATM withdrawing the maximum possible each time. One gang visited 2,000 cashpoints in New York alone.[19] The cost of that pales against the losses suffered by an unnamed British company (believed to be in the high-technology sector) which lost $1.3 billion in a single attack.

The risks to individuals from misuse of their own computers are only part of the problem. Problems with the big computer systems that run modern life can cause even more distress. When computer systems at two British banks, NatWest and RBS, seized up in June 2012, up to twelve million people were unable to pay bills. Some were unable to complete house moves or were stranded abroad. One man due to be released from custody was unable to go home because his bail payment could not go through.

Those problems (probably) were genuine technological breakdowns. We see only dimly the damage done by deliberate attacks. Every year, the big computer-security companies produce reports about the growth of criminality on the internet. They are laden with hype – each of these companies has a product or service to sell. But the trend is clear. Attacks are getting more numerous, more inventive and more damaging.

The boundary between the realm of computers (once dismissed as complicated, geeky but harmless) and the real world of money, food, sex and travel is blurring. Mistakes made online can cost us our money, our happiness and, ultimately, our freedom. We can accidentally give away personal information that will ruin our friendships or marriages, or do irreversible damage to our careers. Data breaches can drive companies out of business or expose them to costly and crippling litigation. Computers can be weapons in conflict between states: so-called 'cyber-warfare'. The dangers that we face because of our reliance on computers may involve some of the most advanced technology in the world – but they affect all of us, and if we are to avoid them it will be only when non-technical people have understood why they need to think and act differently.

As Dan Geer, an American who helped found the internet and is now one of the deepest thinkers about its future, notes, the security of computers and networks is – after a long period of neglect – being taken seriously. But not, he laments 'usefully, coherently, or lastingly'.[20] Much of the thinking and effort which results is costly, but does not make things better.

Experience and instincts honed in real life* are not enough for the world of computers and networks. Anyone who owns or uses an electronic device which can communicate with other machines needs to worry about the risks they are taking. You can harm yourself (financially or otherwise) with a single click. You may also do unwitting harm to other people, either by what you do with your computer, or what it does under the remote control of others.

But this book is not a counsel of despair. Greater prudence in our online behaviour can make us safer. So, too, can legal, commercial and regulatory pressures. Companies that treat our security

---

* I use 'real' in this book as the rhetorical opposite of 'online'.

seriously will gain business and flourish. More importantly, those that fail to do so will suffer. They will lose business, pay higher insurance premiums, see their stock price fall – and face civil and criminal prosecution.

I also highlight the role of innovation. I am the proud possessor of the world's first digital e-residency card, a government-issued document which allows me to identify myself and sign digital documents safely from anywhere. This does not stop me being anonymous when I wish – but it does allow me to prove who I am when I want to. That is a rare privilege now, but will become much more common now that the e-residency programme of the country concerned – the Baltic republic of Estonia – is in operation (it started in late 2014). A famous *New Yorker* cartoon exemplifies the problem: the internet is nice for dogs, but not for people wanting to know who they are dealing with.

"On the Internet, nobody knows you're a dog."

I

Meet the Hakhetts

To see the difficulties and dangers of life online, I invite readers to become acquainted with a fictional but realistic couple. Chip Hakhett runs his own executive coaching firm. His wife Pin works as a human resources assistant in an international media business.[1] Their woes, brought about by a mixture of ignorance, carelessness and bad luck, reflect the real-life costs and misery that attacks on computers and networks can bring.

Pin and Chip think a lot about risk when they travel. They look before crossing the road. They wear high-visibility clothing when they cycle. They keep their cars properly maintained, checking the tread and pressure on the tyres, keeping the windscreen clean and responding promptly to any warning lights on the dashboard. Even when nothing appears to be wrong, they – like most people – have their cars regularly serviced by professional mechanics. They regard people who drive drunk, without insurance, or without a driving test as not just irresponsible, but criminals. Chip, who drives a lot, uses a Volvo, picked for safety over performance. He has also passed the Institute of Advanced Motorists test, giving him a lower insurance premium. Pin uses a small, cheap car for short distances, but dislikes driving it on the motorway. Neither of them would drink alcohol before driving. Their main worries when at the wheel are not mechanical breakdown or their own errors, but accidents caused by other road users who are less conscientious.

Pin and Chip enjoy the convenience and even pleasure that their cars bring, but they have no interest in, let alone enjoyment of, what happens under the bonnet. They would be hard pressed to explain the difference between the petrol engine in Pin's runaround and the diesel motor that powers Chip's saloon. Pin's car has an automatic gearbox, but, like most motorists, neither she nor her husband would be able to sketch even a simple diagram of how it works, or how it differs from the manual gearbox (stick-shift transmission) in his car. Neither of them knows the equations in physics behind the mechanical engineering which means that their cars turn easily at slow speeds, and hug the road when going fast. Why should they?

What they do know is rather more important: the limits and trade-offs of human dealings with cars. Brake too hard and you skid. Slow down in fog. Drive too fast and you crash. If you cross the street recklessly, a car will hit you. Live too close to a main road and you or your children may get asthma. Pin and Chip know how to deal with other road users: they can distinguish between incompetence and aggression. Most importantly, they also know that the skills we exercise do not just affect their own safety and well-being, but those of others.

Pin and Chip rightly judge road transport to be inherently risky, so they devote most of their anxiety budget to it. They worry very little about air travel, by contrast. They assume that planes are built to an extremely high standard, and that the international rules governing air travel are strictly enforced, with safety as top priority. All these considerations are automatic. They do not compare the safety records of airlines because they assume that regulation makes them pretty much the same.

Yet as this book will show, misuse of a computer (with or without the consent of the owner) can be far more damaging than bad driving or sloppy maintenance. At worst, a lone driver can cause an accident in which dozens, maybe at most scores, of people can be hurt or killed. A mistake in aviation can kill hundreds. But a misused computer can help destroy the lives of countless numbers of people, by emptying their bank accounts, plundering their personal data, or cutting off the services on which modern life depends. Though computers are potentially more dangerous, we have not yet learned to handle them as safely as we drive our cars.

None of the instincts and considerations developed when dealing with cars and planes cross Pin and Chip's minds when they deal with computers. Chip uses an old desktop machine that he has had for several years. It is too underpowered to run the latest software, but it works fine with his old version of Microsoft Office: he finds it much more convenient than having to learn all sorts of new tricks. He learned his computer skills in the 1990s, and has not bothered much about keeping them up to date. So long as his computer allows him to print out letters, and keep notes of his customers, it suits him fine. For a login and password he uses his e-mail and his wife's name and year of birth — Pin1962. To save time, he uses this everywhere: on Amazon, Facebook, Twitter and other sites.

Pin is aware that computer security is important. At work, she has to change her password every three months. This rule was brought in four years ago. Her password is now H@khett12 and next month she will change to H@khett13, which she vaguely wonders may be unlucky.

Neither Pin nor Chip worries in the least about being 'hacked'. Why should they? They are not rich or famous. They are not of interest to hostile foreign governments or political activists. They do not know any secrets. They are just two people among more than two billion users of the internet. They think they need take only the limited sensible precautions in their quiet online life as they do in their quiet real-world life.

They are wrong. Our friends are only one click away from falling victim to scams organised by expert international organised-crime gangs. They may also become the target of a gang of hacktivists (politically motivated hackers), or of a nation-state's intelligence service, not for anything they know or do, but because of their proximity to someone who does.

In the world in which the Hakhetts – and most readers of this book – grew up, the most widespread security threat was crime, mostly perpetrated by incompetent and stupid people. Pin and Chip put good locks on doors and windows, avoid bad neighbourhoods after dark, and are careful when answering the door to strangers. They know that organised crime can be more sophisticated and ruthless. But they do not run a casino, or transport large amounts of cash: it is a distant threat, not a practical one. Nor do they worry about political activism. They support controversial causes from the sidelines (Pin, who has had breast cancer, supports animal experi- mentation, while Chip is pro-Israel). But they do not expect this to affect their security. They know that the animal-rights and pro- Palestinian causes, like others, have a thuggish fringe, and that some activists may be unscrupulous or brutal. But neither of the couple engages in public debates or protests.

They worry even less about national security. Chip was born long after his country dropped conscription. They are dimly aware of changes in military doctrine and technology, but happily unaware of the details. Espionage is more distant still. The Hakhetts noted the news stories in 2010 about the Russian 'illegals' living under cover in America, and especially the hard partying and shapely Anna Chapman. But the idea that anything from that world would touch them seems absurd.[2]

In attacks on computers, these dangerous distant worlds become close. A wide range of malefactors, be they criminals, agents of the state, or hooligans, use similar tactics. The same security hole that allows someone to hijack your computer for a criminal purpose can also be used by a more sophisticated attacker. An attempt to knock a website offline can be an extortion attempt, a political protest, or part of an international dispute. All this applies not just to the machines we have traditionally called computers, such as desktops and laptops. Pin and Chip both have modern mobile phones (smartphones) which are in effect small, powerful and portable computers. And their lives are filling up with a range of new devices with chips and software buried in their insides. These include cars, household appliances such as washing machines and electricity meters, and industrial or office equipment such as heating systems or lifts.

In short: anyone who uses, or is dependent on, any sort of electronic device – i.e. just about everyone in the modern world needs to rethink and change their behaviour, and should expect others to do the same. This may seem hard to grasp. How can a single, humble personal computer wreak havoc? Of course in most cases it does not, any more than every car with a bald tyre or worn brakes automatically becomes a death machine.

But the trend is clear and ominous. In past decades, the idea that a house could catch fire because of a computer malfunction would have seemed fanciful. Now it is all too plausible. Similarly unlikely would have seemed the idea that thousands of people could lose their jobs because their employer failed to safeguard company data. That already happens. Nortel Networks, one of Canada's top technology companies, collapsed in 2009 after Chinese hackers stole its designs and business plans during a decade of attacks on its computers.[3] Because we have increased our dependence on computers and networks faster than we have been able to understand what we are doing, we face a much bigger number of what Mr Geer, the security expert, calls 'unmitigatable surprises' – events that do damage from which we cannot recover easily, or perhaps at all.

In truth, just as transport will always involve accidents, perfect security for computers and networks is impossible. A sufficiently determined adversary, with unlimited resources, will always find something which works. If all else fails, he may try the notorious 'rubber hose attack' – a euphemism for making people cooperate through torture, such as beating with a heavy hose.

But that is true of all kinds of security. We do not expect our houses to be fortresses capable of withstanding an artillery barrage – we just want them to be safe enough to deter the kind of burglar who is likely to attack us. We plan our real-world security (largely instinct-ively) on the basis of likely eventualities, practicalities and conse-quences. We need to learn to do the same with our computers. In all other walks of life we trade off freedom, security and convenience. Our dealings with computers and networks should be no different. The fundamental problem is that we have gravely overemphasised the freedom and convenience of using computers, and not thought enough about the security. That has given huge opportunities to malefactors of all kinds, be they spies, criminals or hooligans.

The question is therefore to find the right kind of deterrence and damage limitation. Our aim should be to make the cost for the attacker, versus the benefit of success, prohibitively expensive and risky. Fort Knox, where America keeps its gold reserves, is not invulnerable. But attacking it would require a full-scale military assault (immensely difficult), with no realistic chance of getting the gold away afterwards. If the only way to get the gold from Fort Knox is the military conquest of the United States, then it is not actually the bullion which is at stake, for either the defenders or the attackers.

For individuals, the need is to learn new habits of prudence and caution in the way we use computers. For organisa-tions it requires a thorough rethink of the way they store and deal with data. Recklessness and carelessness must bring severe consequences – from insurers, shareholders, customers, suppliers and regulators, as well as from the criminal justice system.

In particular, three main kinds of attack should be at the forefront of every computer user's mind. Just as we know that coughs and sneezes spread diseases, and that washing hands before cooking is not just polite but essential for the health of those you are cooking for, so computer users need to know about the main avenues of infection.

The easiest way to install malicious programs on other people's computers is to get them to do it themselves. My daughter fell for this on her tenth birthday. I had given her a small £100 ($170) Asus laptop and told her to download Open Office (a free-of-charge program which has most of the functions of the much more expensive Microsoft Office). However, the top entry which came up on Google directed her not to the openoffice.org website, but to another one, where the download came accompanied by some unwelcome search software. This was Mindspark, produced by a legitimate company, but the subject of some controversy because of the way it operates. In my daughter's case it modified her web browser, so that every search produced an avalanche of unwanted information and advertisements. Mindspark's business model is based on funnelling computer users to its customers, and also selling data about browsing habits. There is nothing illegal in that – but it was not something that either my daughter or I had consented to.

We got off lightly. We could have been tricked into installing something worse, such as 'Security Toolbar 7.1', which masquerades as a way of searching the internet, but in fact persuades you to install bogus (and dangerous) security software on your computer. But the little episode highlighted some fundamental vulnerabilities on the internet. A child going into a sweetshop can be reasonably sure that the produce on offer is not dangerous. For more than 100 years we have had food-safety legislation that means that

the purveyors of dangerous products risk heavy fines or even jail.
Moreover, a shop selling food has its reputation to think about. A
responsible shopkeeper will not sell a child liqueur chocolates, or
exotic gourmet confections containing chilli pepper and salt. And
if we do buy something that proves unwholesome, we know what
to do: we can spit it out after the first mouthful. We can buy a
simple remedy for an upset stomach, and we can go to the doctor
for some expert help if it does not get better. A nasty stomach bug
is inconvenient and upsetting, but we know what to do to counter it, and it is unlikely to do life-changing damage. Unless we are
already unhealthy, it is not going to make us vulnerable to other,
still more horrible diseases.

When our computers are involved, the opposite is true. We are
dealing with infections which we may not notice and are unlikely
to understand. We do not know how to deal with them – and the
people claiming to sell remedies may in fact be trying to harm us,
not heal us. Google says it does not allow advertisements from sites
trying to install malware – software which has been deliberately
designed to do harm. But it offers no way of complaining about a site
that does something unpleasant and unwanted to a user's computer.
It does offer remedies, however, for its real customers: those who
think that they are being unfairly barred from advertising on Google.
This highlights an important point. Everyday users of Google are
not, strictly speaking, the company's customers. We are, in fact, the
product that it sells to its customers, who are the companies who
buy advertisements to be displayed on the pages we use.

Even experienced computer users can fall for similar tricks. If a
window pops up on your computer saying that it is infected, and
you need to install some software to deal with the problem, the
natural response is to agree gratefully. Similarly, if you are told that
your software is out-of-date or vulnerable, and that you need to
install a new version, most people will go ahead. People wanting

to plant malware on computers are adept at making their bogus and harmful software look friendly and authentic. They may use the logos and colour schemes of a real product – such as Flash Player, a program which is needed on many computers to play videos – in order to dispel suspicion.

A second easy way to get people to install malware is to get them to open an e-mail 'attachment' – a file such as a picture or document which is attached to an electronic message, or to click on a link that will take them to an infected site. This tactic is known as 'phishing' (as in 'fishing'). The aim is to cast enough hooks in the water that a useful number of victims will bite on them.

It is child's play to fake an e-mail address. To test people's gullibility, I created the e-mail address russian.embassy.london@gmail.com and sent messages to friends and colleagues (adding some logos and other material to the end of the e-mail) to see if they would respond seriously. They did, though a moment's thought should have revealed the unlikelihood of the Russian Embassy resorting to the free-of-charge e-mail service of an American tech giant. With only a little more sophistication it is possible to send an e-mail that really will look as though it comes from someone else.

Few lay people realise that an attachment to an e-mail is in effect a computer program. If you click on it, your computer will follow the instructions the attachment contains. If the attachment is legitimate, then these will be harmless: to use a particular font in a document, for example, or to put a picture on your screen of a particular size and shape. But a cleverly designed bit of malware can contain other instructions, too. These may have a dramatic effect – such as kidnapping your computer with 'ransomware', in which the computer freezes, and you can recover control only by paying a fee to the extortionist. Or they may be quite inconspicuous. You may simply notice that your computer seems to run a little slower, or nothing at all. An infectious attachment may have some innocent name such as 'resume.doc'. You try to open it, but nothing happens, so you shrug your shoulders and forget about it. You are unaware that you have just handed control of your computer to an outsider.

The same is true of the third means of infection – links. When you click on a link to load a web page, you are authorising your computer to follow other instructions. Again, these may be quite innocent: to show a picture, display in a particular font, or to import some material from another source. But something else may be on the website, too. As we will see, this may not even be a complete piece of malware, but just a component of a program which will combine with the other parts at a later date.

We deal with our computers as we used to deal with the security of our cars. In the first decades of the automobile industry, cars did not have keys at all. Then they had flimsy ones, which deterred the casual thief but not the professional. As a child in Oxford in the 1970s, I remember my father going out at night and swapping the cables leading from the distributor to the spark plugs so that if someone broke into the car and tried to 'hotwire' it (removing the lock from the steering column and simply connecting the wires) the starter motor would turn, but the car would not actually start.

For now, most internet users are barely at the stage of locking their cars. This leaves them vulnerable to even the crudest attacks – not from finely tailored software created by geniuses, but from a thoroughly bogus website which grabs your computer with both hands. The cleverness of the fraudster lies not in the design of the infecting software, but in getting people to visit the site in the first place. Some computer users are stupid enough to visit even the dodgiest sites (for example those offering free pornography) and to accept invitations from the most unlikely sources. Others may be prudent enough to decline to respond to e-mails inviting them to visit, for example, bestxxxporntube.com. But even naturally prudent people can be fooled by a link that purports to be something else. One of the commonest scams simply reads 'great picture of you!' Another is: 'seen this?' What follows is a link which on the surface reveals nothing, produced from a link-shortening service such as t.co. I recently received an e-mail from a reputable Swedish politician, which read 'Attached is an important secured document for your review' and contained a link asking me to 'View Document'. Clicking on that would have taken me to a website called premierimoveisaruja.com.br/inc/ (please don't try it) which would have tried to plant the Mal/PhishA virus on my computer, which tries to steal banking details. When I complained, he simply replied that the e-mail was not from him. A similar scam comes through an e-mail that informs you that you have won a lottery prize, or are eligible for a refund. Clicking on the links in these e-mails takes you to a site that will infect your computer.

As well as planting malware – malicious software – on the victim's computer through downloads, attachments or links, the fourth main means of attack is to trick people into giving away their logins, passwords and the like. These can be used for criminal purposes – or to make you an accessory in an attack on another person. Credentials theft, as it is known, may leave no trace on the victim's computer. It has not installed malware which your anti-virus program is going to notice. For now, it is just making a copy of your front door keys, not burgling your house. Only later, when you find the locks on the door have been changed, and strangers are in your house rifling through your possessions, will you understand what has happened.

Prudent and conscientious use of the internet can make all these kinds of attacks less likely and less dangerous. But even the most careful user of computers cannot get round the fundamental problem: the internet was not built with safety in mind.

2

The Unreliability of Computers

It was 10.30 p.m. on 29 October 1969. Leonard Kleinrock, a pioneering professor of computer science at the University of California, Los Angeles, was trying to connect his computer – a costly whirring box the size of a large freezer – with its counterpart at Stanford. Charley Kline, a graduate student, tried to see if he could type the word 'login' into his computer, and make the letters appear on the screen of the distant computer. Amid mounting excitement, the two teams spoke on the phone. As Mr Kleinrock recalled later:

> We typed the L and we asked on the phone, 'Do you see the L?'
> 'Yes, we see the L,' came the response.
> We typed the O, and we asked, 'Do you see the O?'
> 'Yes, we see the O.'
> Then we typed the G, and the system crashed.[1]

The first message sent on a computer network was a product of a different age. In the late 1960s and 1970s, the pioneers were academics wanting an efficient way of sharing time on computers – which in those days were scarce, huge and costly. They assumed goodwill and responsible behaviour, and a high degree of technical competence. Nobody was thinking about privacy or security. Resilience was a priority – the network-of-networks was sponsored by the military, because it was designed to work even if part of it was destroyed by a nuclear attack. But the main point was to experiment and innovate. None of the people in the room in 1969 could have conceived that some fifty years later the same remote communications technology, vastly improved, could be used to take pictures in people's bedrooms, loot their bank accounts, or pester their friends with junk mail. The internet, then as now, functions on the basis of trust. We assume good faith of other individual users. We assume they are who they say they are. Yet impersonation is easy and rife, and detecting it is hard.

Endemic anonymity is both a curse and a blessing. One person can have as many e-mail addresses as they like – or as many websites. There is no central 'telephone directory'. Each computer (or phone or tablet) when it goes online has to identify itself in order to receive and send information. In most countries this addressing system is run by telecoms companies or big internet firms. But it still relies ultimately on trust. There is plenty of scope for confusion – and duplicity. Already the number of devices on the internet is numbered in billions. New changes, which create more addresses, will turn that into trillions. That creates complexity, but it does not help reliability. The identity of any device on the internet can be disguised or blurred, by sending messages via intermediary computers.

One resulting problem is the difficulty of establishing personal identity. Chip Hakhett cannot show definitely who he is, or be sure who he is really dealing with. A second, related problem is navigation. It is hard (though not impossible) to be sure that you are visiting the website you intend to browse. You can easily find yourself visiting an impostor. Thirdly, the networks we use, particularly in big organisations, are rife with dangers to the data we store on them. In short, the internet's founding assumptions work brilliantly in a benign environment. But they create terrible problems when malefactors are at work – and especially when people are unaware of their reach.

Our friends the Hakhetts, both in their fifties, grew up in an age in which things went wrong a lot. Their childhood was marked by toasters which burned out, washing machines which broke down, cars which would not start and telephone calls which failed to connect. But the manufacturing revolution has changed that. The advent of digital telephone exchanges did away with the excitement of wrong numbers and crossed lines. Modern domestic appliances work perfectly – or need only minimal maintenance such as a new light bulb in a fridge or oven. The Hakhetts have little technical knowledge themselves, nor do they need to buy in much from outside. If something does break down, they simply throw it away and buy another one. The only technician they see regularly in their home comes to service the central heating boiler once a year.

But there is a huge exception. Sitting on Chip's desk is a machine which is not designed to be safe or reliable. It regularly breaks down. He does not know why this happens – it is rather unpredictable – but he sorts out the problem by turning it on and off again, or using his laptop instead. Sometimes it wheezes in distress, with a noisy cooling fan suggesting that its power consumption has gone up. If he knew what was really going on inside, he would be alarmed, but he does not. The machine is a computer, and computers are strange beasts: you are happy when they work, and make the best of it when they do not. In any case, you cannot do without them. Chip's computers and their connection to the internet are the heart of his business. He sends e-mails to his clients – high-flying business types who want to polish their people skills – and manages his appointments book, and his company's simple accounts. He makes payments through online banking, and shops for books and other items on Amazon. He uses Skype to stay in touch with his family, and keeps up with his friends by looking at Facebook and Twitter. He likes music while he works, so he downloads his favourite songs from iTunes, and occasionally (though Pin does not know this) glances at online porn sites for a little relaxation during the day.

Pin uses her computer at work only. She processes job applications, creates shortlists, checks résumés, invites candidates for interview and handles the other chores in the recruiting process. She has access to the company's payroll system (when people are hired, she adds their names) and to the health insurance company which covers the firm's permanent employees. On her company's network is potentially life-ruining information: the names of secret illegitimate children covered by the firm's health insurance; disciplinary action for drug and alcohol abuse and investigations into fraudulent expenses claims. All this is just one click away from public view.

The Hakhetts' dependence on computers and the internet, and their rather limited interest in how it works, are typical, excusable and yet potentially disastrous. Computers handle huge amounts of data, with a power and accuracy which previous generations could have only dreamed of. Combined into networks, they enable wealth creation, pleasure, social life and the dissemination of culture and knowledge. They are so embedded in the way we live, work and play that we cannot function without them. The internet – a network of computer networks – has become the central nervous system of modern life. We need it for private lives, for our social lives, for our household banking, transport, health and entertainment, and also (invisibly) to keep our public services and infrastructure running.

Like most users of computers, the Hakhetts find their set-up adequately reliable and efficient. And, indeed, in many respects it works miraculously well. Except in the very poorest parts of the world, anyone can get barebones access to the internet for a cost of pennies through a mobile phone. There is no need to pass a test, or own a computer, or even be literate. Censorship is difficult. It is easy to launch a business, run a campaign, or share something amusing or interesting. Most services are 'free' at the point of use (as noted above, this is a misnomer. The service is not 'free' any more than a commercial on television is 'free'. It is paid for by the real customer, who is the person trying to sell something. You, the user, are not the customer, but the product. The transaction is that your attention is sold to advertisers, while you are distracted by something which you think is 'free'). The internet is decentralised: nobody is in sole charge. Governments can try to regulate it, but they do not run it. Data may slow down when it encounters difficulties, but even in North Korea information rarely stops altogether.

But there is a large and worrying gap between what Chip and Pin find adequate and what we collectively need to be safe. One reason is that because an infected computer can damage other people, while still seeming to work reasonably well for its owner, our incentives are skewed. Another is that we do not understand the risks we are running.

The computers and programs on which we depend are not subject to the same constraints as other machinery. Pin gets into a lift at work and expects it not to get stuck, overheat, or send her plunging to her death. Chip gets in his car, turns the ignition key and would be surprised and annoyed if nothing happened, or it caught fire. If you design a machine which goes wrong a lot, people will not buy it. If, when it breaks, it hurts people, your company will get sued. In some countries, managers will go to jail. The company may go bankrupt. As a result, manufacturers take safety very seriously. Chip and Pin have for many years been subscribers to *Which?*, the British consumer magazine (its American counterpart is *Consumer Reports*). They carefully note how different brands perform in terms of convenience, capability and value for money, and make sure to buy only those that receive good ratings.

But computers which go wrong are regarded as part of life. Chip is quite used to documents which mysteriously refuse to print, websites which do not load properly, and mysterious error messages that appear on his screen. As when his computer simply freezes, he reacts phlegmatically. True, he would be most annoyed if a computer caught fire and burned the house down. That rarely happens (even though the lithium batteries which power his laptop have the power of a firebomb if misused).* But if other less spectacular computer malfunctions leak data, perhaps destroying his life or his business, he would scarcely understand what has happened. Computer professionals tend to react to these vulnerabilities with a brusque impatience. What do people like the Hakhetts expect? They run old computers, badly maintained, and do silly, risky things with them. Of course they are going to get into trouble. This approach is not just unkind, but unfair. The professionals' scorn should really be directed at their colleagues – the people who design and sell computers and software and who run networks. They are portraying their products and services as safe, in the way that aviation or motoring is safe, when in fact it is nothing of the kind.

What Chip and Pin do not know is that the computers they depend on were designed not primarily for safety and reliability, but to be produced as cheaply, quickly and profitably as possible. Inside the machines is a ramshackle mess of improvisation and recycling, the result of hurried work and bad communication. Quinn Norton, a leading computer security expert, wrote a memorable rant about this in May 2014. 'It's hard to explain to regular people

---

* To prove this point I once cut open a laptop battery with a hacksaw. The results were exciting but frightening. I do not recommend readers do the same. I particularly advise against dropping the bits in a bucket of water. Watch it on the internet instead.

how much technology barely works, how much the infrastructure of our lives is held together by the IT equivalent of baling wire. Computers, and computing, are broken.'[2]

Only a few months later, her words seemed all too prescient. News of the 'Shellshock bug' – the worst problem in computer security for a decade – broke in September 2014. This involved a series of errors in a small program-within-a-program, known as a 'shell'. This shell is a way of communicating commands to a computer's operating system. Operating systems are the basic programs which enable a computer to run other applications. Without an operating system, a computer is just a paperweight. The operating systems which most readers will have heard of are Microsoft Windows and Apple's OS/X. In fact there are many more, mostly used on more specialised machines. But all operating systems need a way of obtaining instructions from the computer's user. These may be automatic – if you have Microsoft Word, or Chrome, or some other program installed on your system, it will connect seamlessly with the operating system. But sometimes you will need to give a command directly, typically through the 'run' command in a Windows machine, or the Terminal application on an Apple computer.

This is the so-called 'command line interface'. In effect, it allows you to give the computer a direct instruction. The problem arose in a small program called the 'Bash shell' which had been written more than twenty years ago, but with some overlooked mistakes. These bugs allow outsiders, in some circumstances, to gain control of these machines through the internet – sending them commands which the computer would treat as if they came from a legitimate user. As the computer operating system trusts everything that Bash tells it to do, this is a simple but devastating flaw – computer experts say that on a scale of one to ten, Shellshock scores eleven.[3]

Average home computer users such as the Hakhetts are unlikely to be at risk unless they run websites from their home computers. A much bigger target are the servers – big computers – which run websites for companies and other organisations. After a couple of weeks, software 'patches' – partial repairs – for Shellshock were made available by Apple and other software companies. Computer-security researchers quickly saw attackers using Shellshock to try to gain control of computers, including some servers belonging to Yahoo, the American internet giant. But is almost impossible to know if Shellshock was exploited in the past, by whom and for what purposes.[4] So many different parts of the computer need to access the command line shell that it is hard to be sure if every eventuality is covered. As late as December 2014, a security company found some malware exploiting Shellshock on devices used for storing data.[5] Interestingly the attackers were using the malware not just for a fraudulent advertising scheme, but also to keep other malefactors off the infected computer.

Shellshock epitomises many of the problems with computer security. The scope for damaging attacks is colossal, but what has actually happened is unclear. A well-executed attack using Shellshock would leave few traces. The remedies are urgently needed, yet complicated, slow and at best only partial. Moreover, it is unclear who is to blame. The original program was written by an unpaid volunteer, Brian Fox, in 1989 – a time when the internet was run by enthusiasts – as a replacement for a previous shell, and has been in use ever since. Free software, usually available on an 'open-source' basis (meaning that it is available with relaxed copyright so the code can be inspected, and often updated, by anyone) has been a central part of the development of the internet. Many support it for ideological reasons, as a noble rival to the sordid business of writing programs for profit. Others highlight its practical advantages – errors are more easily spotted and remedied, and innovation is encouraged. Popular open-source software includes the Firefox browser, produced by the non-profit Mozilla Foundation, and the Linux operating system. All those advantages are real – but who do you sue when things go wrong?

A deeper problem is complexity. The microchips which make the logical decisions behind all computer activities, and the computer programs (software) which tell them how to do it, are now so complicated that no one person can understand them. My first electronics set (which I won in a competition in 1973) had four transistors, each of them accompanied by a large piece of paper, bearing a circuit diagram to show how it worked. The first computer I used was a Sinclair ZX81; its chip (the Zilog Z80) had around 8,500 transistors. It was possible, with a powerful microscope, to see how they related to each other and what each one did.

That kind of simplicity is now a distant memory. The latest version of the X-box (a computer gaming console) has five billion transistors. The circuit diagram would be impossible to print out in any meaningful or usable way.

Software is similarly complicated. Computer programs are made up of lines of code. Each one is an instruction. A good way to imagine this is through the analogy with a railway system, outlined earlier. The rails are the wiring of the computer chip. The points are the transistors. The trains are the data and the timetable is the program. If trains follow their instructions, they will move smoothly round the network, with the points switching as required. Everyone ends up where they should, when they should – and there are no crashes.

Writing a simple railway timetable is easy, as anyone who has owned a toy train set knows. In the early days of computers, a moderately able user would write code himself. For example, in the pre-Windows era (when computers responded to typed commands, rather than mouse-clicks) Chip learned this command:

```
prompt $t $d$_$p$g
```

It told the computer to display the date and time on the screen at the command prompt (the line on the screen where the user entered instructions). This minor but convenient feature could be made automatic. Whenever the computer is turned on it runs a small file called autoexec.bat. By putting this line of code in that file, Chip made sure that his computer would always tell him the data and time. In the 1980s and early 1990s, he thought nothing of making such modifications himself: they were the equivalent of a car owner in the 1930s cleaning the spark plugs and carburettor in his vehicle.

A car owner in those days also knew easy ways of disabling a machine. In *The Sound of Music*, Austrian nuns (seeking to protect the runaway von Trapp family from the Nazis) remove the distributor cap from the Germans' car. Few modern car owners could even find that device in their vehicle, let alone remove it. But it is still easy to disable a computer. The three simple lines of code below, for example, are the equivalent of stuffing a sock in a car exhaust pipe. They will bring any Windows computer to a grinding halt, by using up all its free storage space: *

```
@echo off
    copy c:\programs\virus.bat c:\programs
    start c:\programs\virus.bat
```

Modern code is a lot more complicated, which means that carelessness is harder to spot and malefactors' work is easier to conceal. Their programs – malware – can copy data and remove information from a machine or network. It can replace it with bogus data, either to mislead or to sabotage. It can take control of computers

---

* The command '@echo off' means that the program is not shown on the screen as it runs. In other words, the damage it does is invisible to the hapless user. The second line copies the program. The third line starts it again. Within a short while, the computer is hopelessly clogged: there is no space for any real data.

and make them malfunction, or send harmful instructions to the devices they control.

The odds are stacked against the defender. A tiny bit of code, such as the one cited above, can 'brick' your machine – turning it into a useless paperweight. But writing code which is foolproof (or even difficult to attack) is much harder. Each flaw requires a safeguard. Some of the safeguards clash with each other.

Worse, the attacker's malevolent software need not come as one single program. Malware can come in several innocent seeming parts, which fit together to do a job and then separate. It can evolve, taking one form in one part of the machine, and then disappearing, only to re-emerge in another. It can move between machines and devices, lurking on a printer or in a neglected corner of the network. It is best thought of as a biological threat – a bit like malaria, where infection relies on three factors: the malaria parasite itself, an infected mosquito to carry it, and a human with exposed skin that can be bitten.

If you can see a mosquito you can swat it. But malware is hard to spot because modern software is such a swamp. The first version of MS-DOS (the Microsoft software which made Bill Gates a billionaire) had 4,000 lines of code. Even an amateur, with a bit of time and skill, could look at that and understand what each line did. The programs which run in a modern car have 100 million lines of software – more than a top professional could understand in a lifetime. Steve McConnell, a writer on software, notes that for a system with even a million lines of code, even the requirements specification 'would typically be about 4,000–5,000 pages long, and the design documentation can easily be two or three times as extensive as the requirements. It's unlikely that an individual would be able to understand the complete design for a project of this size – or even read it.'[6]

Badly written programs date back to the beginning of the compu-ter age. The derogatory term 'spaghetti code', for an incomprehen-sibly and needlessly cluttered and complex computer program, was

probably coined at least as far back as 1978.[7] Computer experts
reckon that every thousand lines of code – even in the best cases –
will include an error (a rare and possibly unique exception was the
code written by NASA for the Space Shuttle, which cost around
twenty times as much per line of code as normal software[8]). Large
programs have more errors than small ones, because the number
of eventualities increases. One estimate is that the error rate rises
fourfold between small projects and large ones. These flaws are not
necessarily fatal, nor are they necessarily the cause of a vulnerability
that an attacker could exploit. But even if a tiny fraction of them are
exploitable, the danger is there. Some suggest that the rules governing the way software is written should be toughened – perhaps to
the point of applying criminal liability to the manufacturers of inad-
equate software. But even if that measure could get past the hugely
powerful software industry, it would not help remedy the programs
already written, many of which will be in use for years to come.

The number of vulnerabilities is rising, not falling, as new software is written and sold, and new hardware is made. A new product may create a new danger, because of the way it interacts with
hardware and software that at the moment look safe.

The complexity of hardware and software (the computers and
the programs that run them) makes it easy for attackers to find
vulnerabilities – ways of making computers misbehave – and easy
to conceal what they are doing. Computers are far more complex
than a plane or a car. What we call a computer is actually several
different devices. As Ms Quinn put it: 'boxes within boxes, and
each one of those computers is full of little programs trying to
coordinate their actions and talk to each other.'

If anything, that understates the problem. A computer is more
like a house than a box. But it is a house where you do not know
how many doors or windows exist, or how they are secured. You
have tunnels and aerial walkways galore. You do not know how

many rooms there are, or what they are for. You are not alone in your ignorance: the law enforcement authorities do not know either. Even the architect will not necessarily know: your house is constructed from bits of other buildings, which have their own weaknesses and complexities. Someone, somewhere, may have written down the details at the time of first construction. But that may be decades ago, and whether the documentation is preserved or still accurate is something you cannot find out.

Worse, your house is connected to lots of other houses. Countless numbers of people move between the houses. Keeping track of them is hard, and, even when you try to conduct a census of sorts, some of the people are both impossible to identify and clearly malefactors.

You do not know how many houses you are connected to, or where they are, or how the connections work. These houses have their own vulnerabilities, too. Someone who breaks into another house can get into yours. Someone may be living in your house, in a place you cannot see, and moving around all but invisibly. Even if you think you have caught an intruder and expelled him, you may be mistaken. The only absolutely certain way to clean up an infected computer is to smash it to pieces.

So spotting a mistake (deliberate or otherwise) in hardware and software is hard. There are so many places to look, and you do not know what you are looking for.* What may seem like a trivial problem can be fatal when compounded by others. A flaw in the

---

* Another analogy would be like trying to find a single mouse – easy in a prison cell, but not in a rambling old house. You may find evidence of its presence – squeaks, scamperings, droppings and nibbled food. You can try to trap it or poison it. But short of knocking down the house and rebuilding it, you have no way of being certain that you have eliminated the right rodent. Even silence does not mean that the infestation is permanently over: it may just be a temporary abatement.

design of a microchip (assuming anyone spots it at all) can seem quite harmless: perhaps the result of haste or carelessness, or some redundant array of transistors left over from a previous design and copied into a new one (around 60 per cent of chip design consists of reused logic and circuitry).[9] A mistake in a computer program can also seem unimportant: perhaps it does not allocate quite enough memory for a particular function, so the software 'borrows' a bit of capacity from somewhere else.

But that small software glitch can be very serious if combined with another mistake – such as a careless bit of chip design. Attackers often concentrate on the way data flow from one bit of the computer's operations to another: this often involves temporary storage in what are called 'buffers'. These can be easy prey: the data can be doctored as they flow backwards and forwards, and the instructions that allow them to do so can be altered or abused. That can create a chance to take over the computer, steal information from it, hijack it and spread infection elsewhere.

Most people who design computers and write software are used to thinking in two dimensions. They look at their work in terms of what it is meant to do, not what someone else could do with it. If Chip complains that his computer is not working properly, the standard answer (after turning it on and off again) is to try uninstalling different bits of software until it starts working. Failing that, he should delete everything and reinstall his programs. This will often work. One reason that computers go wrong is that data can 'corrupt' over time – an original setting gets changed because of a mistake in the software, or a chance interaction between different parts of the system. Reinstalling everything from scratch can help.

But not always. If you buy software that does not work with your hardware, or vice versa, your options are limited. Consumer protection in the world of computers is limited. Your rights, broadly, are limited to a refund for whatever you have paid. You will not be compensated for interruptions to your business, lost data, or having to buy new products to make the old ones work. Such a punitive regime would kill innovation: manufacturers would not risk selling anything new, for fear of being sued when it does not work.

Vendors do want their customers to be happy, though. If the problem crops up persistently, then – assuming that the software vendor is efficient – he will develop and distribute a solution. These are known as software 'patches'. They are powerful tools – in effect you are handing over control of your computer to an outsider, and letting him make changes. Wise consumer users 'patch' (update) their machines regularly, either by checking to see if the software is the latest version, or by responding to automated warnings. These are regularly issued by companies such as Apple, Google or Microsoft, and by the non-profit foundations and groups which look after open-source software such as the Firefox browser. Chip receives them, but he ignores them. He has had bad experiences with updates. The peremptory messages crop up at inconvenient times. They close the programs he is working on before he real-ises what is happening, and when they reopen, his data is gone. Sometimes his elderly computer cannot install them, and sits there frozen, with a message telling him to wait. Other times, the newly installed software does not work properly. He does not trust manu-facturers to tell him honestly whether an update is genuinely a matter of security, or just a way of installing extra features in a program that he does not want and cannot understand. So he ignores them all: he has a business to run. Pin ignores them, too (though they are installed automatically on her work computer). She feels vaguely annoyed that the home laptop – a product on which the Hakhetts spent several hundred pounds – seems to need constant maintenance.

It is easy to see why consumers do not update their software. It attracts no criminal penalty or even social censure. Yet unpatched (out-of-date) software is a gift for attackers. Chip and Pin would not leave their cars with an unlocked door or open window. Badly maintained software is worse: it is like having bald tyres, a cracked windscreen, no mirrors and bad brakes. Many attackers design their toxic material with unpatched software in mind, and then distribute it widely.

Moreover, putting the onus on consumers to deal with manufacturers' mistakes is not the way other industries work. If a dangerous design or manufacturing flaw is discovered in a toy, processed food, a household appliance, or a car, the makers mind. In September 2014 General Motors announced a recall of 220,000 cars to correct a brake defect that could have caused the vehicles to catch fire – the latest in a series of recalls which affected fifteen million cars worldwide in that year.[10] The company's share price plunged and senior executives resigned. When a battery on the new Boeing Dreamliner caught fire in January 2013, aviation authorities ordered all fifty of the aircraft in service to be grounded until the fault was diagnosed and remedied.[11] Manufacturers who discover that that their products are dangerous have to make great efforts to let people know. They will place advertisements in newspapers telling consumers to bring their products to a shop or dealer for repair or replacement.

Customers expect that designers will make sure that their products work safely, always and everywhere. Chip would be most unimpressed if he bought a new car, but found that when making a right turn while driving downhill in low gear the engine cut out. He would be even less impressed if the manufacturer shrugged his shoulders and said that this was an unavoidable problem and he should try making left turns instead. The earliest computer program was the railway timetable; the acceptable level of accidents there is zero.

Compounding the weaknesses created by insecure hardware and software is the way we expect old and new to coexist.

In other walks of life, we have got quite used to coexisting with old technology. My father drives an unusual car: a 1928 open-topped Humber tourer, called 'Old England'. It does not boast a single transistor. Yet it coexists with modern cars, because it can perform the basic functions of a motor vehicle safely: it can stop, start, turn and indicate. Every few years, it passes a test to show it can meet these basic functions. And although it is slow, noisy and smelly by modern standards (and more dangerous if it were to collide with you), Old England has the same right to use the road as any other vehicle. That would not be true in aviation: a primitive aircraft would not be allowed to fly into commercial airspace, or to land at a modern airport; our definition of airworthiness now means having all sorts of modern safety equipment such as radios and radar beacons, not just for the benefit of the plane and its passengers, but for everyone else.

The internet is much more complicated than aviation, yet it is far more laxly regulated. Almost as a matter of principle, it is open to use by the most primitive and old-fashioned technology. Without any modifications, a computer from the 1980s can, in skilled hands, still get online.[12] This is not because of any particular generosity of spirit, but from necessity. The internet has no central governing body which could deem a particular kind of computer too old or insecure to be allowed access. And it has plenty of powerful voices who want their products and services to be as widely available as possible. If you design the software for an online retailer, your customer will not be pleased if you say that the shop can only be used by someone running an up-to-date computer with the most modern programs installed.

An analogy would be the MOT – the regular test of roadworthiness which British cars undergo. The Hakhetts are admirably aware of road safety issues, and their cars pass easily. They discard old car parts rather than keeping them just in case. Chip would not expect that his new Volvo would be designed so that he can use some filters, seals and shock absorbers from an old VW he used in the 1990s. And if he did for some eccentric reason find and fit ancient car parts on a modern vehicle, he would not be surprised if his car failed the test. When new standards are introduced – for example, the requirement to carry a warning triangle or first-aid kit – he adopts them conscientiously.

In computers our expectations are different. Chip, like other computer users around the world of his generation, expects almost any device or program from the last twenty years to work in combination with every other device. He has several printers – an elderly daisywheel (rarely used now) for forms requiring a carbon copy, a colour printer for photographs and presentations, and a laser printer for most other things. All of them have to run on a computer made in 2005, running a variety of software from different manufacturers, including an antique file-management system called Norton Commander, which he became used to in the early 1990s.

In one sense, this is a reasonable exercise of his consumer sovereignty and choice. The requirement for uniformly up-to-date technology can be irritating, and allow manufacturers to make excess profits on spare parts: Chip was furious when a headlight on Pin's car burned out, and he had to buy not just a replacement bulb, but a costly new sealed lighting unit. But such uniformity reduces the scope for things to go wrong.

Conscientious and regular patching mean that some flaws in old software are more likely to be spotted and fixed, but this is by no means certain. Many mistakes and potential vulnerabilities are not spotted at all, because they seem insignificant in isolation. For the attacker, though, combining two seemingly insignificant flaws may pave the way to a serious breach. Add a third flaw, and they can instigate a catastrophe. Such unknown flaws in software are known as 'zero-days'. They typically come as result of a single mistake or omission by the programmer or chip designer. The most dangerous vulnerabilities come from compounding several. Rather like the malaria parasite mentioned earlier, which needs a mosquito for transport, and a bite to reach the human bloodstream, computer bugs may come as a result of several factors coinciding.

For example, Chip uses the Internet Explorer browser, version 6, which was once dubbed the world's least secure software.[13] That is bad enough, but it is particularly vulnerable if he then visits an infected website. A million people may look at an advertisement booby-trapped with a malicious program. Maybe only 1 per cent of them will do so with the combination of out-of-date and unpatched versions of Flash (a program used to view graphics), Windows, and the Internet Explorer browser. But that will still mean that 10,000 computers get infected – a lucrative haul for the attackers, and dreadful news for those who will be defrauded, impersonated or humiliated as a result.

The problems with individual machines are bad enough. But the security problems get even worse when we hook them together. In particular the internet – a network which links the most modern, powerful, safe and important computers with the most weakly protected, misused and dangerous ones – was not designed for the reliance we are putting on it.

Because nobody is really in charge of the internet, decision-making is slow and cumbersome, and sometimes doesn't happen. This fundamentally flawed system, of ill-designed and incomprehensible technology, hooked together in a network which relies on trust, is one ingredient of a looming disaster. A second is the huge amounts of money and power at stake. If you can disrupt the functioning of a computer or network, or destroy, alter or steal the data it holds, you have a potent weapon. But just as our dependence on computers is growing faster than our ability to understand them, so too the capabilities of attackers – be they criminals, hooligans or spies – to use computers to destroy, disrupt and steal are growing faster than our ability to cope with them.

In real life, espionage, crime, warfare and hooliganism overlap only rarely. A spy may pick locks like a burglar. A burglar may use a firearm like a soldier. A gang of hooligans may adopt quasi-military language and behaviour. But these fields of activity are broadly separate, and we are able to distinguish easily between them. Online, we can't. The same technique that a criminal uses to empty your bank account may be used by a foreign government to steal your employer's secrets. The same jamming tactics used by a gang of politically motivated hackers can also be part of a state's military arsenal.

The techniques involved may display extraordinary sophistication and complexity, but the protagonists are familiar. There is a victim and a perpetrator, an aggressor and a victim. Behaviour is based on the balance of risk and reward. Stupid criminals, spies, hooligans and military types use clumsy techniques for low rewards. Clever ones use sophisticated and expensive means, in search of big prizes, and tend to be detected more rarely.

The danger demands deep changes in the way we behave. As Jarno Limnéll, a Finnish expert, argues, the rise of worries about cyber-security requires a mental shift comparable to that we underwent at the beginning of the Cold War, when we realised that the Soviet Union, our wartime ally against Hitler, was now a foe, not a friend. Another example was the dawning realisation after the terrorist attacks of 11 September 2001 in New York that the world faced a global, elusive and semi-permanent threat from violent Islamic extremism.

The challenge is twofold. The first is to protect ourselves right now. The second is to protect our capability to defend ourselves in future. Attackers do not just interfere with our existing computers and networks. They can make it all but impossible for us to adapt to new threats as well. It is as if you not only lose the keys to your house, but also lose the ability to change the locks. Short of building a new house, you are stuck with permanent insecurity.

The typical response so far to worries about online security has been to recommend stronger passwords, security software and tougher rules. That is rather like dealing with a burglary epidemic by installing a hardened steel front door with enormous numbers of complicated locks on it. These certainly inconvenience members of your household (to the point that they may stop using all of them). But they do little to stop a determined burglar if your back door, windows and roof are all easily accessible.

Indeed, as I showed in Chapter 1, the analogies between physical and online security are only partly helpful. It is not much use having a secure front door if you habitually leave your windows open, live with dishonest housemates, or allow strangers into your basement. But the bigger point is that we need to understand that our computers are not like houses, and the threats they face are not like those in the 'real' (non-computer) world.

While the danger is both grave and only half understood, the answers are not the obvious ones. Security on the internet is a matter for governments, but not only governments, for internet companies (but not only them) and for every individual (but not only for us). It requires profound and difficult shifts, and troubling trade-offs, in the way we understand society and ourselves. The less visible but more pervasive attacks on our prosperity, our safety, our freedom and our happiness come from sources we do not know, use means we do not understand and do damage that we do not recognise.

3

Identity and its Enemies

The single biggest danger we face online is to our identity and reputation. These are what make us people. A name is a person's most fundamental attribute. When you want to dehumanise a captive, you give him or her a number. Reputation – what people think about us – is our currency in society. Without a reputation, you are dependent on the trust people offer to strangers. With a bad reputation, your past misdeeds (real or merely believed) dog your steps into the future. Computers, for all the benefits they have brought in other respects, have eroded the integrity of both.

Our fictional, illustrative couple, the Hakhetts, would be out of business without the internet. If you Google 'Chip Hakhett', he comes up as an executive coach, helping high-level business people improve their skills. He teaches them body language, public speaking and how to conduct interviews (his typical client is someone who has reached the top through being good with numbers, not people). He has a rudimentary website, giving his contact details. But he does not advertise his famous clients. They want confidentiality – it would be a sign of weakness in most contexts for a boss to show that he needs this sort of coaching. So

Chip meets them away from their offices, usually in a hotel room. His reputation comes from his own speeches at conferences, and by word of mouth.

Pin's work, too, relies on the internet. One of her jobs is checking up on job applicants. Before they are invited for interview, she looks at their CVs, and Googles them to see if what they claim on their CV seems to match what the internet 'says'. She uses LinkedIn, a professional networking site, to look for possible hires for her company.

In the pre-computer era, blackening someone's name was possible, but it was cumbersome and expensive. You could write poison-pen letters, denouncing them to colleagues, friends and neighbours. You could persuade a newspaper to print untrue stories about them. In the Soviet Union, the authorities could rewrite encyclopaedia entries (even recalling and pulping versions which praised or decried the wrong person). But in a free society this route would be all but impossible.

Now blackening someone's name is easy. Assume they have a moderately unusual name (Chip Hakhett, perhaps). Then go to Wikipedia and create an entry for them, or edit one if it already exists, adding false but plausible seeming details: last year I created an entry for Mr Hakhett, which asserted that he had been tried but not convicted for fraud, and that his wife worked as a part-time bar hostess.[1] Neither of those would inspire confidence with a potential client.

I then repeatedly typed in 'Chip Hakhett' and 'charlatan'. After just ten searches, Google 'auto-completed' the search for the hapless Chip with the word it thought would be most helpful – 'charlatan'.[2] Top of the search results came the Wikipedia entry, giving a seemingly authoritative description. Assuming Chip doesn't take expensive and difficult counter-measures, his reputation will suffer whenever people search for him.* For a sophisticated internet user, a manipulated Wikipedia entry may be detectable. But such skills are rare. Most people skim-read a Wikipedia page, rather than thinking about how it was constructed, which sources have been used (and not used), who the editors are and what else they have edited, what arguments and controversies may have flared over the page, how long it has been in existence, and so forth. A good start-ing point for the curious is to read Wikipedia entries from the bottom up, starting with the sources listed in the footnotes. Next, read the 'talk page' (available at the top of the entry) and look at the 'edit history'. The context helps makes sense of what is actually written on the topic concerned.

Attacking someone's reputation online illustrates an important point about attacks using computers and networks. They do not need to involve technical wizardry. They are a simple matter of motive, means and opportunity. If you understand the way that the internet shapes our perception of the world – through Google, Facebook, Wikipedia and similar sites and services, then you can shape the world's perception of someone else.

Take, for example, the story of Leandra Ramm, an American singer whose life was all but ruined by an attack over the internet, which she has outlined to me in interviews, and in a book published in 2014. Ms Ramm is beautiful, brainy and talented. In 2006, aged twenty-one, she fell foul of Colin Mak Yew Loong, a Singaporean

---

* I once interviewed a leading government official dealing with organised crime. The interview had an odd atmosphere. Distracting his attention, I used one of the dark arts of journalism – the ability to read upside down – to look at what he had on his desk. It was a print-out of my Wikipedia entry from several weeks ago, at a time when it had been defaced by some critics. He had clearly taken it as gospel truth. He thought he was dealing with a nutcase. I decided that I was dealing with an incompetent.

who initially presented himself as a potential sponsor of her career, though he was in fact on trial (and subsequently convicted) for arms trafficking. First his e-mails turned from 'creepy to scary'. Then he bombarded opera companies with threatening messages, falsely claiming that Ms Ramm had defrauded him. This effectively 'squelched' her career. Almost all the opera companies involved decided – shamefully – that they did not want to have anything to do with the 'girl with the stalker'. In all she received around 5,000 e-mails from him, mostly copied to her friends and colleagues, depicting her as a talentless 'thieving whore'. He invented hundreds of new identities to lure her into opening e-mails – and in some cases impersonated her, even writing letters under her name to her management company terminating their contract. He set up a blog 'Divas gone Wild' which described her as an 'undercover prostitute'.

Using spurious citations of copyright violations, he sued YouTube and Google to make them take down material which Ms Ramm had legitimately posted there. That harmed her career, too – she wanted to advertise herself. The companies concerned do not have the time to check up on complaints. It is simpler just to act on them. As with so many other things on the internet, that gives the noisy and obsessive an advantage over the quiet and decent. Mak Yew Loong tracked down her family, friends and colleagues and pestered them by phone, fax and e-mail. Her relationship with her boyfriend came under strain, and finally ended. Her parents no longer answered their phone. 'He knew more about us than we did about him,' she recalled. He made chilling threats of violence against her and her friends and family, involving truncheons and knives, rape, beatings, disfigurement, castration, blinding and murder.

If this harassment had happened in the real world – say, on the streets of New York – the police would have been quick to act. But the internet has enabled malefactors on one side of the world to reach victims on the other. For Ms Ramm, help was scant. Nobody in the United States cared what was being posted on the internet in Singapore. 'We deal with real murders . . . not e-mails,' she was told by the FBI when she sought their help. Nobody in Singapore cared about a reputation traduced in the United States. Only when I commissioned a story about her case in *The Economist* did the wheels start to turn.[3]

In December 2013 Mak was jailed for three years, for what District Judge Mathew Joseph called an 'abhorrent case of cross-border cyber-stalking'. Handing down the sentence he told Mak that he had used the internet as 'a weapon of massive personal destruction in the real world of your hapless victims'.

Most people are unlikely to have a reputation of sufficient profile to warrant a deliberate attack. It would be easy to tarnish Chip as a fraudster, or his wife as a prostitute. That could be the result of a grudge, a prank, or business rivalry. But they are more vulnerable to another form of attack: impersonation. Be it for prankish fun or the most sinister reasons, impersonation is easy on the internet. We are used to trusting people online whom we have never met in person, on the basis of fragmentary clues which can easily be reproduced by a third party.

Impersonation is sometimes called 'identity theft', but I dislike that term. The identity is not stolen: it still belongs to the person concerned. Just because someone steals Chip's keys, credit card, passport and driving licence does not make him into Chip: the thief does not then become married to Pin. It means he has stolen things which allow him to pretend to be Chip.

In the real world, impersonation is quite difficult: we rely on plenty of real-world clues to back up the physical objects that confer identity. If someone sees a suspicious-looking person unlocking the Hakhetts' front door, the fact that he has the right key does not make him less worrying. If he is then seen driving Chip's Volvo, a good neighbour will be more, not less, inclined to challenge him. A stolen passport works only if nobody checks the photograph. The stolen credit card works only so long as the spending pattern is not unusual, and so long as Chip does not report it missing. None of these safeguards is foolproof, but it is hard to evade them all, and certainly hard to do so for a sustained length of time.

But impersonation on the internet is a lot easier. Chip's gait, demeanour, appearance, voice and other hard-to-fake elements help other people recognise him. But online Chip is judged by bits and bytes – by digital data: a string of 1s and 0s. Perhaps (if he is lucky and careful) these will be encrypted and complicated, backed up by other factors of authentication such as a physical gizmo which issues codes, or by the answers to cleverly designed questions. Or (if he is unlucky or careless) his online identity consists of a simple login and a short password. Anyone else who can generate the right digital signal can pretend to be Chip, and most people will believe him.

Successful impersonation involves stealing information and privileges. Each stage reached makes the next one easy. Access to Chip's computer gives control of his e-mail account. Authentic seeming e-mails sent from that can change his address (or redirect his mail). Then the attacker can apply for new documents on his behalf. Once he has the new documents (for example a driving licence or utility bill) registered to a new address, he can start applying for loans or credit cards in the purloined name. The first Chip may know about this is when he finds that his credit rating has collapsed, or that debt collectors are hounding him for unpaid bills which he never incurred.

All that has become a lot easier thanks to our dependence on computers and networks. Long ago, intercepting someone's communications involved physical proximity (hence the 'eaves' in eavesdropping). In the early electronic age, bugging a telephone or planting a microphone was risky, complicated and conspicuous. It was well beyond the capabilities of a private citizen: only government agencies or professional detective agencies had the know-how, and the risk of detection was severe. Anyone wanting to trick or snoop on the Hakhetts in the 1980s, for example by infiltrating their network of friends, would have to spend many months monitoring their social life, perhaps intercepting mail, steaming it open and resealing it, or going through their rubbish looking for old correspondence. Only a professional private investigator or a government official would be able to undertake such costly and risky tasks.

Now you can look at the Hakhetts' Facebook pages, which lists all their friends in plain sight. Facebook gives their biographies, hobbies, holidays and peeves, as well as their dates of birth, the schools they attended and the names of parents and siblings. It even lists their pets, alive and dead. This matters: all these details are useful for someone trying to guess a password, or answer a security question (which may be something like 'give the first and third letters of your first pet's name').

In my fictional depiction, the Hakhetts are not just on Facebook but also LinkedIn – a huge social-networking site for some 300 million professionals. Both of them have a policy of accepting all requests for connections – for Chip, it might be a possible client, and for Pin, a possible hire. LinkedIn gives their past employment and all the colleagues they have worked with. Neither of the Hakhetts, or the tens of millions like them, have given much thought to the way such information could be misused. That is not LinkedIn's fault – it just provides a platform where its users can share information. It does not claim to have verified the people who provide information, or those who read it. But providing information to total strangers is risky. And so is trusting what you see on your screen.

A report in May 2014 by iSight Partners, a computer-security firm, uncovered 'Newscaster' – an operation in which Iranian attackers had since 2011 used more than a dozen elaborate fake identities on sites such as Facebook, Twitter and LinkedIn to trap at least 2,000 victims, including senior American military, diplomatic, political and media figures, as well as notable pro-Israel voices.[4] The phonies claimed to work in the media, defence industries or government, and had carefully constructed biographies with plausible sounding details (including links from a fictitious media website, newsonair.org, which plagiarised content from genuine outlets such as the BBC).[*]

These people, invented but credible seeming, then befriended their targets. In many 'networking' sites such as Facebook and LinkedIn, once someone counts you as a friend, they then share a swathe of biographical and other information – ranging from home addresses and phone numbers to names of family members, details of holidays and hobbies, and work-related matters. The attackers then sent e-mails to their targets to trick them into giving away their usernames and passwords for these services, and planting malicious software which could steal data from their computers. The aim of this attack – which iSight dubbed 'unprecedented in complexity, scale, and longevity' – may have been to gain insights into American military capabilities and alliance with Israel, perhaps to gain a negotiating advantage on issues such as sanctions or nuclear proliferation, or perhaps to prepare the ground for a future disruptive attack.

Both the Hakhetts are vulnerable to this sort of attack. At a minimum, by accepting contact requests from people they do not know, they can help give the makers of invented identities an appearance of legitimacy. Once you are connected with Chip, you can start targeting his customers – who just happen to be the

---

[*] This has nothing to do with newsonair.com, which is an entirely above-board news website based in India.

chief executives of powerful and interesting companies. Once you are connected with Pin, you can start work on her colleagues at work – a big media conglomerate full of interesting targets.

Yet the abuse by 'Newscaster' of LinkedIn, like the hounding of Leandra Ramm by Colin Mak Yew Loong in Singapore, was both brazen and low-tech. It did not involve skilful use of technology or any specially developed software. Its main weapon was ingenuity, and it exploited the greatest vulnerability in any security system: people.

Even leaving gullibility and trickery aside, computers have changed the way publicly available data can be searched and processed. The Hakhetts' home address and home telephone number were never, strictly speaking, fully private information. They have not bothered to go 'ex-directory', so for a small fee you can find out their phone number if you know the address. The address can be obtained from the electoral registration service. Both Chip and Pin are directors of Chip's company, and so its address – which is their home address – is also available from a corporate registry.

Now all that information is available online – sometimes free of charge, sometimes for the payment of a small fee. In theory, it is possible to conceal some of it – using an accountant's address for your company, having an unlisted phone number and so forth. But few people make the effort, any more than they worry about what they put on Facebook.

Perhaps they should. Providers of vital services such as health, banking, or online shopping use it to establish who you are. They all too often begin a phone call (or a session on the internet) by asking for your date of birth, mother's maiden name, last four digits of your phone number, or home address. By making that information public, and by doing business with online companies which allow users to put convenience over security, the Hakhetts, and countless others, are making life easy for attackers.

A paradox of the internet is that the Hakhetts hand over so much information about themselves for very little in return. Chip and Pin are thrifty. They use 'free' e-mail and other services. Why pay for something which you can get for no cost? What they do not realise is that Google, Facebook and other companies sell the data that they gather about the Hakhetts, to advertisers who want to reach them. If they write e-mails about dogs, then they will find advertisements for kennels, dog food and other canine paraphernalia cropping up on their screens. If they share an interest in holidays in Latin America with their friends on Facebook, the advertisements that appear on that site will be tailored towards what it presumes are their interests – and future purchases. As explained earlier, the users of 'free' services are not the customer, but the product.

It is true that we consent to this. Nobody forced the Hakhetts to use Google or Facebook. There are less intrusive alternatives, although they may be less convenient. But a central point of this book is that the fictional Hakhetts, and millions of their real-life counterparts, are getting a poor deal. In exchange for giving up a great amount of detail of our lives, we are not getting things that would make us safer, particularly the ability to identify ourselves, and make binding decisions, smoothly and securely. Nor do we have the ability to identify other people and authenticate their decisions. Not only are we liable to impersonation, we do not know if the people we are dealing with are real. It is rather as if we could travel free of charge, in return for handing over all our privacy to people who want to sell things to us, and sacrificing a great deal of personal safety. Like hitchhiking, we might do that when we are young, bold and carefree. More likely, if we knew what was really going on, we would chose a bit more safety for a rather higher cost.

It gets worse. Not only are the Hakhetts' online identities open to attack, they are also not useful for the two things they most need:

to be able to show who they are, and to see whom they are dealing with. Anyone who has Chip's login and password can pretend to be him. Anyone who has his colleagues' and friends' credentials can pretend to be them. Both sides are losers.

This quasi-anonymity is haphazard. Sometimes we are right to think that we are operating without scrutiny. Other times that may be a delusion – every keystroke, mouse-click and action on the internet may be tracked by someone hoping to make money from us, to whom we have given consent without really realising what we are doing. Sometimes we may have given our identity details to someone we trust, but who is in fact too careless to store them properly. Or we may give our identity details to someone we assume will keep them, but who scrupulously discards them. We think we are being observed, but we are not.

Either way, this messy anonymity is a pernicious anomaly. In the real world we engage in anonymous interaction only in very specific cases – at a Venetian-style masked ball, or perhaps in a darkened room in a swingers' club. In such cases, we know the etiquette, take appropriate precautions, and are ready to leave if we feel uncomfortable. But these are private spaces, entered for a specific purpose. In public spaces, the social consensus about anonymity is ambivalent. We are not forced to identify ourselves in everyday life, but must do so in some circumstances. Deliberate concealment of identity is frowned upon. In some countries driving a car with heavily tinted windows, or demonstrating in a mask, is actually illegal. Germany, Denmark and Canada are among the countries which ban demonstrators from covering their faces. France prohibits the public wearing of Islamic female dress: niqabs and burqas.[5]

Yet in most of what we do on the internet we are visitors to a masked ball, but without the ability to take our masks off, or to see if others are doing so. This undermines the concept of identity which underpins our political, legal and economic systems. Contracts are between physical or legal individuals. You cannot sue or prosecute someone with an assumed or invisible identity. Only real people can vote and be elected. Yet on the internet identities are transient, varied and dangerously weak.

To see the depth of the problem, compare it with what we expect on the roads. To drive a car, you need a driving licence and your vehicle must be roadworthy, insured and identifiable. None of those requirements is trivial. A foreign driving licence may be easy to obtain (or buy). A number plate can be faked. But if you get caught driving an untaxed, uninsured car, with fake number plates and without a valid driving licence, you face a criminal trial, a large fine and perhaps imprisonment.

At a masked ball, we at least have a choice. We can tell when people are wearing masks and when they are not. It is easy to remove masks, either unilaterally or by mutual agreement. The difference between a mask and a real face is instantly evident. And we have plenty of other clues to someone's identity besides their face: gait, size, dress and tone of voice. None of those apply to identity on the internet – at least not yet. An e-mail or a website contains only one obvious identifier: the address. Are we dealing with the real thing, or an impostor? For most users, it is hard to tell.

Anonymity has great uses. The ability to browse the internet anonymously, and to share information on it, is a boon for freedom lovers and the bane of autocrats. But anonymity should be a matter of choice both for the person concerned and those who have to deal with him. Chip should have the right, when he chooses, to identify himself unambiguously and definitively on the internet, just as he does in real life. Similarly, he should be able to identify the people he is doing business with to the same degree of confidence that he enjoys when he meets them face to face. The way that the system works now makes that difficult or impossible.

This is changing. Some countries, such as the Baltic republic of Estonia, have long had secure electronic ID systems. These still allow anonymity for those who want it – but they also make it possible to prove who you are and to verify the identity of those you are dealing with. Worries about a 'Big Brother' system have derailed the proposed system of ID cards in Britain. But digital ID does not need to be compulsory; it just needs to be attractive. In countries where it is in wide use, digital ID is voluntary, but the vast majority of the population chooses to be involved. Crucially, it puts the user in charge. You are not dependent on other people's whims about what to accept from you and what to disclose about themselves. With a secure digital ID you can prove who you are – whether to a government, to a business or to another person. In turn, this makes it much easier for them to trust you. It dispenses with the rigmarole of multiple passwords, security questions, dongles and other paraphernalia. If you lose your digital ID card, you can instantly disable it. It works only with two PIN codes, one for identification and one for authorisations. If you forget your codes, you apply for replacements – but you have to turn up in person. If you think they have been compromised, you can cancel them instantly. The combination is extremely secure.

For now, though, knowing who people really are online is hard. Someone wanting to defraud the Hakhetts can go to an internet cafe and pay cash to use a computer there. He can buy a 'smart-phone' – a modern mobile telephone with internet access – and a SIM card, giving him data and a phone number, all for cash. Some countries require identity documents before allowing the purchase of a mobile phone, but these checks are easily circumvented. Once the attacker has access to a computer (even someone else's) he can set up an e-mail account, or even (with a bit more trouble) a website. Much of this can be done for cash, or by using a pre-paid debit card, which can be bought over the counter at a newsagent's.

At no point, in most countries, would he have to show a passport or give any other verifiable information about his identity. Nobody thinks this is odd. The attacker would not be able to drive a car or pilot a plane, or travel abroad, or open a bank account, with this level of anonymity. But he can do whatever he likes on the internet – the electronic nervous system of modern life.[6]

The contrast is striking with other global systems, such as maritime and air transport. Identifying a ship or a plane outside national jurisdiction is fairly easy (though admittedly finding out who actually owns it is more difficult). If you are a new country wanting to become part of the world's postal or telephone system, or to open an international airport, you have to meet a whole range of difficult standards. You have to handle payments for the difference between incoming and outgoing mail or phone traffic, to run a suitable air-traffic control system, and so forth. These rules are enforceable because these systems are largely based on national boundaries. With a handful of exceptions such as satellite telephones (which have their own dialling code) every phone number is linked to a particular country.

Even the international high seas have a well-developed body of law and practice to stop dangerous shipping practices. In theory you can launch a hideously dangerous vessel with a toxic cargo, man it with slave labour and sail around the world's oceans. But you will find it hard to make money. Your rust-bucket will not be able to dock in a civilised port, or use routes such as the Suez and Panama canals. It may have difficulty gaining access to treaty-governed waters such as the Black Sea. If you start bothering other law-abiding vessels, you may find a rich-world navy paying you intense or even lethal attention. The internet has no body to enforce such standards – it has no central authority, just a loose and squabbling collection of non-profit bodies with contested legitimacy and limited enforcement powers (see Appendix Two).

In the real world, you are likely to know if you are involved in misbehaviour and our carelessness principally affects only ourselves. As the next chapter explains, one of the most difficult features of the computer age is that we may have no idea of the damage that our computers are wreaking on others. If Chip or Pin lose their wallets or purses, or keys, or allow intruders into their house, or fall prey to a confidence trickster, they bear the responsibility themselves. At most their families or house guests may suffer, too. But once the attack is on their computers, then many others are at risk as well.

4

Collateral Damage

Pin and Chip are at home when they receive an anxious phone call from a friend, wanting to know if Pin is all right. She insists indignantly that she is not in Penang, and not penniless. The friend reads out an e-mail she has received and Pin hurries to check her account on Chip's computer.

But when she tries to log into her Gmail account the password has changed. She tries to reset the password – a process that normally involves an e-mail which is sent to Chip's account. But no e-mail comes. The hijacker has changed the account settings so the e-mail goes elsewhere. Pin cannot get into her account to warn her friends to ignore the messages. She would like to e-mail them from Chip's account – but her contacts are kept on her Gmail account, so she cannot reach them. She has a few contacts stored on her phone – but that has gone on strike because it is locked out of her Gmail account, too.

When Chip checks his e-mail, he too reads this startling missive.

I'm writing this with tears in my eyes. I was in Penang, Malaysia, for a short holiday. Unfortunately we were mugged at the park near the hotel. Our cash, credit card and mobile were stolen but luckily we still have our passports.

We've been to the embassy and the police here but our flight leaves in less than 3hrs from now and the hotel manager won't let us leave until we settle the bill.

I'm emailing all my friends in the hope that someone can help.

XX Pin

A bit of thought suggests that this is a scam – and not just because Pin is in the next room talking to her friend on the phone. Hotels in civilised countries do not prevent people leaving before they have paid the bill (they take credit card details when you check in). But there is just enough detail to sound plausible. If Pin's phone has been stolen, there is no point calling it. The 'we' makes it sound as if Chip is there, too, so no point calling him either. It sounds all too likely that the embassy and police have not been particularly helpful. The admission that the supposed Pin is e-mailing everyone she knows, in a hurry, explains the lack of a salutation and the generic XX sign off. Anyone who is tempted to reply will be sending a message to the fraudster, who will then ask for a quick money transfer via Western Union. The cash will never be seen again.

The advantage of this sort of scam is that it can be automated. You can buy e-mail accounts with working logins and passwords on the internet, or crack them yourself using off-the-shelf software. Then you start sending messages. Even if only one in a thousand produces any money, it adds up to a nice hourly rate if you have access to hundreds of accounts and are sending thousands of messages a day.

Meanwhile, Pin is trying to work out what to do. Google does make it possible to recover an account, even if everything has been hijacked – Pin has to submit her previous passwords and phone numbers. But the process is necessarily slow and arduous – otherwise it would enable attackers to hijack accounts, instead of helping victims recover them. Unfortunately, Pin has not set up some of the security features that might help her. But while she wrestles with a problem she has never previously encountered, her friends are wiring money via Western Union to help her out. When she eventually recovers her account, she has a lot of explaining to do. She also feels duty bound to repay a couple of friends, including an elderly and cash-strapped aunt, who sent money she could ill afford.

Pin's e-mail address book can be scooped up and misused for other reasons, too. It can be analysed to see if she has any particularly valuable contacts who can be exploited in some other attack, perhaps on her employer, or its suppliers or customers, or other business contacts. In that case, the intruder is not trying to lock Pin out by changing her password. He just wants the ability to send and receive e-mails in her name. This can be done subtly – incoming

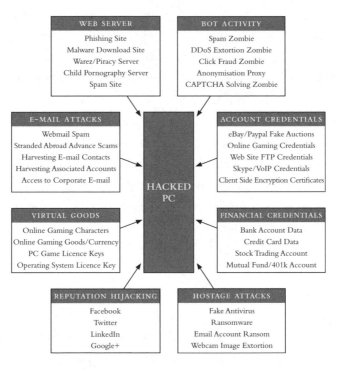

Figure 1 The uses of a hacked computer – in ruining your life, or other people's[1]

and outgoing e-mails can be instantly deleted and emptied from the trash. There is no need to change the password. In that case, Pin will not realise that someone is now able to impersonate her.*

The graphic on the previous page is based on the work of by Brian Krebs, an American computer security expert who runs an invaluable blog called 'Krebs on Security'. His diagram highlights all the uses to which a hijacked computer can be put, endangering both the owner and other people. He writes:

> nearly every aspect of a hacked computer and a user's online life can be and has been commoditised. If it has value and can be resold, you can be sure there is a service or product offered in the cyber-criminal underground to monetise it. . . . I haven't yet found an exception to this rule.

Almost everything on that diagram should be of concern to Chip and Pin Hakhett, though the crooks' prime target is the e-mail account. This is not just a way of sending and receiving messages. For many people it is the gateway to all their life online. Passwords and usernames for other services are sent to your e-mail. In much of the world, the e-mail address is (crazily) the single most important way of identifying someone. Far too many other forms of security, such as Apple ID (used for purchases on iTunes), Amazon accounts (used to buy anything), Facebook and Twitter accounts, and most other e-commerce applications, work at least in part via e-mail.

---

* There are clues: if she is sharp-eyed, she may notice a line at the bottom of the screen on her Gmail page telling her when someone last logged in to the account. If she clicks on 'details' she will find a screen showing the address of every computer which has recently logged in. If that shows a location she does not recognise, it will be a sign that someone else is using her account. But few people bother with such a level of scrutiny.

A more sophisticated version of the hijack comes if the attacker can perpetrate crimes in the Hakhetts' name, sending out spam from their genuine e-mail address – or using the messaging facilities in social media and networking sites such as Facebook, LinkedIn or Twitter. Such e-mails may be peddling dodgy goods, or spreading malware, with the added authenticity of coming from someone whom those receiving the e-mails are likely to trust. Or they may play more heavily on the presumed contact between them and the people in your e-mail address book. If you receive a message from a friend on Facebook, Twitter, LinkedIn or other social media site you may be more likely to overlook mistakes in grammar or curious turns of phrase. A simple message reading 'take a look at this' and a link can wreak devastation on those unwise enough to click on it.

If someone gets control of Pin's e-mail account, they have not just access to her communications, but also to a kind of time machine. He can look back through her sent mail, inboxes, junk mail, and 'trash' (waste bin) to see what she has been doing in past days, weeks and years. The attacker has an address book of far greater significance than its real-world equivalent: if Pin loses her old-fashioned leather-bound notebook full of scribbled addresses and phone numbers, it is inconvenient. But the lost property does not tell the finder or thief how often she writes to or telephones the people whose names are in it. And it does not allow someone to impersonate her. For Pin losing control of her e-mail account is like losing not only her address book, but also an unlimited supply of blank signed personal station-ery, plus details of every letter she has sent and received for months or years. Pin may be locked out of her account, facing a difficult or even impossible task to recover all this vital data, and warn her friends that she is being impersonated. Or (which can sometimes be worse) the intruder is stealthy – harvesting as much data as possible and biding his time until he can make the most of it.

All accounts linked to an e-mail have value and can be sold on criminal black markets. As Mr Krebs notes:

> One prominent credential seller in the underground peddles iTunes accounts for $8, and fedex.com, continental.com and united.com accounts for $6. Groupon.com accounts fetch $5, while $4 buys hacked credentials at registrar and hosting provider godaddy.com, as well as wireless providers att.com, sprint.com, verizonwireless.com, and tmobile.com. Active accounts at Facebook and Twitter retail for just $2.50 apiece . . . some crime shops go even lower with their prices for hacked accounts, charging between $1 to $3 for active accounts at dell.com, overstock.com, walmart.com, tesco.com, bestbuy.com and target.com, to name just a few.

Chip's accounts at shipping companies – UPS, DHL and FedEx – are particularly valuable to a fraudster. A whole criminal industry exists around buying expensive items on the internet using stolen or fraudulent credit cards, and having them shipped to addresses where accomplices then repackage them and send them off using stolen shipping company accounts. His account may be used to send a stolen computer, or drugs, from an address in Denmark, say, to Lithuania. The police may eventually come knocking on his door – but he will have little to show them except surprise. Another scam is to use a hijacked shipping account to send fake cheques to people, with an instruction to transfer some of the money back to the sender. Oddly, people fall for this. What they are actually doing is sending money to a total stranger in exchange for a bogus cheque that their bank will eventually reject. They are out of pocket, but the criminal cashes in. As with the 'penniless in Penang' scam, an important feature of these crimes is that even if the success rate is very low, the internet allows the crime to be automated on such a scale that it becomes lucrative.

Most security measures involve sending e-mails to confirm changes and to recover lost information. For example, if Pin or Chip forgets their password or login, the default setting for most of the websites and services they use is to send an e-mail either containing the password, or including a link where it can be reset. That may seem fine – but it is astonishingly sloppy given the ease with which an e-mail can be compromised. In that case the fraudster simply clicks on the link himself, and resets the password to one that he knows and the victim doesn't. When Pin tries to recover access to her account, at Amazon, or Apple, or wherever, her login and password are not recognised. Worse, the fraudster can change the e-mail to which the account is linked, change the security questions and change the main credit card.

When this happened to the Hakhetts, it created a Kafkaesque catastrophe, in which Pin and Chip tried in vain to explain that they were really themselves. When they managed to reach someone from Amazon by phone, they failed the security checks. Chip was asked for the last four digits of his credit card. He gave it – and was told it was incorrect (the fraudster had changed it). On another website, he was asked for his memorable word. That proved 'incorrect', too (it had been changed). Pin was asked to give the last four digits of her home telephone number – incorrect again (ditto).

It is as if the Hakhetts had come home to find themselves locked out of their house, and a party going on inside. But with a twist: not only does their front door key no longer fit, when they call the police they find they are unable to prove that it is their house: the land registry and electoral roll have been altered, too, and the people giving the party denounce them as impostors, even as they are drinking their wine, eating their food and wrecking their home.

But the Hakhetts' computers are at risk even if they maintain control of their e-mails. Just one careless or misplaced click can make the law-abiding couple accomplices to crime, by bringing their computers into a botnet. This remotely controlled network of computers – a network of 'bots', as in robots – is one of the most important concepts in security. Botnets are not always illegal or malevolent. There are reasons why you might want your computer to be under someone else's remote control – if you have programmed your computer to install software updates automatically, then you have in effect made it part of a botnet.

But for the most part botnets are an internet plague, largely overlooked by the owners of the infected computers. There is no easy real-world analogy. One way of understanding this is to think of a parasite which leaves its host alone in order to attack other victims. Examples of this in the natural kingdom would be the malaria parasite, which barely troubles its mosquito host, but uses it to reach its human victims. Like mosquitoes, botnets are a swarm. Each individual infected computer is only a tiny nuisance. But in thousands, or millions, they become a menace.

Another analogy would be if a terrorist planted a bomb in someone's car, in the knowledge that he would drive it unwittingly to the target destination. This happens more often in Hollywood thrillers than in real life. Imagine that someone can by automated means plant hundreds, thousands or even millions of identical bombs in the cars of unwitting strangers, and that they will never notice they are carrying these devices, and that they can be used not just once, but again and again. Imagine also that these bombs are infectious: if one person's car carries a bomb, then soon his friends and colleagues will have one, too.

That, in short, is what botnets are: vast networks of zombie computers which can wreak havoc on strangers, silently and invisibly, without their owners' knowledge. In his testimony to the Senate Judiciary committee, Leslie Caldwell of the US Department of Justice portrayed this danger in unvarnished terms.

> The threat from botnets – networks of victim computers surreptitiously infected . . . controlled by an individual criminal or an organised criminal group – has increased dramatically over the past several years. The computers of American citizens and businesses are, as we speak, under attack by individual hackers and organised criminal groups using state-of-the-art techniques seemingly drawn straight from a science fiction movie.[2]

The first big use of botnets is in swamping attacks on others. In the dirty world of British parliamentary by-elections, in which I spent some years in the early 1980s, it was possible to disable the opponent's campaign by placing a small classified advertisement in a local newspaper. This would offer a good quality used car for sale at a remarkably cheap price, and giving the victim's headquarters' telephone number as the one to call. Such an ad could be bought untraceably, paid for in cash over the counter at the newspaper office. The result would be hundreds (sometimes thousands) of incoming calls, which – in the days when a typical office had only one phone line – would make it all but impossible for the adversary to function. (A disadvantage of this tactic is of course that the other side could do it, too.)

A 'denial of service' attack is the online equivalent. The target is not a phone line, but a website or a server (a computer which runs a network or machinery). Instead of a few hundred phone calls, millions of bogus, automated requests for information swamp the target computer so genuine ones do not get through. This can happen as part of a political campaign, or as part of an extortion attempt, or out of sheer random malice. It is easy to do, and the defences are expensive. Anyone who has read Daphne du Maurier's story *The Birds*, or seen the eponymous film, can visualise the effect.[3] A single bad-tempered seagull is a nuisance. In large numbers, they are a disabling, even lethal menace.

In 'denial of service' attacks normal visitors to the website find a blank screen or an error message. The possible results range from the inconvenient to the catastrophic.

One such attack, mounted by extortionists, closed down Code Spaces, a company that hosted websites. When it declined to pay off the attackers, they extracted devastating revenge: a plaintive message on its website reads 'most of our data, backups, machine configurations and offsite backups were either partially or completely deleted'.[4] It has ceased trading. Among other victims of such attacks has been Feedly, which helps internet users collate updates from their favourite websites (in internet-speak an 'RSS news aggregator'), and the archiving service Evernote. A 'denial of service attack', also mounted by extortionists, meant that the company's customers were unable to gain access to their data.[5]

Such attacks are simple acts of criminality. But they can also be politically motivated. In June 2013 opponents of the ruling South African party, the African National Congress, knocked its website out with a 'denial of service attack', in protest at its support for the Zimbabwean dictator Robert Mugabe.[6] In 2012 a preposterous and amateurish anti-Islam film called *The Innocence of Muslims* prompted protestors to jam the websites of American banks. Political protest can easily shade into state-sponsored activity. For a country, a 'denial of service attack' on a wide front can feel like an act of war. Estonia was hit by such attacks in 2007 after it moved a Soviet-era war memorial from the centre of the capital, Tallinn, to a cemetery in the suburbs. The attacks which followed are often seen as the first example of what is often (but misleadingly) called cyber-warfare. Estonia's online banking system stopped working. Its government ministry websites were unavailable. The emergency phone numbers for fire, police and ambulance services were briefly unavailable.[7] This attack did not require sophisticated digital weapons or breaking into the victim's computer. Such attacks can be organised and paid for from far away, and they are hard if not impossible to attribute, because the attackers typically do not use their own computers. That would be far too cumbersome, conspicuous and costly. Instead, they steal other people's – or, to be precise, their computers' capabilities.

To see how difficult this is to counter, let us go back to the Hakhetts. Their computers could take part in such an attack, but entirely without their knowledge. Their passwords and logins would work as normal, their programs would load, and their data would not be harmed. Thanks to the botnet an invisible program is at work, whose job is not to steal money from Chip and Pin, or to block their computers, or to do anything else malevolent or noticeable. The aim is simply to purloin a tiny part of the computers' processing power, and a sliver of their internet connection, to serve a distant master.

The vast majority of the offending infected computers which engage in swamping attacks have innocent, unwitting owners. On each machine the botnet typically consumes only a tiny amount of electricity and computer processing power. The instructions – when to stop, when to start and whom to target – come in over the internet, all but invisibly, and usually leave no permanent trace. Even if the owner of the computer can be traced and notified, he has little incentive to clean up his computer. Nor does the internet service provider need to worry much if its clients have infected computers. The data being directed at the Estonians, or any other victim, is only a tiny share of the overall traffic.

All the effective ways of dealing with a swamping attack involve spending money, chiefly by buying or renting more powerful computers and a bigger connection to the internet (the equivalent in the real world of installing more phone lines). Other solutions include special scrubbers to filter out the bogus traffic. But the bill for these lands on the victim, not on the perpetrator and his countless, unwitting accomplices. Denial of service attacks using botnets are increasing in number, size, duration and sophistication. The latest twist is to hijack servers – the big computers of the kind that run websites. These have large amounts of processing power and can send lots of data to the internet.

As companies improve their defences, attackers become wilier. Swamping attacks now concentrate on the weakest point of the site, such as the little boxes where users type search terms or their passwords. Freeze those, and the whole site may go down. Another weakness buried deep in the architecture of the internet is the computers known as DNS (Domain Name System) servers. With the right tools, these can be tricked to fire huge quantities of bogus information around the system, jamming it.

The second big and crude use of botnets is to send other kinds of 'spam' e-mails. The 'Penniless in Penang' ones spewed out by Pin's hijacked account are just one kind, relating to a real person, from an otherwise real address, and with a time-limited and specific scam. Spam may also be junk mail promoting a real product or service (such as pharmaceuticals which should be available only on prescription). It can promote sinister and illegal products such as drugs or pornography. In both cases the product or service may truly materialise, or the money may be sent in vain. The e-mails can also contain links or attachments which, when clicked on, will infect other victims' computers – the equivalent of electronic letter bombs.

Spam can be sent from wholly fictitious addresses, and simply uses the power of the hijacked computer and its connection to the internet – in both cases the bigger the better. If the powerful servers at Pin's workplace are infected through her carelessness, they can be used to send these e-mails – millions of them, twenty-four hours a day, seven days a week. Nobody will write back to her – the address given in the e-mails is a fake and the links it contains have nothing to do with her employer. Those who open, read and act on these spam messages may if they are lucky get the dodgy products they order. Or they may be making a terrible mistake, opening themselves to a criminal attack in which their computer is an unwitting accomplice. Pin – and the IT people who run her company's network – may never see the program which is sending these e-mails. The only hint may perhaps be that their computers seem to be making heavy weather of things, running a bit more slowly than they should. Most users are unlikely to notice this. Unless they thoroughly disinfect their computers, it will continue indefinitely.

Cleaning up an infected computer is an arduous, intimidating and frustrating business.[8] Installing and updating anti-virus software may not be enough – the malware is most likely hiding as 'root-kit' – meaning that it conceals its activities from the rest of the machine, and subverts software that tries to find it. Installing a 'firewall' which alerts the user to anomalous incoming and outgoing traffic may help identify the source of the problem. But the main way of dealing with this kind of malware is to wipe the computer completely and install everything from scratch. Even that may not be enough when dealing with a sophisticated threat. The only completely safe way of proceeding is to throw away every electronic device (not just computers, but also printers, routers, storage devices, keyboards, etc.) and start again.

Botnets are a big and growing business. You can make money by infecting computers, and by acting as a broker: botnets can be rented by the hour, with whatever size and purpose the customer likes. These can be sending spam, or mounting swamping attacks – or can be customised to mount more sophisticated crimes. Older versions of software for use with botnets are typically available free, while more modern ones cost several thousand dollars (and come complete with aftersales service from the criminals who design and distribute them).

Between September 2011 and May 2014, another botnet called Gameover Zeus infected between 500,000 and a million computers and caused more than $100 million in financial losses, including a fraudulent $7 million bank transfer. This malware was sufficiently costly and damaging to prompt an unprecedented joint operation between the FBI and Microsoft.[9] Gameover Zeus was an unusual botnet in that it worked on a peer-to-peer (P2P) basis, rather like the Skype internet telephony service. In other words, it was more like a swarm of bees than an army of attackers under a single command. Instead of having a single central computer to run the network, command and control was shared among the infected machines. Microsoft's technical expertise helped unravel the intricacies of the P2P system, notify the users of the infected computers and help them clean their machines.[10] In June 2014 the Justice Department named the mastermind behind the network as a Russian citizen, Evgeny Bogachev.[11] At the time of writing he was on the FBI's Most Wanted list, but seemed in little danger of extradition from Russia.

Computers were infected through 'phishing' e-mails containing doctored attachments or links to infected sites which infected visitors with 'drive-by downloads'. As with the predecessor, Zeus, a 'key-logger' on infected computers, recorded passwords and other credentials typed into web browsers, and sent them to the attacker. Gameover Zeus, however, was more sophisticated. It could modify websites to trick victims into giving even more detailed credentials.

Whereas a legitimate banking website might ask a customer to provide the first and third digits in a code number, Gameover Zeus would modify the page (an attack known as 'web injects') so that it would demand the complete number. The user would think that the bank had simply changed its procedures, and trustingly provide the information – thereby making it easy for the attacker to impersonate him. Gameover Zeus also hijacked the victims' computers into taking part in other attacks, making them unwitting accomplices in creating misery for others.

Another example of this is when a hijacked computer can be used to help hackers probe other people's websites for weaknesses. This typically involves a kind of attack called an SQL injection, in which the attacker types a malevolent instruction into a web page. The simplest example of this comes from fiddling with the address at the top of your browser window. Every time you visit a website, your browser sends an address – for example, edward-lucas.com/contact would bring you to the page with my contact details. But this address may not just open a web page – it can also be used to send an instruction to the computer that runs the website.

https://www.google.com/search?q=sql+injection, for example, tells the Google server to do a search for the two terms sql and injection.

On a badly configured website, these instructions can be used to reveal information which should not be made public, either leaking information (such as all the passwords and usernames stored on the site), or else clues about other vulnerabilities which can be exploited. Or it can plant malicious code on the website so that anyone visiting it is at risk of infection.

The problem for the attacker is that finding these vulnerabilities is time-consuming. It may be necessary to try a great many combinations of instructions to find one that works. That is where hijacked computers come in. They do the work auto-matically. A botnet called 'Advanced Power', which Mr Krebs investigated in December 2013, appeared to have been working since May in that year.[12] It had infected 12,500 computers, and used them to scan websites for vulnerabilities, reaping a harvest of at least 1,800 pages. Here Pin and Chip's own browsing habits can be used to the attacker's benefit. Every site they visited can be probed for several potential vulnerabilities – and a report of them sent back to the botnet's owner. Neither of them will know that their computers are being used in this way. It does them no damage – but they are still aiding and abetting criminals, albeit unwittingly.

The Hakhetts' computers can also make money for an attacker if they are used to simulate a genuine customer. 'Click Fraud' is a form of internet crime which generates seemingly legiti-mate internet traffic for malicious or illegal reasons. Just over one third of all ads viewed on the internet are seen not by humans but by other computer programs.[13] In other words, one third of the money that advertisers are paying in the hope of attracting potential customers is wasted – and goes into the gangster-run underground economy. The profits can come in different ways. Some advertisers will pay a website owner a tiny amount for each time that a visitor to the site clicks on their advertisement. This creates a temptation for an unscrupulous website owner to generate a lot of bogus, artificial clicks. Again, the Hakhetts will not notice: only a thorough examination of their computer would show that an invisible browser window is hard at work in the background.

A more sophisticated fraud involves trying to hurt a competi-tor by clicking on a link which will require him to pay some-one. This is promoted by, among others, a criminal group called Goodgoogle (which obviously has nothing to do with the search

engine firm).[14] It exploits the way in which advertisements work
on the Google site. If you type in, for example, 'buy edward lucas
book' you receive not only the search results created by the giant
company's computers and algorithms but also some advertisements from bookshops. Prices for these vary. Advertisers will pay a
lot to be in first place. To illustrate, try a Google search for 'whip-
lash' and see the advertisements from law firms which sprout at
the top of the page. If you click on one of those links, the firm
which has posted the ad will pay Google.

To be prudent, advertisers also cap their daily spend, so that a
sudden eruption of clicks does not bankrupt them. For example,
Chip might pay so that anyone entering 'Chip Hakhett book'
into Google will see a link which allows people to order his
tome on executive psychology, *Sunshine in the Boardroom*, paying
him a small commission in the process. He has to pay a small fee
each time someone clicks on the advertisement – whether or
not they actually order the book. As Chip does not want unlimited liability, he sets a limit, perhaps a few thousand clicks, after
which the advertisement no longer appears and he no longer
pays.

That gives great scope to an unscrupulous rival. By automat-
ing a flurry of clicks, he can quickly exhaust Chip's budget. The
money has been wasted and customers will turn elsewhere. That
is the service that Goodgoogle offers, with the (slightly garbled)
marketing pitch: 'Are you tired of the competition in Google
AdWords that take your first position and quality traffic? I will
help you get rid once and for all competitors.' Prices range from
$80 to $1,000, paid for in untraceable digital currencies such as
Bitcoin.

Other frauds involving automated clicks abound: a particularly
clever one is to place blame on a rival company by staging a flurry
of clicks which make it look as though it is manipulating the system.

The rival will then be punished for the apparent abuse, when in fact it has done nothing wrong. But it will have difficulty proving its innocence: the botnet is untraceable without expensive forensic work (and possibly even with it). The network of hijacked machines could have been hired by anyone. In the rough world of internet justice the most likely suspect tends to end up with the blame.

These scams and crimes have the advantage that the cost of generating a click from a hijacked computer is almost nothing, but multiplied by many millions the impact is substantial. Hijacked machines also make it far harder to detect what is being done. Generating a huge number of bogus clicks from a single computer would be conspicuous. But doing so from a huge network of legitimate machines means the activity can be manipulated to look like a natural pattern.

The next form of remote-control attack is using the victim's computer to help make the attacker appear anonymous in some other form of malfeasance. Your machine's processing power and internet connection is used to give another computer an untraceable presence on the internet – useful for all manner of nefarious purposes such as pornography, trafficking illegal materials or fraud.[15] This capability is switched on and off remotely, and the effect on your computer's performance will most likely be negligible. But you are still an unwitting accessory to all manner of crimes.

A computer can also be hijacked to solve puzzles. Both Pin and Chip have come across the 'captcha'. This aims to distinguish between human beings and computers – not least to stop the kind of 'click fraud' outlined above ('captcha' stands for 'Completely Automated Public Turing test to tell Computers and Humans Apart')

The website you are visiting will ask you to type in the letters you see. For a human, reading the graphics above as 'smwm' is not hard. For a computer it is. This presents a problem for crooks. One way they can solve it is by hijacking other people's computers. Chip and Pin will notice this because their computers freeze briefly at odd moments, presenting a 'captcha' in a pop-up window which is labelled as a 'security check'. Perhaps with some puzzlement or irritation, they type in the answer and resume work a second or two later. This need not happen very often. It is most useful for the criminal, and seemingly of only trivial inconvenience for the Hakhetts. But they are the unwitting accomplice in a crime, just as surely as if you were being conscripted to help to try every combination on a combination lock.

The next group of attacks involve stealing credentials – the username and passwords – that the victim uses on sites that may be of interest to an attacker.

Both Pin and Chip have eBay accounts, which gives access to the online auctions staged there, either as a buyer or seller. Chip has not used his for years. It is linked to an expired credit card. That might seem of no value. On the contrary, it is extremely useful to a

Captchas typically look like this:

Figure 2 Licensed under Public domain via Wikimedia Commons - https://commons.wikimedia.org/wiki/File:Captcha.jpg#mediaviewer/File:Captcha.jpg

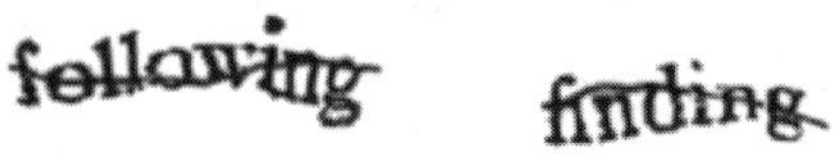

Figure 3 'Modern-captcha' by B. Maurer at English Wikipedia – own work. Licensed under Public domain via Wikimedia Commons - https://commons.wikimedia.org/wiki/File:Modern-captcha.jpg#mediaviewer/File:Modern-captcha.jpg

fraudster. Chip's account can be used to participate in or stage fake auctions. These can sell bogus goods and defraud buyers. After a lot of complaints, eBay will disable Chip's account, and he will have some explaining to do. But not for some time.

An even more powerful attack is to use stolen eBay accounts which have real credit card information to buy goods which can be sold elsewhere. In an attack in June 2014, criminals used more than a thousand stolen accounts at StubHub, a ticket reseller owned by eBay, to make $1 million.[16] The tickets, to big sporting events, shows and concerts, were sold by touts for cash, which was then laundered.

If the Hakhetts, or anyone using their computers, have played an online game, then your credentials can be valuable. Pin's nephew Roger is an avid gamer, and when he comes to stay she thinks nothing of letting him use the laptop. For convenience, he stays logged in. But if her computer is hijacked, every identity on it is prey to attackers. Roger's character may be used in some other scam. His hard-won points can be sold to another gamer. In the illegal marketplaces for stolen credentials game accounts fetch between $5 and $1,000.[17]

Chip's website is another target. He posts pictures of himself, links to speeches he has given and other promotional material there. He does this using File Transfer Protocol – FTP in computer jargon. This is an old-fashioned and rather insecure way of fetching and sending data to a remote computer over the internet. But if Chip's FTP credentials are stolen, an attacker can plant malicious software on his website. He will never know. The pictures, videos and other material look no different. But any sort of image, graphic or similar material on a website can be used for concealment. This is called 'steganography', from a Greek word meaning 'concealed writing'. A picture which appears on a website is a computer file – containing a string of data determining the colours, size and content of the image. But the file can contain other data, too – for example, something that

installs malware on the computer, or communicates with an existing program, giving it instructions. The web browser obediently
loads the image and to the user all will appear normal. A researcher
called Jérôme Segura found an example in February 2014 in which a
seemingly innocent picture of a sunset, once loaded on the victim's
computer, was used to steal banking credentials and empty the
victim's bank account.[18] In short, once an attacker has control of a
website he can plant malware – perhaps disguised as a graphic, or
some other small feature such as a clock – meaning that an innocent
third party visiting the site risks a devastating infection.

Both Pin and Chip have Skype on their computers. As with
e-mail, this can be used to send authentic seeming messages,
to every contact. Such e-mails – and the links to toxic sites, or
malware-laden attachments that they carry – are also much more
likely to get round the spam filters that now come as standard in
most e-mail software.

Chip has set up his Skype account so that it can call real phone
numbers, paying a modest amount every couple of months for the
privilege. He has set this to 'auto top-up' so that his credit card
is automatically charged when his balance drops below a certain
level. But this is the equivalent of leaving his wallet open. For a
start, the hijacked computer can be used to dial expensive numbers,
which pay the owner every time someone calls them. The bill goes
to Chip, the money to the fraudster.

Chip's hijacked computer can also be used to generate spam
phone calls (also called 'robocalls'). These peddle goods and
services (often bogus ones) over the phone, typically with automated messages, in defiance of laws which try to prevent unwanted
telemarketing. Those dialled may be his friends, or just random
strangers. These phone calls cost Chip money, too.

A final kind of this sort of attack is theft of security information held on your computer. This can be complicated – it is a

fair bet that few lay users of computers are familiar with x.509 security certificates – but the principle is simple. For all sorts of interaction on the internet we need to make sure that the data we send and receive are encrypted. Otherwise anyone monitoring our internet traffic (for example, by snooping on our home internet connection) could read what we do as easily as if it were on a postcard. As I explain later, the system of setting up secure channels of communication on the internet has huge flaws. But in essence it involves two keys – one held by the website you are accessing, the other held by you. By using both keys, you create a kind of secure tunnel between the computers at each end. Compromising your computer means that one set of keys is stolen – which can make it easier for an attacker to see anything you do online. That can be a springboard for a whole range of other crimes and nastiness.

So far these attacks have not cost much money, if any. But the next category – involving your financial data – spells disaster for the Hakhett family. Their credit card numbers (the long one embossed on the front) plus the farcically short three-digit card security codes printed on the signature strip create a potent combination. In a shop or restaurant, a card user must enter a PIN into a terminal before a transaction goes through (or in some cases provide a signature). But online, the Hakhetts just have to give the three-digit code to identify themselves. That is easy to steal. During an online purchase, Pin enters her card details in what she thinks is a secure website. Oddly, the site freezes and she starts again, mildly cross at the inconvenience. What she does not realise is that her credit card number and the PIN, plus her address and other details have been stolen, either because her computer is infected, or because she is visiting a bogus website. It is as if she had just handed her card over to the fraudster.

Tighter procedures have made the most blatant scams more difficult. If Pin or Chip order something unusual over the internet, or want it delivered to an address they have not previously used, then the computers at the credit card company may sound an alarm. They may require extra verification – for example, producing a list of addresses and asking which if any is a real, previous residence. The company may phone to ask if the transaction is legitimate. Such precautions make some kinds of fraud harder, but not others. Chip does not check his credit card statements properly. Pin does, but ignores unexplained charges below a certain level. The $49.95 annual 'membership' she is being charged by a mysterious site in Florida is not the leftover from a nice holiday which she vaguely thinks she ought to cancel. It is a lucrative racket. Multiplied by tens of thousands of compromised credit cards, those charges add up to a nice sum for the attacker.[19] If Pin does complain to her credit card company, she will get her money back. But for small sums, many people do not bother. In another scam Malaysian criminals, armed with nothing more than a shed, an internet connection and a good quality printer, placed a tempting sounding job advertisement, using the applications to harvest a wealth of personal data. They then used the applicants' details to open bank accounts, form companies, submit false accounts and claim tax refunds. This had earned them £220,000 before they were arrested in 2012.[20]

The value-destruction in crime is colossal. Trading in stolen goods is illegal, so expensive goods are bought for full price with fake credit cards, but then sold at a discount of 50 per cent or more.[21] But a gang in New York indicted for using stolen store-card accounts, obtained with insider help, to buy luxury goods at Saks Fifth Avenue got round that – they returned the stolen goods to the shop and exchanged them for gift vouchers, which are much closer to cash.[22]

But these are the tiny minority of cases where the authorities have actually managed to get to grips with what is going on. Most online fraud is never prosecuted; the banks, credit card companies and retailers who are defrauded simply regard the cost of crime as a business overhead. Among the public, complacency abounds, thanks to the extensive legal protection given to the card user (who in America is liable only up to a rarely collected $50).

Credit card companies have sophisticated algorithms to spot sudden, unusual spending patterns. But bank accounts are less well protected.

If someone uses the Hakhetts' online banking details, it is as if Pin or Chip made the transaction. This is inherently unfair. If someone puts on a wig, goes into a bank and takes out money from Pin's account using her signature, she has at least a chance of proving that it was not her. If her alibi stands up, then the bank is at fault for not having spotted the impostor, and she will get her money back. But if something similar happens online, she usually have no recourse. Banks have shifted the responsibility for spotting fraud from themselves to the customer – a good example of how computers have eroded rights we once took for granted.

Pin fell foul of a typical online fraud: a bogus e-mail, seemingly from her bank but in fact from a fraudster, well-formatted and peppered with convincing looking logos and banking jargon. The message read:

Dear Megabank Customer

In order to make your online experience even more secure, we have introduced a new security feature which allows us to detect unusual activity on your online account.

Please login **here** to activate this feature and update your account.

Please note that accounts not activated within 24 hours of this notice will be suspended for security reasons.

Yours sincerely

Nancy Turner

Nancy Turner
Head of Customer Communications
Megabank internet banking

As with the 'penniless in Penang' e-mail, there are some clues in this message that all is not well. It does not give a phone number. Closer scrutiny of the 'from' field in the e-mail might show that it did not in fact come from 'no-reply@megabank.com' but from a quite different address.

It is well-crafted nonetheless. It tells a plausible story and creates a sense of urgency. Pin clicks on the link, and sees what appears to be her bank's website. Again, if she were looking closely, she might see that the address is subtly different. The security certificate (if she knew how to check it) does not come from a reputable source and is missing some vital details. But she trustingly types in her username and password – which is now in the hands of the fraudsters.

Minutes later they are looting her bank account. It is as if she had simply allowed the keys to her car to be copied, instantly and irretrievably. Financial catastrophe looms. Loss of online banking credentials is far worse than losing your ATM card and PIN. In that case the thieves are limited by daily withdrawal limits. Stolen credit cards can be blocked and their victims are usually reimbursed for anything spent on the card after the loss has been notified. But bank accounts are less well protected. Individuals and companies alike can be ruined if their bank accounts are drained. Unless they can prove that the bank was negligent, they may never get their money back.

Pin should be protected by some new bank security rules, which send a text message to her phone, which she has to type into the website before a new payee can be created. Her bank has incorporated that. But unfortunately, the thieves are one step ahead. When she was logging in to the bogus site, it asked her for her mobile phone number as a 'security check'. When she entered this number, her phone buzzed: it was an SMS, purportedly from the bank, asking her to click on a link in order to 'update' her mobile banking software. Her screen went dark for a while, and then her phone continued as normal.[23]

But what actually happened was catastrophic. The link Pin clicked installed malware on her phone. It now intercepts and redirects her text messages. Those from Chip, Roger and her friends go to her as normal, so she does not notice anything wrong. But those from the bank go to the fraudster, who now has everything he needs to empty her bank account. First, he logs in using Pin's credentials. Then he starts spending Pin's money. One option is simply to transfer money to an account he controls. But he will have to empty it quickly, before the authorities finally start investigating. Another option is to buy goods online and have them shipped to another address. But many online stores no longer dispatch goods to foreign addresses, especially to countries which have been used by criminals, typically in the former Soviet Union and West Africa. A whole criminal industry has grown up around this, involving people who will accept goods sent from a stranger and for a modest fee ship them abroad.

The estimable Mr Krebs has tracked down a real-life example of this, while investigating profsoyuz.biz, a (now dormant) Russian-language site which appeared to provide services to people wanting to turn stolen financial credentials into cash.[24] He spotted that a credit card belonging to a woman called Laura Kowaleski was being used to buy a toy for $189, plus $56 in shipping. She had already noticed the bogus transaction and was in the process of contacting the police when Mr Krebs called her. The toy – a Lego set – was sent via FedEx to a thirty-seven-year-old man in Los Angeles called Oscar Padilla, who had responded to an online job advert and believed he was working for Transit Air Cargo, a legitimate shipping company in California. In fact he was working for criminals, who had created the site transitac.com, whereas the legitimate company is transitair.com. Moreover, he did not notice that the e-mails he received from his manager came from the slightly unlikely transitaircargoinc@gmail.com. He was promised $1,000 for his first month of 'work' which involved sticking pre-paid labels on the packages he received, and sending them off, with a $2,500 salary thereafter.

Before Pin's bank allows a new payee to be created, it sends an SMS to her phone and asks her to type in the code it contains. That, the bank assumes, is a strong security precaution – it is quite unlikely that a thief will have both the security details needed to log into a customer's account, and also the customer's phone. But this thinking is out of date. The thief has hacked Pin's phone, so that the message with the security code never reaches her – instead it goes to the fraudster, who types it in as requested. He then empties Pin's account.

When Pin finds out what happens, she is distraught. Not only is her personal current account empty, but so is the joint household account she runs with Chip, and also a savings account she has opened for her nephew Roger. In all, many tens of thousands of pounds have gone. But her bank is unsympathetic. The transfers were made in accordance with the rules. If she gives away her banking details, it is not the bank's fault. They sent the right codes and demanded the right passwords. They are no more to blame than if Pin's post is intercepted, they argue. But this argument is disingenuous. If a chequebook is stolen from the mail, a customer like Pin – in most cases – is not liable for any resulting fraud. When the theft is of electronic data, she is. Her gullibility in clicking on a link may seem like a minor lapse, but it has major consequences.

Clearly a crime has been committed, but the police are not much help. They have a lot on their plate. They may track down one of the 'mules' used by the fraudsters – someone like Mr Padilla in California. But these people, who shift money and goods for the criminals, are rarely prosecuted. The most likely outcome is that their credit rating is damaged.

A far stronger standard involves the use not of messages but of physical objects, such as card readers that generate a code. If only Pin were an Estonian, she would be a lot richer. The lucky residents of that Baltic country use a government-issued ID to identify themselves in online banking, and to authenticate transfers (as outlined on page 227–38).

The next category of attack involves direct misuse of your computer for extortion. One of the most insidious forms is rogue anti-virus software, sometimes known as scareware or rogueware. This is the real-world equivalent of a crooked locksmith – someone who comes to your house claiming to improve its security, but actually sabotages it, either so that he can rob you or so that he can sell keys to other criminals.

Anti-virus software is widely available free of charge. Installed on a clean computer and regularly updated it plays a useful role in scanning your machine regularly for odd or sinister behaviour. It can prevent you installing malevolent programs or opening toxic e-mails (the two main means of infection). In order to function, these programs have a lot of power over your computer, rather like a security guard who is able to visit every room in a building.

Rogue software uses that power in order to rob you or ruin your privacy. Chip's computer displayed a convincing seeming warning box which appears on his screen, telling him that his machine was infected because of 'pornographic material' and asking him to install some 'security software'. Being a busy, gullible and rather guilty man, he hurriedly clicked where requested and ignored warnings produced by his computer.[25]

That was a mistake. The 'rogueware' disabled Chip's anti-virus software (which was in any case not up to date, and therefore not working properly). It also prevented him from getting help. Even if he wanted, he could not install new anti-virus software. If he tried to delete the new software, his computer would not let him: the buttons he wanted to click would refuse to work.

The business model behind this is based on a kind of affiliate marketing scheme, in which the people who push the rogue software are paid a commission for each successful installation and a share in the proceeds of any subsequent looting. This can be highly lucrative. A study a few years ago showed that members of such a scheme could make $150,000 in ten days.

Once the software is on Chip's computer, it gets to work. He does not use online banking, so his finances did not meet Pin's fate. Instead, the attackers did something potentially worse.

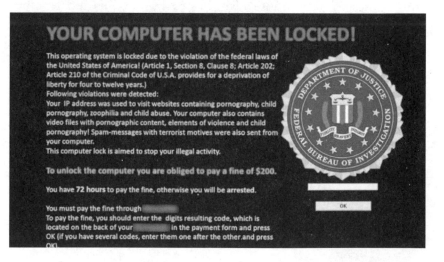

Chip was guilty, cross and baffled. Yes, he had looked at pornographic websites – but nothing illegal and certainly no child pornography. On the other hand, his business was crippled without files on the computer. It contained his calendar, e-mail, customer list and all the coaching materials he had developed over many years.

Chip poured himself a large whisky and considered his options. He did not want to go to the police. Supposing someone, or something – he was unclear about how these things worked – had actually planted something illegal on his computer. That would lead to shame and perhaps prosecution. He called a friend who fiddled around with the computer but to no avail. He used his laptop to search for the wording of the warning notice on Google. Clearly he was the victim of a scam. Clearly he would not get his data back unless he paid. He got his credit card, and after some tedious false starts, managed to buy $200 of digital currency, which he sent to the address provided. Shortly afterwards an e-mail, in slightly broken English, appeared on his screen, giving a long password: NRaAndcnyaBsl1taaCdk1eitWt.

He typed it in. His computer whirred. His files were again open and accessible. Chip poured another whisky and breathed a sigh. He had got off lightly. But he had also encouraged the wrongdoers in their trade. If nobody ever paid a ransom, the criminals would give up.

The best-known form of ransomware is called Cryptolocker, which locked victims' computers and told them they had three days to pay a ransom (paid in untraceable digital currency such as Bitcoin) ranging between $300 and $750. Between mid-2013 and May 2014 Cryptolocker infected more than 260,000 computers worldwide. Victims included the police department in Swansea, Massachusetts, which paid some $750 to recover its investigative files. A Pittsburgh insurance company refused to pay and spent $70,000 on recovering its data. A business in North Carolina was not so lucky. It refused to pay, sacrificing its most important data (despite hiring a computer security company). It lost $80,000 and told the FBI it might have to lay off some workers as a result.[26] An analysis of the scam by Dell, the computer manufacturer, estimated that the criminals responsible made $30 million in 100 days.[27]

Earlier versions of Cryptolocker are now vulnerable. In an interesting twist of events in August 2014, security vigilantes hacked into the criminals' computers and stole (or abstracted) the keys used to lock the victims' files. Two security companies now offer a free online service for victims hoping to decrypt their files.[28] New versions of ransomware are even harder to deal with.

Ransomware can freeze almost anything that people will pay to protect. Simply locking someone out of their e-mail account can be enough to make them pay up, particularly if the demand comes with a warning that within twenty-four hours all the contacts and e-mails will be irrevocably deleted. This is the online equivalent of a real-world extortionist who changes the locks on your house. He then dangles the new keys in front of you – and says that if you don't pay up, he will throw them in the river. Faced with such a stunt, you would in most countries be able to call the police. Online, you can't.

As with other kinds of ransomware, this kind of extortion is almost wholly automated. The criminal will be attacking tens of thousands of machines simultaneously. All he has to do is buy a list of e-mails online for a few dollars, and load the file into a program (also available easily) on his computer. He either drafts or copies a convincing sounding e-mail (for example, one which says 'next year's proposed salaries – please comment', and includes the toxic software in an attachment). Then he presses a button and sits back. The computer pumps out e-mails by the million. Perhaps one in a thousand, or one in ten thousand, people are foolish enough to click on the link. But once they do, their computers freeze and they are presented with the ransom demand. Once they decide to pay, the money, paid via some form of untraceable electronic cash, arrives in the crook's account. All he has to do is to count it and move it somewhere safe. If he is running an 'honest' scam, he will also send the decryption key so that his victims get their data back.

A final kind of extortion is closer to old-fashioned blackmail. It involves taking control of the camera on your computer (and perhaps the microphone). Most modern laptops have a built-in camera (often called a webcam) and there is no easy electronic way of making sure it is not working (one old-fashioned way of disabling it is to put a yellow sticky 'Post-it' note over it).

Having hijacked the webcam and camera, the criminal can try to catch the victim in a compromising position (perhaps triggered by noticing that he is visiting a pornographic website). Chip is meticulously careful about his habit. He makes sure he is alone in the house and draws the curtains before he starts indulging in sexual fantasies. But he does not bother to cover up his webcam. An e-mail demanding a payment, and threatening to send pictures of him enjoying a pornographic video to Pin would probably bring him to pay up instantly. This is an unpleasant crime, but it has a big disadvantage from the perpetrator's point of view. It cannot easily be automated. You may be able to turn on thousands of webcams, and have them record huge amounts of material – but the vast majority of it will be innocuous. Searching for something with the potential to embarrass, and working out how to use it to extract money, requires human intelligence. For most criminals on the internet, the defining feature of an attractive business is that the computer should do all the work.

A more promising crime is stealing credentials to social media and networking sites such as Facebook, LinkedIn and Twitter. The aims can vary. One is spam, of the kind discussed above. The terse and informal style of social media messages makes them particularly easy to fake: a message reading 'seen this pic? t.co/qwerty' gives few clues to authenticity. An e-mail, with its longer format, offers more to scrutinise before you choose to believe it. Another aim is extortion. If your social life depends on Facebook, you may be prepared to spend some money to regain your account. You may also be willing to pay to stop someone spreading lies about you. But the account may be valuable for other reasons.

As mentioned in the Introduction, short, snappy Twitter 'handles' (nicknames) can be worth a lot and are in scarce supply. Naoki Hiroshima has one of the best: '@N'. Or at least he had. As mentioned earlier, Mr Hiroshima had turned down an offer of $50,000 for it, but an attacker, exploiting some security flaws in other companies' procedures, managed to seize control of Mr Hiroshima's websites, Facebook account and other parts of his online life. He then warned him that unless he handed over his Twitter handle, he would arrange for the websites to be destroyed. Mr Hiroshima complied.[29] Only after he wrote about the scandal did Twitter intervene and restore his property.

A similar attack happened in 2012 against Mat Honan, a journalist.[30] In the space of an hour, he wrote, his 'entire digital life was destroyed':

My Google account was taken over, then deleted. Next my Twitter account was compromised, and used as a platform to broadcast racist and homophobic messages. And worst of all, my AppleID account was broken into, and my hackers used it to remotely erase all of the data on my iPhone, iPad, and MacBook.

The missing files included, among other things, irreplaceable photos of deceased relatives and his daughter's early years. This was not random hooliganism. The criminal simply wanted to play pranks using his @mat Twitter handle. He was eventually able to recover much of the data, thanks to speedy and well-informed remedial action.

Next come things stored on your computer which are worth money elsewhere. These could include online gaming credentials, mentioned above (such as characters who have built up points which can be used), and also the digital keys used to access paid-for software. If you buy software, you will be given a long key to show that you have paid for the programs. This can be on the back of the disc (if you buy it in physical form). You have to type it in to show that you are the legal owner of the software and have the right to install it on your machine. But for just that reason it can be valuable for someone trying to pirate the software (i.e. to copy it illegally).

In the real world we take great care, with procedures developed over hundreds of years, to make sure that fraud like this is kept to a minimum. Important transactions require the involvement of lawyers or notaries, who have a legal duty to make sure that the person they are dealing with is indeed who he claims to be, and that he really does have the title to the property he is selling. In the haphazard world of the internet, your fate, and those of others, hangs – with scandalous danger – on the slender thread of your access to an e-mail account. And as we shall see, that is now a matter not only of individual security, but of the fate of nations.

5

The Geopolitics of the Internet

Computer networks are a great leveller. Complex criteria of trust-worthiness, familiarity and predictability give way to simple binary questions: are the 1s and 0s in the right order to make a transistor switch one way or another? And so it was that in the 1980s some ingenious West German computer enthusiasts, hoping to raise money to pay for cocaine and high living, were able to gain access to some of the most secure computer networks in the United States on behalf of the Soviet KGB, in an episode known as the 'Cuckoo's Egg' attack.[1] With more sophisticated tools, but exploit-ing similar weaknesses, thirty years later a bunch of Chinese mili-tary hackers, known as APT1 (of whom more later), were also able to run riot through some of America's most important computers and networks, involving what officials say is the theft of intellectual property to the tune of $300 billion.[2]

In the real world either stunt would have been much harder. Defenders have an inherent advantage over attackers. The more steel, concrete and guns you have, the harder it is for an outsider to breach your security. But on the internet money and power count for less, and other factors count for more. The West German hack-ers in the mid-1980s did not have great technical skills. They did not spend large amounts of money. They certainly did not need

to use physical force. Their main assets, like their Chinese counterparts thirty years later, were persistence, ingenuity, the weakness
and complacency of their targets – and invisibility.

Lack of retribution is the modern-day equivalent of the Ring
of Gyges – the magical Greek token mentioned in the introduction, which confers invisibility. Plato could not have foreseen the
internet, but he was all too aware of the weak foundations of moral
behaviour. What would we do, he wondered, if we were able to
do wrong with impunity? Would our moral instincts keep us from
misbehaviour, even if we faced no danger from doing so? In the
real world, retribution follows attribution: if you attack someone,
they notice, and will respond if they can to deter or punish you.
On the internet, distance is irrelevant: your attacker can be on the
other side of the world. Most victims of attacks do not notice they
have been attacked, and when they do find out that something is
amiss, they do not know exactly what has happened or who has
done it.

In the Cuckoo's Egg case it was a tiny accounting anomaly that
launched an unusually stubborn young researcher down the long
and frustrating trail which would eventually unearth the hackers'
work – usually regarded as the first attack waged by one country
against another's computers. And it was only when an exasperated
American government decided to go public with its investigation
of the Chinese attack that the Western public began to realise the
full extent of the efforts being mounted against them.

A second feature of attacks on networks and computers, true at
the dawn of the cyber age and perhaps even more important now,
is that the hardware and software were not designed to be secure.
We would never build a bullion repository out of cheap crumbly
concrete and flimsy metal. But we rely on gimcrack chip design
and spaghetti software even for our most vital computer systems,
mostly because we have no alternatives. The academic networks

which the KGB hackers used to attack America were designed to help researchers to collaborate, not to keep secrets safe. Surprisingly little has changed since then in the way the internet works. This makes everyone vulnerable to attack – but the strong have more to lose than the weak.

These factors level the playing field. The underdog can threaten, challenge and steal from the strong and rich in a way that would be unimaginable in the physical world. Autocratic countries do it better than democratic ones. The more opportunistic and unscrupulous you are, the easier it is to use the internet to attack others. The more constrained you are by bureaucracy, legality and public opinion, the harder it is.

In recent years this has tended to favour rising powers over established ones. China in particular, which has mounted the greatest espionage operation in history, sees electronic spying as a crucial part of its plan to overhaul the West. That, in many Chinese eyes, is justifiable. The West despoiled and colonised China, and showed no compunction in stealing Chinese intellectual property in past centuries – such as the secrets of sericulture (silk making). But this is little comfort for Western companies which fear that they are going out of business because of the systematic plunder of their most closely guarded commercial secrets.

Three hundred billion dollars is a Fort Knox-size lump of money. But China would be unlikely to deploy its spies to attack the bullion depository where the United States stores a large part of its gold reserves. It is not a tempting target. Built with 16,000 cubic feet of granite, 4,200 cubic yards of concrete, 750 tons of reinforcing steel, and 670 tons of structural steel, it has armed guards and admits no visitors. If anyone did trick their way in, it is hard to see what they would do: gold is heavy and hard to move. An armed attack on Fort Knox is all but unimaginable, and the US Treasury Department, which runs the bullion depository, devotes little thought to that contingency. By the time enemy tanks are blasting at the gates, the United States will have other problems. But the US Treasury worries a great deal about attacks on the US banking system. In an exercise named 'Quantum Dawn' in 2013, the department organised a war game in which hackers managed the equivalent of breaching Fort Knox – getting into the secure networks of banks and government agencies.[3]

A similar exercise in Britain, involving dummy attacks by a team of hackers, shocked the Bank of England, which found that its networks were nothing like as secure as it had believed. Waking Shark II, as it was called, was a three-day exercise which explored a 'concerted cyber-attack against the UK financial sector by a hostile nation state' aimed at 'causing significant disruption/dislocation within the wholesale market and supporting infrastructure'. The final day of the exercise coincided with the so-called 'triple witching' day, when three kinds of financial contracts, for stock index futures, stock index options and stock options all expire on the same day. An anodyne official report gives only a diluted flavour of what the participants discovered.[4] But the UK financial system was subjected to a panoply of disruption. These included DDoS (swamping) attacks, which caused websites and other internet-facing systems to be 'unresponsive or intermittently available'; attacks of the kind that hit Sony, penetrating the firms networks for 'disruptive and destructive' purposes; corruption of the data for share prices at the end of the day, affecting overnight risk and margin calculations; disruption of the perpetrator clearing processes for bonds, which produced 'significant liquidity and funding issues'; and disruption of the bank payment systems. The exercise highlighted a number of weaknesses – not least that none of the participants remembered to contact the law-enforcement authorities.

Whether such an attack in real life would be perpetrated by pranksters, criminals, activists or the Chinese government is not the main point. For a start, these categories are not mutually exclusive. The attacks on American computer networks in the 1980s were carried out by hackers who were neither hardened criminals, nor people of strong political convictions – they had stumbled on something which they thought might be lucrative, and eventually made contact with the KGB through East Berlin. Nowadays a terrorist group or foreign government trying to disrupt the US financial system might use criminals or activists. Gangsters trying to steal money or extort a ransom from banks can buy in legitimate expertise from outside. The same people may work for a business that does jobs for governments, while also engaging in criminal activity.

Cuckoo's Egg – the Soviet-sponsored attack by West German hackers on American computers in 1986 – highlights dilemmas and weaknesses that have barely changed thirty years later, and also many ways in which the defenders' job has got a lot harder. Just as with the most breaches nowadays, the intrusion by the Cuckoo's Egg hackers went undetected for many months. It was discovered not thanks to millions of dollars' worth of research and detective work, but to a chance discovery and a notable amount of personal effort.

In August 1986 a young astronomer called Clifford Stoll noticed a tiny ($0.75) discrepancy in the billing for time on the computers at his workplace, the Lawrence Berkeley Laboratory in California. Computers were in those days rare beasts, and time spent on them was billed to the user. But Mr Stoll noticed that slightly more time was being used than billed. It was a tiny clue, and there was no particular reason to be suspicious. No classified work took place at the lab. Mr Stoll had no security clearance – indeed, he was rather suspicious of government, big business and the intelligence services. But he objected to the idea that an outsider was trespassing on the trust of the academic community. At his own expense, with the disapproval of his bosses and with precious little help from the government agencies from which he sought help, Mr Stoll organised one of the most impressive pieces of detective work in the history of computing. Over the next ten months he tracked the mysterious electronic intruder – which initially he assumed to be just one person, though in fact there were several. He also assumed the culprit was a student prankster, motivated perhaps by the desire to get free time on the computer, or simply by the satisfaction of breaking the rules.

But whoever the malefactor was, he was skilled at covering his tracks. Mr Stoll proceeded cautiously. He did not disable the intruder's access. Instead he tried to examine his methods and motives. He hooked up a printer to the network, which printed out, line by line, details of his comings and goings. Mr Stoll made no mention of his enquiries in electronic messaging – it was clear that the intruder was reading all such material to see if he had been spotted. It also became clear that this was not the work of a normal prankster. The uninvited guest was only mildly interested in Lawrence Berkeley. But he was using the laboratory's connections to other computer networks to move around the world, not just America but far afield, such as military bases in Japan and Germany. His targets were military networks and those at organisations involved in classified technological research, such as missile-defence work.

Over ten months, Mr Stoll and his allies saw the intruder attack about 450 computers and successfully get into thirty of them. Though a competent programmer, the attacker did not employ sophisticated new means. The intruder simply used a range of existing flaws and holes in the software to see if they would work. If one failed in one place, he tried another approach or another target.

The combined blunders of the people who used and managed the networks, and of the people who sold them equipment, meant that the intruders' chances of success were good. For example, many networks allowed outsiders to log in with usernames such as 'anonymous' and passwords such as 'guest'. Even those using slightly stronger security were vulnerable. Having broken into the network, the first target of the intruder was typically the file containing the encrypted passwords. He then used a 'dictionary attack' to see what they were.* He then had access to every set of credentials used on the network. The intruder no longer had to break in – he could simply impersonate a legitimate user.

But tracking down the source of the intrusion was hard. Whoever the attacker was, he was gaining access to the Lawrence Berkeley network by leapfrogging between the telephone system and computer networks. In those days it was possible to connect two computers over a telephone by using a device called a modem. Speeds were low, but the flexibility was great. A modem would work almost anywhere in the world, and could call any phone in the world. Crucially, most networks which were fitted with modems left them unsupervised. The assumption was that only those with the correct login and password would be able to gain access to the network via the modem. But there was nothing to stop someone dialling up hundreds or even thousands of times and trying different combinations. Once in, users could, on some networks, then dial out. In this case, the attackers seemed to have dialled into the University of Bremen, and then used its connections to other computer networks

---

* If your password is 'Wednesday' it may be stored in encrypted form, say as 5xGk71y92. If an intruder breaks into the network, he can steal the encrypted passwords and the encryption program. Then all he needs to do is put every word in the dictionary into his copy of the program and look at the results. If he wants your password, he will look for 5xGk71y92 and see it was 'Wednesday' – and then use it, together with your login, somewhere else. It is not much harder for him to check all the words in the dictionary including variations such as Wednesd@y and Wednesd@y01. So please never, ever, use a password based on a single word in a dictionary, or a variation of it, or on anything else (such as a postcode) which is stored on a list somewhere on the internet. And never use the same password on different sites.

to reach a defence contractor in Virginia. By a clever series of tricks and disguises, they were able, in effect, to cross the Atlantic invisibly. As a convenience for customers, the defence contractor allowed people on its network to use modems for outgoing calls to other modems within the United States. None of the networks involved in this had any idea they were being used: the intruder had either given himself permission to do what he was doing, or disabled any monitoring system that might have highlighted it.

But Mr Stoll faced then a problem which plagues internet security then as now: getting others to take it seriously. The authorities were intrigued by the breach, but not alarmed. The material on the networks was not itself secret (though the military installations they served were). It was unclear what crime was being committed, or how the offender would be prosecuted. International cooperation in criminal justice involves laborious bureaucratic toing and froing. Why would the German authorities start tapping phones because seventy-five cents was missing from an American laboratory's accounts? In any case, the intruder was not on the network long enough to be traced easily. Most of the accomplices involved in the attack were unwitting, and even when they were alerted did not see why they should get involved. If your phone is mysteriously dialling a number which you do not recognise, and the cost is trivial, you are unlikely to make a fuss.

Breaking into a computer network now is, if anything, a lot easier than in the days of Cuckoo's Egg. There are many more users and computers, meaning that the attacker needs to find only one point of weakness to get started. Mr Stoll was able to visualise quite easily the way in which outsiders could connect to his laboratory network, and what other networks they could then reach: it was like a railway map. Nowadays, mapping a network is a formidably difficult task — more like trying to keep track of a galaxy. Connections with other computers and networks can easily be numbered in tens of thousands, not a few dozen. They may open and close for all sorts of different reasons. Many of them may be automated, and be created for reasons (a now discontinued project involving some faraway computers) which have long been forgotten. All that offers huge scope for attackers, and makes the defenders' task much harder.

Modern-day attackers — whether hackers, activists or spies, or a hybrid of these elements — use a similar approach, but have far more tools at their disposal. These are discussed in detail elsewhere, but they include the 'toxic e-mail', with an attachment or link that infects the recipient, of the kind that snared Pin and Chip Hakhett, and also the use of a USB stick (a small portable device used to store electronic data) which can introduce malicious software on to a computer. As in the days of Cuckoo's Egg, any network connected to the outside world can be reached. Hackers then typically made their first breach by finding a modem with a weak password (or none) which would give access to a network. That rarely works now. But it doesn't need to. Other means of breaching a network do more damage and leave less trace. Whereas in those days the main vulnerability was the theft or corruption of data, now all computers on a network are vulnerable to more sophisticated attacks, including the installing of malware.

If the target computer hosts content that is accessed through a web browser, it can be attacked with the doctored commands of an SQL injection attack, discussed in the previous chapter. Conversely, a computer can be infected by making it visit a website that has been infected, where it unwittingly downloads software disguised as a harmless picture or diagram (the so-called 'watering hole attack'). Even machines that have little to do with humans — such as computers that run automated industrial systems — can be sent bogus commands disguised as instructions. If you can get physical access to a computer you can put a memory stick in the USB socket. This can quickly and invisibly copy malicious software on to the computer. Any computer even connected to the internet is vulnerable to an attack if a chink in its hardware or software can be found. Even networks not connected to the internet are vulnerable – modern malware will jump on to the network from an infected mobile phone, or via a computer storage device. Having done its work, it can then send the data back home by similar means.

APT1's preferred method was to send 'spear-phishing' e-mails, well written and well targeted, to people in the organisations they were trying to breach. These – in effect electronic parcel bombs – were sent from Gmail accounts set up in the real names of people who could plausibly be sending e-mails. In one case, APT1 even targeted Mandiant, the security firm which later exposed its work. It sent an e-mail to carefully selected staff members, purporting to be from the chief executive, which read as follows:

Date: Wed, 18 Apr 2012 06:31:41–0700

From: Kevin Mandia <kevin.mandia@rocketmail.com>

Subject: Internal Discussion on the Press

Release

Hello,

Shall we schedule a time to meet next week?

We need to finalize the press release.

Details click **here**.

Kevin Mandia

This is a notably more sophisticated effort than the e-mail supposedly sent to friends by Pin Hakhett ('penniless in Penang'). It is written in the crisp business English that a busy chief executive would be likely to use. Many people reading it would assume that Mr Mandia, for reasons of convenience, was using his private e-mail account rather than his office one. In any case, it is better not to ask too many questions when you get an e-mail from your boss. Anyone clicking on the link in the e-mail would have downloaded a file called Internal_Discussion_Press_Release_In_Next_ Week8.zip.* Anyone unwise enough to try to extract the 'internal discussion' document would have in fact unleashed a sophisticated piece of malicious software on to their computer known as a 'backdoor'.

Unlike the spear-phishing e-mails sent by criminals, these messages were from real addresses, monitored by real people. If the recipients answered, they would get a reassuring reply. One cautious soul actually wrote back to say 'I'm not sure if this is legit so I didn't open it' – only to receive a terse reply from his purported colleague (in fact a member of APT1) saying 'it's legit'.

This is a good example of what in security speak is called 'social engineering' – otherwise known as confidence trickery – a

---

* Zip files are a way of compressing a large lump of data so that it can be e-mailed conveniently. They are a treacherous format, because they can be used to compress anything: a picture, a document – or a program. Other filenames used by APT1 to tempt e-mail recipients included:
  2012ChinaUSAviationSymposium.zip
  Employee-Benefit-and-Overhead-Adjustment-Keys.zip
  New_Technology_For_FPGA_And_Its_Developing_Trend.zip
  North_Korean_launch.zip
  Oil-Field-Services-Analysis-And-Outlook.zip
  POWER_GEN_2012.zip
  Proactive_Investors_One2One_Energy_Investor_Forum.zip
  South_China_Sea_Security_Assessment_Report.zip
  Telephonics_Supplier_Manual_v3.zip
  Updated_Office_Contact_v1.zip
  Welfare_Reform_and_Benefits_Development_Plan.zip

centrepiece of the Cuckoo's Egg attack thirty years ago, and still vital now. The intruder combines his electronic attack with a bit of human contact to convince the victim to take the necessary step. In the days of Cuckoo's Egg, hackers wanting to use telephones free of charge would simply call up the telephone company pretending to be engineers who had forgotten the necessary codes, but the scope is much greater now. Moreover, in those days e-mails were simple messages, like postcards, not parcels. It was not possible to attach a toxic payload to them.

Once installed, the 'backdoor' opened. In other words, the malicious software made contact with its 'command and control' server. This communication would bypass most security procedures. Companies often build electronic 'firewalls' round their network, which are meant to stop an intruder creeping in over the internet. But firewalls are not designed to deal with an intruder who is already inside the network, and communicating out. The security software would assume that the communication came from a legitimate source – and also allow it to receive a reply.

Such 'backdoors' are a favourite tool of attackers. The more basic versions are available in the criminal markets on the internet. More sophisticated, bespoke ones can be ordered. APT1 used forty-two families of backdoor,* ranging from the simple kind to purpose-built models. The most basic backdoors do just one thing: they will open up an internet connection to the attacker's server, download a file and start it running. After that job is completed they are programed to go to sleep (or they may even delete themselves).

More sophisticated forms of backdoors will obey a range of instructions, which they typically receive by forcing the host computer to go to a particular web page, where the commands

---

* Malware versions that share 80 per cent of the same code are said to belong to the same 'family'.

may be disguised as a picture, or hidden in the 'comments' section of a news site. This neatly gets round any security provisions which the managers of the network may have installed. To anyone monitoring incoming and outgoing data, it simply looks as though the user of the computer is browsing the internet. Even if someone does look at the doctored website, nothing will seem amiss – the commands it contains are only for computers with that specific backdoor program installed.

Nor – at least initially – will the owner of the computer find anything wrong. His machine will seem to run as normal. He will not even notice that it is visiting the doctored website to receive instructions. But the backdoor can run programs, upload and download files, create and delete the directories where data are stored, log and copy anything he types on his keyboard – and even create a 'remote desktop' – meaning that anything he sees on his screen, say in California, is visible to the APT1 snooper in Shanghai – who can then take control of the computer using his own keyboard and mouse.

Most of the companies attacked by APT1 did not know anything was amiss. They did not suffer immediate financial loss: the aim was not sabotage or theft, but espionage. What was interesting for the Chinese was the intellectual property, business plans and other information which would tilt the outcome of future business competition. The danger is particularly acute when attacks involve several stages. If you are trying to target a high-technology company with good defences, you may start off with a customer or supplier who takes fewer precautions. That is where victims such as the Hakhetts come in. If you have the ability to send e-mails in their names, you can then reach people whom they trust who will then open the attachments or click on the links those messages contain. A simple message saying 'thought you'd like this' and an amusing picture will arouse no comment and will be soon forgotten.

If the recipient does mention it, Pin or Chip will look blank, but neither side is likely to think anything more of the matter: it is just a memory lapse or misunderstanding. The picture may indeed be amusing – but by clicking on the link, or unloading the attachment, the recipient has just compromised all their business partners and colleagues.

This new twist since Mr Stoll's day is the development of these costly and complicated digital weapons. These are designed to steal, destroy or corrupt data; they give the attacker the ability to disable or disrupt the adversary's computers remotely and untraceably. These weapons are costly by the standards of computer enthusiasts. But they are still a great deal cheaper than conventional ones. They are bought not from big arms manufacturers, with enormously complex defence procurement agreements reached by lengthy negotiation, but simply and quickly.

Some of them are created in-house by government spy agencies, which devote huge efforts to trying to find holes in software and hardware which they can use in espionage and warfare. Many others are also discovered by individual hackers, with a mixture of luck and skill. And a growing band of private-sector companies develop them as a commercial product. A 'zero-day' vulnerability – a flaw in a computer program or chip that nobody has noticed – can be sold for hundreds of thousands of dollars, depending how ingenious and useful it is.* That is a lot of money for the hacker who discovers it, but small change for governments. A single precision-guided missile, such as the BGM-109 Tomahawk, cost

---

* A 'zero-day' vulnerability is one that has not yet been announced, meaning that there is almost no chance that it has been patched: it will work everywhere, every time. Once the manufacturer is aware of the flaw in the product and offers a remedy, the clock starts ticking. Other vulnerabilities are still useful for mass attacks – even if only a handful of users fall victim, the exploit can still bring a useful haul.

$1.65 million in 2014.[5] 'Cyber-weapons', as they are often called, offer much more bang for the buck.

Digital weapons can be used in espionage or sabotage. This corresponds to the real-life division in the spy world between intelligence collection (finding things out) and special operations (making things happen: chiefly blowing things up and killing people). Both kinds of work involve breaking into another country's networks and computers and will use mostly the same techniques and methods to do so. But the aims are different. The spies simply want to know what is going on, as invisibly as possible. The saboteurs want to develop the capability to disrupt the network, degrade the data on it, or deny access to those who need to use it. A debate rumbles on about how much sabotage shades into cyber-war, and how it should be defined and regulated. I deal with these issues in the next chapter. But there is much less controversy about espionage over the internet. This may seem paradoxical, as espionage is inherently secret, and scandalous when details come to life. But the reality is more banal. Almost all countries engage in some kind of intelligence work. If you have secrets, you try to keep them. If you have internal or external adversaries or rivals, you need to find out what they are doing. Signals intelligence – creating codes to conceal your own secrets, and cracking those of others – is an ancient capability, too. But the internet has transformed both spying and spy-catching, not least because of the overlap with means normally used by criminals.

This kind of online spying shades into warfare. It prepares the ground for a future conflict, and for its outcome, in a way that the victim may never realise. If you know the lie of the land inside your opponent's political and economic institutions, you can see the places to apply pressure, and the hidden strengths which you must avoid encountering. You gain military, diplomatic, political and economic advantage, while he loses it.

In the past, this was the job of conventional espionage – the placing of human intelligence agents and the collection of radio signals for code-cracking and analysis. But this kind of espionage had its limits. If you are being spied on in the conventional way, you have some chances to unravel what is going on. Perhaps you see that a key official is acting strangely, so you can follow his movements, see whom he meets and then check them out. Eventually you will find the next step in the chain. Here the advantage is increasingly with defenders over attackers. It is harder to use human sources, and easier to spot them, in a world where every movement leaves a digital trace which can be scrutinised and examined.

Online espionage is booming. A distant descendant of the Cuckoo's Egg attack was a sophisticated operation called Dragonfly, unearthed by the Symantec security firm in June 2014.[6] It targeted dozens of companies in vital industries in Western countries, chiefly energy and pharmaceuticals. It used bogus e-mails and rogue websites to plant malevolent software on computers, which could then be used for both spying and sabotage. The group behind the attack (also known as Energetic Bear) is thought to be sponsored by Russia; it had previously attacked North American defence and aviation companies.

Even more sinister in mid-2014 was the news of Uruboros (Snake). A variant of an earlier attack launched against NATO defence and foreign ministries in 2007 (known as agent.btz), Uruboros is invisible except under the most expert scrutiny. It allows an outsider to control a computer remotely and steal files from it.[7] Earlier, in January 2013, came news of another series of apparently government-sponsored attacks dubbed 'Red October'.[8] The security company Kaspersky Lab, which uncovered the attack, believes it dates back at least to 2007. The victims were 'diplomatic and governmental agencies' plus 'research institutions, energy and nuclear groups, and trade and aerospace targets'. The attackers had developed a unique and complex malicious program called 'Rocra' which hopped from network to network, using identities stolen from one victim to gain access to the next target. It was controlled from Germany and Russia – though that does not mean that the masterminds behind the attack were there. It stole all sorts of documents, but had an interesting ability to abstract encoded files created with the 'Acid Cryptofiler', a French-designed system widely used in NATO and the European Union.

Red October used many of the techniques and vulnerabilities discussed elsewhere in the book. The means of infection was 'spear-phishing' – an innocuous-seeming email sent to a victim which included a concealed toxic cargo. This exploited weaknesses in the widely used Microsoft Office software (a clutch of programs which includes Word, PowerPoint and Excel) in order to gain access to the victim's computer – and the network to which it was connected. Kaspersky Lab found several hundred infected systems, mostly in Eastern Europe but also North America. The software was persistent – if a machine was cleaned and updated, it had a 'resurrection' module, which lurked in Microsoft and the similarly widely used Adobe Reader software. This would set the machine up for reinfection. It also stole data from mobile phones and could even recover deleted files from removable disk drives plugged into an infected computer. It seems likely that Red October originated from Russian-speaking attackers – perhaps a Kremlin-sponsored outfit trying to find out about American activities in Europe, or perhaps from Americans trying to find out about Russian dealings there.

Red October came at the same time as an attack on the Council on Foreign Relations (CFR) website.[9] The CFR is America's most reputable think-tank dealing with international affairs, set up in the aftermath of the First World War to prepare the country for greater responsibility in world leadership. It is broadly comparable to the Royal Institute for International Affairs (Chatham House) in London. The CFR website is one of the most informative in the English-speaking world for anyone wanting to find out what the American foreign-policy elite is thinking, reading or discussing. But this attack was not directed at the pundits and thinkers of the CFR, but at the people who might be interested in them.

This was a watering hole attack, which exploited a previously unknown weakness in Microsoft's notoriously vulnerable Internet Explorer browser (a 'browser' is a computer program used to visit internet sites). The attackers had planted a small, invisible computer program on the CFR website. This checked which version of Internet Explorer the visitor was using. It also checked if another notoriously vulnerable program, Adobe Flash, was installed, on the visitor's computer. Then it checked to see which language was being used: targeted were Chinese (the simple version used on the mainland, as well as the more complex variant used in Taiwan), American English, Russian, Japanese and Korean). If any of those three criteria were not met, the victim was merely redirected to a blank page. Otherwise, their computers were infected with malicious code which could then steal documents or create other vulnerabilities.

Few if any of the users would have noticed this. Why should they? They were visiting a reputable website. Their computer loaded apparently legitimate content. They had not installed any new program or done anything out of the ordinary. They would not necessarily notice anything wrong with their computer. But these users – and everyone they had dealings with – were at risk as a result.

All these attacks highlight a central problem for defenders: attribution. Assume that you realise that your network has been breached (most victims don't). Assume, even, that you have identified what the intruder did there – the documents he stole, the

malware he used (most victims can't do that either). Assume even
that you have worked out the route which the stolen information
took after it left your network (also highly unlikely).

None of that helps very much. If you are American, you may
guess that the attacker is likely to be Iran, China or Russia. But what
then? All these countries have an interest in weakening America.
Commercial and state interest overlap. The same hackers work for
different clients. Maybe your attacker was a contractor, based in
China, but working for Russia. Or vice versa.

Any clues that defenders do find can be misleading. Malicious
programs, when examined, can give some idea about their origins.
Software writers usually leave time stamps in their work, which
show which lines of code were written when. They may forget to
take them out. Hackers who habitually do not work on Fridays are
more likely to be from the Islamic world. If they do not work on
Saturdays, they may be Israelis. If they work Chinese office hours,
that gives a clue, too. Sometimes they may reuse bits of code seen in
other attacks. Or they may leave a few words in the text which hint
at their background (for example, Cyrillic text suggests that Russian-
speakers are at work). But all these clues are indicative, not decisive.
If you want to give the impression that you are Russian, it is quite
easy to do so. And if you are determined not to give that impression, covering your tracks is not difficult either. The attack on Sony
Pictures was widely blamed (not least by the American authorities)
on hackers working for the regime in North Korea. But security
professionals were sceptical.[10] The people claiming responsibility for
the attack had not initially mentioned the comedy film featuring the
assassination of the North Korean leader. The techniques – especially
the use of social media, and the reconnaissance carried out on Sony's
networks – seemed too sophisticated for North Korean hackers.

Even in the Cuckoo's Egg attack, the breakthrough came only by
accident. Mr Stoll created what would now be called a honeypot – a

bogus set of documents containing material that would be of interest to a foreign espionage service. The aim was simply to lure the intruder into staying connected long enough to trace at least part of his route into the network. But the ploy had another benefit. These documents – mostly a mixture of jargon and waffle – included a letter from a fictitious secretary, called Barbara Sherwin, saying that because of their size some of the documents could be posted on request. Mr Stoll had drafted this only as supporting material. But to his amazement, a few weeks later a letter then arrived addressed to Miss Sherwin, asking her for a price list for the documents. The letter came from a Laszlo Balogh, a Hungarian American in Pittsburgh. When the FBI investigated him, he turned out to be working for a Soviet-bloc spy agency.

At that point the wheels started spinning fast. The German authorities were able to trace the original source of the intrusion – a computer company in Hamburg, and a private flat. They made arrests among a group of German hackers called the Chaos Computer Club. Their motive had originally been a confused mixture of anarchist sentiment and annoyance at the high cost of getting online in Germany. But once they realised how vulnerable the American military networks were, they began offering their services to the KGB, in return for money and cocaine.

Mr Stoll returned to astronomy – though his account of the story, *The Cuckoo's Egg*, remains one of the most interesting and informative books ever written on computer security. But the lessons remain valuable to this day. Perhaps the most important is that the most dangerous feature of any network is the right to control it. In modern computer parlance, gaining control of a network is called 'root'. Once you have 'root' you can not only steal and compromise data, you can cover your tracks. You can disable or alter the systems that are supposed to log and monitor the way that data moves around the network. You can give yourself new legitimate credentials. In short, you can change the rules, so that you are no longer breaking them.

For all the huge investments in computer security since Cuckoo's Egg, this fundamental weakness has not changed. The anonymity the internet offers makes it easier for attackers and harder for defenders. Computers and networks allow far more detailed and sophisticated forms of intelligence gathering. They are ideally suited for the deception, camouflage and stunts which come naturally to spies. But they bog down the spycatchers.

For obvious reasons, countries do not like talking about specifics in espionage. Failures are embarrassing, and advertising successes may hinder the chance of another one. American, British and other Western officials had been grumbling about Chinese espionage for several years with increasing irritation. In 2011 America's National Counterintelligence Executive published a report specifically criticising China, among other countries, for its industrial espionage.[11]

But few specific details emerged until 2013. In that year the security firm Mandiant* released its sensational report on Chinese attacks on Western companies and organisations.[12] These were not run-of-the-mill tricks of the kind used by ordinary criminals but 'advanced persistent threats', or APTs – jargon for attacks launched by or on behalf of governments. Mandiant identified a group it called APT1, which it said was one of at least twenty such groups in China, active since at least 2006. They tracked its attacks on nearly 150 victims – while admitting that this was probably only a small part of the group's activities. In terms of the quantity of information stolen, Mandiant reckoned that APT1 was perhaps the most prolific internet espionage group in the world.

It was not just a bunch of talented students having a lark on the internet. APT1's behaviour, size and clout left no doubt that it

* Mandiant has since been bought by another security firm, FireEye.

was in fact the 2nd Bureau of the 3rd Department of the General Staff of the Chinese People's Liberation Army, more conveniently known by its internal designation of Unit 61398.

The story the Mandiant report told was shocking. Unit 61398 had a staff certainly of hundreds, and perhaps thousands. It had special fibre-optic cables laid to its building by China Telecom. It had stolen hundreds of terabytes of data – 'technology blueprints, proprietary manufacturing processes, test results, business plans, pricing documents, partnership agreements, and emails and contact lists' – from at least 141 organisations in twenty major industries. Most were in English-speaking countries, and engaged in business areas that China has identified as strategically important. The data thefts were repeated over time. APT1 typically had access to its victims' networks for just under a year – 356 days, though in one case it had managed to maintain its breach for four years and ten months. The APT1 group does not attack networks using addresses in China. It hops through many stages before it reaches its targets. The 'hub' is typically in the United States – and may be a network breached only in order to reach other victims, in what is disguised as legitimate traffic.

In many respects, network security is now harder than in Mr Stoll's days as a detective. In order not to give any clue to the attacker that he was being observed, he used an effective but primitive set-up, connecting a printer to the network with home-made wiring. The line-by-line record of each step the intruders were taking filled several large boxes in his office. A modern-day version of that would be impossible. Modern printers are far too delicate and sophisticated to use in this way. The danger that the attacker would spot the scrutiny would be higher, not lower.

Another big difficulty for Mr Stoll was balancing the need of detection against damage limitation. If you spot an intruder on your network, simply shutting off his access may not be the wisest course.

You may never see him again. You will have no clue to his motivation, or his methods. But if you let him roam, he may steal something that really matters. This bothered Mr Stoll a lot, but he came up with a useful dodge: when the intruders were about to get hold of something important, he jingled his keys across the bare wires that connected his printer to the network. The resulting crackle frustrated the attack – but in those days, noisy connections between computers were a fact of life. The intruders put their failure down to bad luck, not interference. That would be a lot harder now.

So is maintaining secrecy. Mr Stoll was able to slow down the intruders by creating false trails. That is a good tactic – but everyone involved has to know of the deception, and not talk about it. A well-placed attacker can search every e-mail sent in a company for mention of something he is curious about. So if people are exchanging puzzled messages about some mysterious documents or directories on the network, he will soon find out. Mr Stoll was able to keep this secret by telephoning his colleagues from coin-operated call boxes, or simply meeting them face-to-face.

That, too, would be far harder these days. If you are facing a skilled intruder, anything that happens in your office is vulnerable – he can listen to what you say, get into your telephone system to see whom you are calling, and even listen to the calls. Running an amateur counter-espionage operation of the kind that Mr Stoll managed so brilliantly would be risky, and quite possibly do more harm than good.

Excitement about KGB spying on American networks soon waned. It was hard to see that Cuckoo's Egg had made much of a difference. The Soviet Union was already collapsing at the time it was under way. Five years later it ceased to exist. The research that was at risk was interesting – but America has yet to build the full-scale 'Star Wars' missile-defence system that Ronald Reagan dreamed of, and the Kremlin feared. It has proved too difficult and expensive. Espionage makes decision makers better informed. But it does not mean that they make better decisions, or that those decisions will have better outcomes.

In the case of APT1, worries about Chinese espionage faded from the headlines after the Mandiant report. One reason was the revelations of Edward Snowden, a contractor for America's National Security Agency who is now a fugitive in Russia. Based in Hawaii, at the Regional Security Operations Centre, he had access to his country's most highly classified secrets, which were supposedly protected by a formidable range of physical and electronic security measures. Anyone trying to break into the facility would risk being shot. But Snowden's job involved moving secret material from one network to another – an ideal position for someone bent on stealing secrets.[13]

The disclosures caused by Snowden in 2013 focused public attention far more sharply on the alleged abuses perpetrated by the National Security Agency (NSA) and GCHQ than on attacks on Western countries by China (and Russia). It was not until 2014 that the story revived, when the FBI issued arrest warrants for five Chinese officials it believed were behind attacks on Western companies.[14]

This investigation has many similar features to the APT1 report. The indictment shows that the FBI started work in 2006. One of the companies concerned, SolarWorld, received a warning in July 2012 that it was under attack. Hackers were stealing material which would help Chinese competitors undercut the company's business. In particular, they were interested in documents that SolarWorld had provided to its lawyers, who were representing it in a trade dispute about rocketing levels of cheap Chinese solar panels. In the course of that dispute the company had to provide the Commerce Department with detailed information about its costs and customers. That would have been of great interest to the Chinese.

Western officials now hope that their campaign to curb Chinese spying is back on track. They argue that what distinguishes Western espionage activity from that of Chinese government hackers is the target. Britain, America and their allies spy on companies in foreign countries – for example, on Russia's gas giant Gazprom. But they do so for reasons of state not commerce. Gazprom, though nominally a private company, is in effect an arm of the Russian state. It is used to reward Russia's friends and punish its enemies. At home it acts as a cash box for the regime, supplying below-cost gas to domestic consumers and industries. It is hard to imagine a worthier target for espionage.

America also admits that it spies on foreign companies which pay bribes. American companies face formidable criminal penalties if they do this. They object to being undercut by European and other competitors who are able to break the law with impunity. In a pithy commentary called 'Why we spy on our allies' in the *Wall Street Journal* in March 2000 James Woolsey, the former head of the CIA, made his case with admirable bluntness:

Yes, my continental European friends, we have spied on you. And it's true that we use computers to sort through data by using keywords. Have you stopped to ask yourselves what we're looking for?[15]

European companies habitually win contracts by bribery, he maintained. In most cases their products are too backward or costly to win any other way. By finding out about the payment of bribes by Europeans, and complaining about it, the American government levels the playing field. He added that America also spies on European sales of dual-use technology to rogue states and on other sanctions busting. And he pointed out that France is a mighty practitioner of industrial espionage.[16]

But the biggest difference is in the use to which intelligence is put. Critics of British and American intelligence contend that the NSA and GCHQ are spying on those countries' commercial rivals in order to benefit their own companies. If so, that would certainly dent any claim to the moral high ground in computer espionage. America does not complain about other kinds of Chinese spying, such as on political and military targets, for the good reason that America itself spies hard on the leadership in Beijing. If spies are caught, they are arrested and then jailed or deported. But the rules are the same for both sides.

Both evidence and logic suggest that on commercial espionage the British and American spymasters are telling the truth. One reason is practicality. In a closed society, where business and government work hand in hand, it is easy to see how a state spy agency would pass on commercially sensitive information to favoured companies – perhaps state-owned, or run by government cronies. But in a competitive and litigious society like America, it is much harder to imagine how this would work in practice. Assume that the NSA did spy on Chinese solar panel makers, and gained some commercially sensitive information. How would the agency then decide to distribute it? Any company that gained access to intelligence gathered at taxpayers' expense would have an unfair advantage over its American peers. If those companies found out, they would complain vociferously.

In theory, one could imagine a lawless or self-interested spy service in Britain or America that would distribute nuggets of information to favoured companies, but do so with such discretion that news of this practice never leaked out. It is impossible to prove a negative, and those who take a hostile and conspiratorial view of the work of GCHQ and the NSA will never believe that they are not just the puppets of the corporate state. But it is striking that no hint of such a programme has leaked out in the media, and that no business executive has ever mentioned such a practice, even obliquely.

The really conclusive point is that even the huge trove of documents stolen by Mr Snowden gives no sign of this. For someone bent on exposing illegality and wrongdoing in American intelligence, any sign of collusion with commercial interests would have been a prize catch, and one which his supporters would have trumpeted as proof of their contention that Western espionage is out of control. Mr Snowden scoured the computers of the NSA for every sign of deliberate law-breaking and wrongdoing, but with little result. He found an isolated instance where people had abused their position to further their romantic interests, and one instance where some intelligence officers had pondered (but rejected) the idea of discrediting some propagandists for extreme Islamism by highlighting their fondness for pornography and deviant sex.

But he did not find any sign at all of what many people in his circle of supporters would assume was self-evident: that the NSA and GCHQ are the handmaidens of big business. He found evidence of American spying on Gazprom and similar entities. But he found no sign that this intelligence was used to further the interests of American oil or gas companies.

Complaining about Chinese espionage alerts not only the victims but also the perpetrators, who can then try different means. Similar dilemmas beset Mr Stoll when dealing with Cuckoo's Egg. In any environment involving lots of people, there are practical difficulties in being honest and open where any kind of security is concerned. If you discover a glaring security flaw, immediately announcing it in public may not be the best thing to do. For a start, you want to avoid panic. More importantly, not everyone will act on your advice. But potential malefactors may. Imagine that you discover that a particular make of car has a lock that can be picked by some trivially easy means – for example, by sliding a metal ruler between the window and the frame of the door. It will be weeks or months before every car owner affected has time to go to the garage and have the necessary security feature fitted. But in the meantime, thieves will have an open season.

Another dilemma for defenders is whether to copy the attackers' techniques, rather than expose them. When Mr Stoll started explaining what was going on to the NSA, he was horrified by their reaction. This agency – then, as now, responsible for America's computer security, as well as espionage – was fascinated by the methods the intruders were using. But from the questions they asked it was clear that they were just as interested in how to use these techniques against another country as in defending America's own networks. Mr Stoll saw the issue primarily as a breach of trust. He liked the idea that the same values reigned on the network as in personal interaction: good faith, openness, shared endeavour. Cheating on the rules, even for the trivial amount of seventy-five cents, was a sign of something annoyingly wrong – just as if a colleague were to steal money from the honesty box next to the biscuit tin. He did not like the idea that his country would be more interested in copying the intruder than foiling him.

But from an espionage point of view, access to a network or computer is morally neutral. If you believe that your country is a force for good in the world, and that your instructions come with legitimate political authority, you will pick locks, steal things, lie and cheat with a clear conscience.

As result, two fundamental priorities clash. The prime duty of government is protecting its citizens from harm. From that point of view, if you know that if they are running unwitting risks you should tell them. But suppose that your country's enemies are also running those unwitting risks – meaning that you can spy on them? The internet sharpens this dilemma, because attribution is harder, distance irrelevant and the threat more ubiquitous. An attack is scalable – if you wage it against one computer, you can do it to thousands or millions.

To see the difference, consider the way espionage agencies use lock-pickers and forgers, adopt disguises and tell lies. They can do things that in normal life would be regarded as disgraceful. But when they break the rules, it is for a specific purpose. If a spy agency, in the course of an operation to crack an organised crime gang or a foreign spy ring, picks a front-door lock, plants a bug, intercepts a phone call or impersonates a schoolteacher, this is a one-off. Only that particular lock is picked, only that particular victim is duped.

When it comes to these techniques on the internet, everyone is vulnerable. If you find out that a particular combination of hardware and software allows you to take control, in the right circumstances of someone else's computer, that is true not just for your target, but for everyone in the world who has the same configuration. You cannot know who else may discover the vulnerability – or what they will use it for. The techniques that you may be using to breach a network for a little bit of quiet espionage can also be used by another adversary to wreak havoc or terror.

This is the second part of the threat: attacks on computers and networks for sabotage. Working out the rules and priorities in warfare poses even greater difficulties for policymakers than computer espionage.

6

Spies v. Warriors

Spying is inherently illegal. It is not governed by international laws or convention. You do what your political masters tell you to do, and try to stay undetected. But warfare is different. Armed conflict between states is governed by international law. Wars of aggression are illegal. Combatants are treated differently from non-combatants. Military force must be used with the risk to civilians in mind. Some weapons – biological, chemical and some kinds of mines – are banned. Civilised countries may cheat on these rules on occasion. But nobody wants to renounce them completely.

In the event of war – or as a means of intimidation – digital weapons offer useful capabilities. Attacks on computers and networks could cripple the adversary's financial system, close down critical infrastructure, induce public panic, paralyse communications, and ultimately break the will of the political leadership. The saboteurs will necessarily reveal their hand when they use their tools, so they want to stay secret as long as possible.

Fear of a catastrophic attack on vital computer systems – sometimes termed a 'Digital Pearl Harbor' – has made internet security companies rich. But it is worth noting that this has not actually happened. International conflict on the internet so far has consisted of limited sabotage attacks, such as the American–Israeli interference with Iran's nuclear programme (using the Stuxnet malware, of which more later), and the Russian swamping attack on Estonia discussed on pages 79–80.

Digital weapons are changing the face of international conflict as profoundly as gunpowder did in Europe in the Middle Ages. The ability to deal death at a distance changed not only warfare but society. But whereas gunpowder took two centuries to spread, the internet has taken only two decades.

Military planners now have to cope with a new battlefield, marked by baffling and unpredictable features. All the problems which Pin and Chip Hakhett face in their personal and business lives are also national security problems. Government computers are vulnerable to swamping attacks and toxic e-mails. A single breach can lead to catastrophic damage if internal controls are weak: once hacked, Chip's computer gives attackers his entire online life.

One example of the vulnerability of big systems to a single breach was the data stolen by the NSA contractor Edward Snowden, discussed in the previous chapter. But even before that the weaknesses in American military systems had been abundantly highlighted. A disillusioned army intelligence clerk, Bradley (now Chelsea) Manning, was able to download 700,000 classified documents from a military network, by the simple expedient of putting them on a CD which she labelled 'Lady Gaga' while working unsupervised in an office in Iraq in 2010. The files included a devastating video of an American airstrike on a civilian convoy in Baghdad, in which American pilots apparently mistook journalists' cameras for weapons. Published by the activist group WikiLeaks, the files created an international furore. Manning was sentenced in July 2013 to thirty-five years in jail. The documents also included tens of thousands of diplomatic cables, many of which were based on confidential conversations held by American diplomats with local contacts. WikiLeaks appeared to be careless about their security.

These threats are asymmetrical, for individuals, governments and businesses alike – in other words, attackers need to get lucky only once. Defenders need to be lucky all the time. Moreover, attackers can make large numbers of automated attacks until they get lucky. Their costs are low. Defenders – who have much more at stake – cannot rely on automation, and must spend more time and money. Attackers can research their targets. Defenders cannot visualise what they are defending, they will find it hard to know their attackers' motives and means and they often do not even know they are under attack. As Richard Danzig, an American government adviser, has noted in a report called 'Surviving on a Diet of Poisoned Fruit', all this comes as a big shock to his country's defence planners, who are used to unquestioned technological hegemony, quantifiable risks and enemies whose tactics and aims can be studied exhaustively. Nobody ever questioned America's technological lead in the 'war on terror'. Facing enemies on the internet brings back long-forgotten memories of inferiority, dating to the days when the bleep of the Sputnik satellite alerted Americans to the danger of losing the space race. America could, and did, cope with the Soviet Union eventually. But that was a single and very conspicuous adversary. Now it has too many to count, with capabilities that are 'fluid, egalitarian, distributed and dynamic'.[1]

Big military powers are far from helpless. Unlike Pin and Chip, they have enormous amounts of money available to them. They have military discipline available to enforce their security procedures. In a culture where having a dirty weapon is a punishable offence, it is easier to make people take computer hygiene seriously. The military is used to war games: it can form teams of hackers and deploy them to test its defences, just as it rehearses attack and defence on real-life training grounds. America's Defence Advanced Research Projects Agency (DARPA) has pioneered some important technical breakthroughs as well, together with Microsoft and others. Networks are increasingly designed with the assumption that they will be breached, but with the aim of making life as difficult and fruitless as possible for the intruder (I give more details of this in a later chapter). All this means that attackers have to work harder – finding the right combination of vulnerabilities and useful ways of exploiting them.

But it is still a losing battle. As Mr Danzig notes in his report, 'We are increasing our vulnerabilities faster than we are closing them.' One big reason is miniaturisation, discussed in a later chapter. Our evolutionary heritage has equipped us to deal with weapons we can recognise, but not those that are too small to notice. Another is that warfare on the internet includes attacking non-military targets: if you can cripple your adversary's financial system (by wiping out all the data), or destroy his electric power grid, you have probably brought about his defeat before the shooting starts, if indeed it ever does.

Digital weapons are already in use for sabotage. Stuxnet, an ingenious computer bug developed by the American and Israeli governments and launched in 2010, destroyed many hundreds of Iranian centrifuges used to enrich uranium. That set the Iranian nuclear programme back several years – something that otherwise would have been possible only by launching a full-scale military attack. Stuxnet had several features which exemplify the way nations can wage war on networks and computers. For a start, it attacked machines which were not connected to the internet. They were in computer parlance 'air-gapped' – there was no electronic connection between them and machines connected to the internet.[2]

It is thought that Stuxnet reached its target through one or more USB sticks, either carried by a saboteur, or given to people who would be likely to use them on the machines in question. That was the first phase of the attack. The second was that the malware – technically speaking a 'worm' then moved from computer to computer, invisibly and unstoppably, using a series of 'zero-days' (previously unknown flaws in operating systems and other programs). It exploited the vital and most vulnerable part of computer security, security certificates. Certificates are issued by specialist computer security companies to give a rock-solid guarantee that a piece of software or other interaction is genuine. Stuxnet was able to change the configuration of the computers it infected, and used two genuine but stolen certificates in the process. That gave it 'root-kit' control over the computers – operating them as if it were a legitimate user. But these machines, running Microsoft Windows software, were not the real targets. The software was looking for computers running a specialist form of software called a 'Programmable Logic Controller' used to control machines that need to operate according to a particular routine. These could be anything from a fairground ride to a centrifuge.

On any computer that did not run this software, a specialist product made by the German technology giant Siemens, the virus did nothing. But when the software was present, Stuxnet changed again. When, and only when, it detected a centrifuge running at a particular speed, it went into action, sharply varying the rotations from high speeds to low ones. It also disabled the monitoring systems which should have alerted the operators of the system to the fact that something was amiss. This maltreatment – running the machines at the wrong speeds, with intolerable variation – destroyed a large number, supposedly 1,000 out of 5,000, of the costly, high-precision Iranian centrifuges installed at the Natanz nuclear facility.

America has all but boasted about its role in Stuxnet, with a well-sourced leak to a *New York Times* journalist, which later prompted a (fruitless) leak inquiry from outraged national-security professionals.[3] Gary Samore, at the time the White House official charged with dealing with the Iranian nuclear programme, said, 'we're glad they are having trouble with their centrifuge machine and that we – the US and its allies – are doing everything we can to make sure that we complicate matters for them'.[4] Another leak (to many intelligence professionals a shocking instance of self-aggrandisement by politicians) led to the *New York Times* printing a story in 2012 in which it said Stuxnet was part of something called Operation Olympic Games, started under George W. Bush. One commentator said it was the most important advance in electronic warfare since the breaking of the German Enigma encryption in the Second World War.[5]

In one sense, Stuxnet (and a related program called Flame)[6] exemplified the advantage of using computer software as a weapon. Nobody was killed, and nobody was exposed to risk. It is entirely possible that the doctored USB stick was actually put into a computer by someone who had no idea what it contained. The success of the operation reduced the pressure from Israel for a military attack on Iran, which would have been dangerous and cost real lives.

But Stuxnet was not risk-free. For a start, it spread. It was not meant to appear on the internet (indeed, this is what initially led to its discovery). It affected other industrial control systems, too. According to Kaspersky Lab, the Russian computer security company, it was found in nuclear power plants and even on the international space station – though apparently with no deleterious effect.[7]

Second, it was not kept secret. The Iranians knew that their centrifuges were breaking down. They did not know why. The public discussion over Stuxnet may have done something for the egos of the American and Israeli computer experts involved. But it has also made it far harder to pull off a similar stunt in future. Flame, which activated microphones and webcams, copied every stroke made on the victims' keyboards and everything that appeared on their screens, and used Bluetooth wireless technology to attack other devices, was an exceptionally powerful and useful piece of software – until the Iranians discovered it while investigating a unilateral Israeli attack on oil-industry computers. Worse, Flame was in part disguised as a Microsoft software update. That makes many users of computers distrust these vitally important patches. It raises suspicion (strongly denied by Microsoft) that Microsoft had cooperated with the attack, putting its shareholders' and customers' interests in second place to those of the government.[8]

Third, it invited retaliation. Soon after news of Stuxnet emerged, an attack named Shamoon wiped the data on tens of thousands of desktop computers at the Saudi Arabian oil company Aramco. If there was any taboo about using digital weapons to attack another country's industry, it is now breached.

The question now is when an attack on another country's computers turns into an act of war. There is no easy answer. Modern military conflicts do not involve a tidy declaration of war, followed by attacks, counter-attacks, escalation, second and third fronts, and at the end an armistice followed by a peace treaty. Warfare in the modern age is shapeless. It is hard to know when it begins and ends. And it is hard to know where economic competition and propaganda shade into real hostilities.

The internet is particularly suited for this kind of conflict. As Jānis Bērziņš, a Latvian defence expert, has shown in his study of the Russia–Ukraine conflict, modern warfare targets willpower and decision-making abilities, long before it resorts to high explosive, hardened steel and rocket fuel.[9] A precision-guided information bomb – which spreads panic through rumours – can do far more damage than a warhead if it hits the right place at the right time.

Digital weapons sharpen the questions about when war starts and stops. They also raise profound questions about the definition of combatants. It is legitimate in warfare to bomb another country's infrastructure. So is it lawful to attack the computers and

networks that control it? And the civilians who operate them? By
what means? What laws and norms apply? The resulting confusion
is troubling, and could be dangerous.

Imagine that someone has hacked into your power network and
planted some bugs on the computers that control the electricity supply
network. In theory, if those bugs were activated, the breakdowns
could lead to mass blackouts, causing economic damage, human
suffering and the danger of civil unrest. Is that an act of warfare?
Yes – because if another country bombed the power grid in order to
do similar damage, it would be a clear instance of aggression.

But attacks on computers are closer to terrorism than warfare.
You may guess who the attacker is – in some circumstance there
may be only one plausible culprit. But if they do not accept
responsibility, what do you do? The United States has said that it
will respond to a cyber-attack with 'kinetic' (i.e. real-world) means.
That is an effective deterrent statement. It would justify (at least in
theory) hunting down hackers on the other side of the world and
killing them.

In practice, though, this is much more difficult. In September
2011 an American drone strike killed two US citizens, Anwar
al-Awlaki and Samir Khan, who were living in Yemen. Khan
was editing the al-Qaeda magazine *Inspire*. Editing a magazine –
however obnoxious and inflammatory – is a long way from what
most people would call warfare. And how can you be sure that
you are hitting the right person? If you launch a drone strike
against a hacker – even one who has caused terrible damage on
behalf of a hostile government – how many other people is it
acceptable to kill at the same time?

Over the past centuries we have gained some pretty clear ideas
about what is acceptable and unacceptable on the conventional
battlefield. Even in the Middle Ages, when torture and rape went
unchecked, rules developed on the taking of prisoners (at least

among the nobility). The Geneva, Hague and Vienna conventions created a body of international humanitarian law which has guided most international conflicts since. Even when the laws are broken, they still have some purchase – for example, through the activities of the International Committee of the Red Cross, a scrupulously neutral Swiss-based organisation which is the custodian of the Geneva Convention.

These give guidance on when it is legal to go to war, and how war may be fought: for example, the dividing line between combatants and non-combatants, and what targets are off-limits. It is in both sides' interest in a conventional conflict to treat prisoners of war decently, for example. During the war Germany's Luftwaffe was keen to protect captured Allied pilots from the Gestapo, because they wanted their own pilots, shot down over Britain, to be treated decently, too. Both sides in war try to avoid attacking hospitals, out of a sense of common humanity. The Red Cross symbol is protected by international law – abusing it (for example, to disguise a military object) is a war crime.

Espionage, by contrast, is almost wholly unregulated. Spies are prosecuted if they are caught in peacetime, and may be shot in wartime. To show you are not a spy, it is important to wear uniform when you are on, or over, enemy territory. But when war is waged against computers and over networks who is a combatant? What is off-limits? How do we arrange arms control? A provisional set of answers comes in a manual produced by a NATO-linked centre of excellence in the Estonian capital, Tallinn. It proposes ninety-four rules, drawn from the existing body of international humanitarian law, which it suggests should guide war waged between and on computers and networks (so-called 'cyber-warfare').[10] Its main argument is that an attack from computer to computer is essentially no different from any other offensive action: the country carrying out the attack is subject to international law, and the one being attacked can react accordingly – including retaliating via computer or in other proportionate means. In other words, the basic principles of necessity and proportionality which govern other armed conflicts apply.

Among the other important points the manual makes is one of responsibility: a country has jurisdiction over the computers and networks on its territory, so therefore if they are used to attack another country, then the state can be held responsible. If a country is harbouring terrorists or pirates, and does nothing about it, it can expect to suffer a military attack. Similarly, those involved in warfare-by-computer can commit war crimes, for example by gratuitously targeting non-combatants.

But what is a non-combatant? Here things get tricky. According to the Geneva Convention, a combatant must meet four conditions. He must be under command, wear something distinctive and recognisable from a distance, carry his weapons openly and act according to the laws of armed conflict. Anyone who does not meet these conditions is a 'non-privileged belligerent' and liable to be tried as a criminal (and possibly shot as a spy). Working out what this means for those involved in 'cyber-warfare' is difficult. What happens, for example, if a country sends special-forces units to raid a computer company in a foreign country which has been making and deploying malware? Are the workers there – who may be unarmed in a physical sense – entitled to be treated as soldiers? What happens if they try to surrender?

The Tallinn manual does not aim to be definitive (let alone authoritative). Even its own experts admit that working out what the rules mean in practice is difficult. How negligent does a state have to be before it can be deemed responsible for attacks waged from its territory? And what about the countries which have only indirect involvement – for example, because cables run across their territory, which carry the malevolent software or stolen data? It is also unclear how far intention matters. If one country unwittingly causes catastrophic damage to another – perhaps in a computer-espionage operation gone wrong – does that really give the victim country the right to counter-attack as if the offence was intentional?

In a sense these problems are not completely unfamiliar. Each new kind of weapon creates new difficulties for the conduct of warfare. Shooting civilians on the battlefield is unacceptable. Killing them by dropping bombs on them is allowed. But digital weapons are a new form of armament for several reasons. Their development is inextricably linked to criminality. Organised crime gangs may use military equipment, but it is not developed with them in mind and the authorities may assume that it is unlikely that gangsters will get their hands on, say, a new kind of tank. The conscience of a weapons developer is fairly clear: he may find a new way of hitting the adversary, but it does not make his fellow citizens more vulnerable. If he fails to make the discovery but the enemy does, then his side is weaker and at greater risk. The 'bouncing bomb' which allowed the RAF to breach the dams on the Ruhr in May 1943 had nothing to do with Barnes Wallis's family finances, or his ability to lock the door at night.

But the modern digital weapon is not like the bouncing bomb. It bounces back. Every digital weapon uses weaknesses in the way computers work. You need to evade security controls to get your program on to the enemy's network in the first place. Then you need to evade more controls to get it to the place where it can do the intended damage. If possible, it should cover its tracks at every stage, evading yet more controls in order to do so. Then it will gain the authority it needs and start messing up the enemy's data, or destroying his power grid, or making his nuclear centrifuges spin wildly out of control – all the time maintaining as much invisibility as possible.

For those dealing with warfare, espionage and security this creates a triple dilemma. If you come across a vulnerability in hardware or software, you can do only one of three things with it. You can exploit it for intelligence purposes. You can stockpile it for use as a digital weapon. Or you can let the manufacturer know in order that the problem is solved, for the sake of public safety.

If computer security was our top priority, then anyone discovering a 'zero-day' anywhere in the world would immediately report it to the company that made the software or hardware concerned. We apply this kind of thinking to public health: if a government scientist comes across a new virus that is making people dangerously ill in some obscure part of the world, he would not think that the most important thing was to see if it would be useful for his country's germ-warfare programmes. The responsible reaction would be to examine the virus thoroughly to see what the vaccine or treatment might be and see what other public-health steps, such as quarantine or disinfection, might be necessary.

With digital weapons the authorities are torn between two incompatible priorities. One is the protection of their own people, which requires them to make sure that all hardware and software flaws are dealt with as speedily as possible. The other is the attempt to gain an edge over adversaries.

Trying to do both rests on a form of thinking called 'security through obscurity'. The idea is that if you find some sufficiently rare exploits, and combine them in an ingenious way that nobody else would think of, you can still attack the adversary, while minimising the risk to your own side. That is a comforting approach but not a realistic one. For a start, you do not know how long your exploits and their combination will stay obscure. Secondly, there may be other combinations involving just one of the exploits, plus some others that you have not heard of.

Digital weapons are therefore even more dangerous and peculiar than biological weapons. If you develop a nasty bug to use against your enemy you can aim to have a vaccine in place for your own side (though you will still be breaking the international treaties that ban the development of biological weapons). With digital weapons you cannot deploy the vaccine, because the moment you do the other side will know about it and adopt it, too.

The second problem with digital weapons is a related one. You cannot be sure that they are going to work. At the time you develop the digital weapon, it may indeed be totally unknown to the other side, and every element in it will work perfectly. But how long will that last? If you have bought the exploit, you cannot be sure that the hacker who discovered it and sold it to you will keep it secret. If you discovered it yourself, you cannot be sure that someone else will not find it, too. As explained earlier, most advanced digital weapons involve several different exploits – one to get the malware on to the target machine, another to keep it invisible, a third to help it move around, a fourth to do the damage and a fifth to report back when the job is done. But if just one of those fails to work, then the others are useless.

This creates an inherently unstable balance. If you discover a digital weapon, you had better use it while you can. At the moment you discover it, it is at its most powerful. Every day you wait raises the chances of its being useless. No other weapons are like this. Conventional real-world weapons ('kinetic' in military jargon) go out of date, too – but only slowly. And they rarely lose all their effectiveness at once, even if the enemy is developing countermeasures. You may have to use rather more of them, but some will get through.

Real-world weapons have another big advantage. They are intimidating when displayed. Rather than actually attacking another country, it can be enough just to test-fire a missile, or hold a military exercise on his borders. You may even parade your heavy weaponry on your national day, as Russia does in Red Square in May.

Digital weapons are not like that. If you give even the slightest hint of the capabilities they have and how they work, then you greatly increase the risk that your weapons will not work when you need them. Put at its simplest, if the exploit involves Internet Explorer, then the adversary will switch to another browser. If you are using a vulnerability in a particular computer chip, then the adversary will make sure that his computers use a rival version. You may hint that you have an awesome arsenal of digital weapons. Countries such as Britain, which used to keep strict silence about any offensive digital capabilities, now are happy to say publicly that they are working on them. You may hint that your digital arsenal will freeze any adversary's communications, disable his power grid and bring his banking system to a halt. But the effects are unpredictable. He may feel you are bluffing. Or he may be so scared that he reacts in ways that make you worse off.

This makes arms control difficult, too. Over the past decades, the world has become quite good at dealing with all sorts of other weapons. We have verification regimes, inspections (surprise and announced), and careful categories for working out what role different weapons play in the size of the overall arsenal. We have a test-ban treaty on letting off nuclear weapons in the air. We are also stumbling towards an outline of how to deal with space-based weaponry, such as satellites which can destroy other satellites (or attack targets on the ground).

None of that works with digital weapons. Just as we have no idea what is fair and what is not fair, we have no real way of knowing whether we are superior, or inferior, to our adversary. We cannot test our weapons to see if they work, because by doing so we greatly increase the chance that they will not work next time. We may resort to human intelligence (trying to infiltrate old-fashioned spies into his digital-weapons arsenal). But even that is unlikely to give a proper answer.

In a world where rival countries tend to think the worst of each other, this is a dangerous position. As Martin Libicki of the Rand Corporation notes:

The normal human intuition about how things work in the physical world does not always translate well into cyberspace. The effects, and sometimes even the fact, of cyber-operations can be obscure. The source of the attacks may not be obvious; the attacker must claim them, or the defender must attribute them. Even if the facts are clear, their interpretations may not be; even when both are clear, policymakers may not necessarily understand them.[11]

If you think you are weaker than the other party, you may decide to make your digital weapons exceptionally damaging – for example, by developing new means of attacking the civilian infrastructure. You may think it is better to launch a disabling surprise attack now than wait until you are attacked with overwhelming force.

Reading the other side's intentions is hard. Probing the other side's defences may be seen as prudent reconnaissance – or an act of war. The boundary between espionage and warfare is blurred to almost nothing. Is the adversary trying to read your communications – or preparing to sabotage them? As Mr Libicki notes:

Perhaps the frequency and volume of exploitation crosses some unclear red line; or the hackers simply make a mistake tampering with systems to see how they work and unintentionally damage something.

Add to that another difficulty mentioned earlier: attribution. You may be aware (if you are lucky) that your country's computers and networks are being interfered with. You are not sure if the interference is intrusive espionage or low-level warfare. And you do not know who is to blame. The command and control of the attack may come from a computer in a country you regard as an enemy – but you cannot be sure that it is happening with that country's consent. It could well be that another adversary has simply hijacked a computer there.

Dealing with this is difficult. Demands for transparency and de-escalation may be directed in the wrong direction. In October 1962 President John F. Kennedy knew that Soviet naval vessels were steaming towards Cuba. There was not the slightest chance that they were Chinese. He could talk to the Kremlin and with a mixture of threats and concessions try to defuse the crisis. In a war waged by computers, that would be much harder. Maybe the Russians have hired Chinese hackers. Or maybe China has hired Russian hackers. Or maybe it is the Iranians using a mixture of both. Who is to know?

Prudence pushes in both directions. On the one hand, it would be unwise to respond to an intrusion by tightening security, or trying hard to investigate. If the other side has already misread your intentions once, then your behaviour will seem like a further act of aggression, confirming his suspicions. But if you do not react quickly, you are taking a big risk: suppose the intrusion you have detected is indeed the first stage in a disabling attack. You may have only minutes to respond before it will be too late forever.

Mr Libicki makes seven suggestions. First is to be clear if an attack is really an act of war. This, he notes wisely, is a 'decision, not a conclusion'. If you decide that you are at war, then esca-lation naturally follows. But not all attacks from another coun-try are necessarily categorised as military. As noted above, the line between espionage and attack is blurred. But espionage is also part of economic and commercial competition. It may include steal-ing intellectual property in order to give your own companies a competitive edge, or trying to find out what another country is doing with financial decision-making, such as monetary policy – interest rates, the trade in government debt – or exchange rates.

Even if the effects of the attack on computer networks are physical, they are not necessarily an act of war. Disrupting computers may make normal life in your capital city impossible, but it is not the same as a foreign occupation. It does not necessarily topple a government, or kill people. It would be possible to respond to this kind of attack by fixing the vulnerabilities that it exploits. If your power network, phone system and government communications are either robust, or repaired quickly, then the attacker's weapons are useless. Normal life can go on. In this sense an attack waged over computer networks is quite different from one involving high explosive and hardened steel, where physical destruction and human casualties are immediate and inevitable.

Clearly this is not an easy decision. Countries are entitled to go to war even before a shot is fired: blockading a harbour, or mining it, counts as the opening of hostilities. So does jamming another country's air-defence radars. But the point is that the decision-maker does have discretion: you can respond to a provocation, or not.

The second point is not to hurry. In theory a first strike in war on computer systems could be utterly debilitating. But this is actually highly unlikely. It is not like a nuclear strike, where a sufficiently massive attack could destroy a country's ability to launch any nuclear retaliation. Defending against a nuclear strike is hugely costly and disruptive. Even if you build fallout shelters for the entire population, the damage from an attack is dreadful. But defending against a cyber-attack, as we shall see, is about good housekeeping. An extremely robust and resilient array of computers and networks in everything that matter may be expensive and a bit inconvenient, but it is not a complete waste of money in the way that a fallout shelter most likely will be. It will, for example, make a country much safer against other threats, such as from criminals and hooligans.

This kind of warfare, Mr Libicki notes, is about telling stories. You have to explain to your own people what is happening, and also to shape the way in which the other side (or sides) understands what is going on. Sometimes that involves secrecy (as in the exact nature of your digital arsenal, what you think is most vulnerable to attack, and so on). So it is important to see – and explain – what you are actually hoping to gain, and what you see as being at stake. Are you, for example, worried about the initial attack or (more likely) what might follow it?

If someone probes the computers and networks that run your electricity supply system, that is annoying. But if they find out that your defences are robust, that is a good message for them to learn. It may deter them from trying to wreak havoc. An initial attack may even teach people in your country a useful lesson. They will take your own warning more seriously if they see that their carelessness has cost them money, for example.

Similarly, governments have to decide how much they wish to make the attack an affair of state. If you treat an attack on your computer systems as a national catastrophe, then you are creating an expectation among the public that you will do something dramatic in return: national pride and credibility are at stake. It may make more sense to say that the attacks are a nuisance, but that they are an expression of weakness, not strength, by the other side. A strong country can cope with an attack on its computer systems, just as it can cope with political and economic competition.

Telling the story carefully and well also helps shape the way events develop and end. Governments need to explain why the attack happened – is this essentially an attack by criminals and hooligans, or by a country with a political agenda or grievance? Is it perhaps the result of a miscalculation? Offering the attacker a way of backing down gracefully may be more sensible than responding in kind, or by escalating the use of what in military parlance are known as 'kinetic' (real) weapons.

The rules of computer warfare are still being written. But the most useful conventions are the ones that work before war actually starts. As East–West deals on the verified limiting of nuclear arsenals showed during the Cold War, they build trust and transparency. One sensible route is to agree to cooperate in the investigation and prosecution of crime on the internet. That may help determine whether what is perceived as an attack was actively sponsored by the other side's military, launched by someone else but tacitly tolerated by the government concerned, or is in fact a freelance effort with no government connection backing. A country which wittingly harbours criminals deserves a lot less trust than one which tries to catch them.

Another useful step would be an agreement not to spy aggressively on public infrastructure systems, such as gas, power, water or sewerage networks. These are potential military targets, but breaking into the networks and computers that keep them going in order to prepare the ground for a future attack could – by accident – cause them to go wrong. Or it could create weaknesses that other attackers such as criminals or hooligans could exploit.

In computer warfare, what the attacker actually does, what he thinks he did, and what the defender thinks has happened may all be different. Similarly, what the defender thinks he has done in response may be different from what the attacker perceives as happening. As Mr Libicki notes, a defender may think he has replied in a calm and sensible way to an outrageous attack. But the attacker may think that his gentle probing has brought a savagely disproportionate response.

Imagine, for example, that you are in charge of the defences of, say, Russia and you notice that someone has broken into one of your most important networks – say, the one that communicates with your nuclear arsenal. The intruder has messed around with the programs that make it work, in a way that is hard to understand. But your investigation leads you to believe that he has planted a bug that will sabotage the entire network in a crisis. As a result, you are furious. You assume that the Americans are responsible. You introduce emergency procedures, switching over your nuclear command and control to a more primitive but less vulnerable network which gives you less flexibility, but which you can depend on. You also respond by aggressively probing their network and launching some modest attacks to show them that you can do exactly the same to them.

But the Americans do not see it that way. Indeed, the military commanders are baffled by your behaviour. What has actually happened is that some American spies – working quite independently of the military – have installed a secret early warning system on the Russian network, so that they will know if you have put your nuclear forces on alert. That is, in their eyes, an entirely normal bit of espionage – no more threatening than planting a microphone in a bunker under the Kremlin.

This American espionage operation on the Russian network was so secret that nobody in the military knew about it. As a result, American generals are furious and worried about what they see as an unprovoked Russian attack on their computers, and the sudden switch to a network which they cannot monitor. That looks like the behaviour of a country preparing to launch a nuclear strike against the United States. They respond by putting all their forces on alert – after all, they do not want to be vulnerable to a disabling Russian attack on their communications network.

From the Russian point of view, that is still more threatening behaviour. First the Americans break into the most sensitive military network in Russia and make preparations to sabotage it. Now they are putting their forces on alert. Surely the right thing for

Russia to do is to respond in kind – perhaps also test-firing a missile for good measure.

It is easy to see how this sort of misunderstanding could result in a terrifying escalation. In the days of old-fashioned 'kinetic' weapons, such misunderstandings were possible, too. But an elaborate array of confidence-building measures, agreements, hotlines and observers all helped to reduce the scope for dangerous misperceptions. We have yet to do something similar with digital weapons – those aimed at, and launched from, computers and networks.

The answer to this lies only partly in elaborating how far international law applies. It is much more important to develop 'norms' – commonly accepted codes of behaviour – governing the way countries interact in this new domain of warfare. But it is not just international relations that have to adapt to the potential of new technology. We should start with our daily lives. The visionary physicist Nikolas Tesla wrote in 1926:

> When wireless is perfectly applied the whole earth will be converted into a huge brain . . . and the instruments through which we shall be able to do this will be amazingly simple compared with our present telephone. A man will be able to carry one in his vest pocket.[12]

But those pocket-sized devices are not just a boon from the point of view of convenience. They are a bane when it comes to security.

7

The Spy in Your Pocket

The mobile phone enables probably the most sophisticated and pervasive attacks on privacy and anonymity yet invented. The benefit is greatest for governments. If you can use the force of law to gain access to the phone company's computers, your target's phone is a tracking beacon, pinpointing his exact whereabouts. With a few simple tweaks it can also be a microphone picking up his conversation. With more sophisticated means it can be a way of infecting any computer he is close to. It does not even matter if the victim switches off his phone, so long as he does not remove the battery.*

John Bayliss, a former senior official at Britain's GCHQ spy agency who is now a security consultant, tours conferences to give an eye-popping demonstration of what is possible even with commercially available products. He starts by showing how a phone can be turned on remotely, giving no sign that the microphone is live. It can either transmit what it picks up via a phone call, or (on some devices) record it and e-mail it secretly to the person organising the bugging. At a presentation in London, I watched Mr

---

* It is also possible to doctor the actual battery so that it carries a tiny bug or tracking beacon.

Bayliss, an amiable, rotund figure with a mop of unruly grey hair, pass a phone to a member of the audience. He asked him to check it was switched off, and then to speak quietly into it. The audience member's voice blasted from a speaker on the stage. Next he showed how he can track his wife's movements, using a commercially available product designed to help locate stolen phones. He installs it on his wife's phone, but disables the feature that tells her that it is installed. As far as she is concerned, her phone is operating as normal. But Mr Bayliss can see her movements on his computer whenever he likes.

This software requires regular authorisation, sent by text message. But Mrs Bayliss never gets those messages. Her husband has set up another piece of software which diverts messages to him first. He then decides whether to forward them on to her. He can also read her outgoing messages, which are forwarded to him for review. Again, she will not notice anything, except perhaps a slight delay. If Mr Bayliss forgets to forward an SMS, she will blame the phone company. We do not expect our electronic devices to be completely reliable. Mr Bayliss has one more feature installed – every time his wife's phone makes or receives a call, he gets an SMS telling him about it.

Mr Bayliss concludes his demonstration of wizardry by confessing that he does not actually do this to his wife. But he stresses that none of his exploits involve secret, advanced software of the kind that is available to his former employer, GCHQ. It is all possible using off-the-shelf commercial products. The only hurdle for the attacker is to get it installed on the target's phone. This can be delivered by sending a picture, or even a doctored text message. Simplest of all is just to gain access to the phone for a few minutes under a pretext and download the program from the internet. Think of that next time a stranger with a sob story asks if he can make a quick call from your phone.

Phones can be used not only to intercept messages, but also to make sure they never arrive. Recall the way in which the attackers looted Pin Hakhett's bank account. She had prudently arranged with her bank that, as well as using a password, she also receives a code by text message to authorise any new payee – the so-called 'two-factor authentication'. But the attacker evaded that by infecting not only her computer but also her mobile phone – sending an SMS, purportedly from the bank, telling her to click on a link to install new security software on her phone. That allowed the attacker to divert the security code. Only when Pin turns up at a branch of her bank, armed with her passport and other real-world documents, does she find that her bank account has been plundered.

This may sound like science fiction, but it is all too real. At the same conference where I heard Mr Bayliss make his presentation, I also met the legendary hacker Kevin Mitnick. That designation is something of an understatement: it might be better to say that he is the person who invented hacking. He cut his teeth in the Cuckoo's Egg era, initially amusing himself by playing tricks on the American telephone system. He found that simply by impersonating telephone engineers, and with a few technical tricks, such as sending a whistle down the line with the right frequency, he could make free phone calls. When mobile telephones arrived on the scene, he worked out ways of making free calls on them, too. He was eventually sentenced to five years in jail – a punishment which many of his fans thought unfair, as he neither vandalised the networks he had breached nor had he stolen money.

Mr Mitnick has plenty of party tricks. His visiting card is a sliver of metal, which, when you break it into pieces, becomes a rather useful set of lock picks. His main speciality is 'social engineering' – tricking people into giving away personal information (either their own, or others). He illustrated this in dramatic form. He asked me if I had a mobile phone number on my phone that I would particularly trust. Slightly pompously, I said I had one belonging to someone I could not name, but which was listed in my phone simply as 'Buckingham Palace'. He asked me for the number, and, with some trepidation, I gave it to him (he promised not to dial it). He fiddled with his keyboard for a moment and told me to look at my phone. There was an incoming SMS message – apparently from my 'Buckingham Palace' contact. It read simply: 'please give Kevin all the passwords.'

This was not as magical as it appeared. There are sites on the internet which offer these tricks as a commercial service. One of them is fogmo.com which advertises as follows: 'With our anonymous SMS service you can choose exactly who you want your SMS message to appear from, it really can be from anyone. You can even choose to send from a name instead of a number. Some people call this spoof or fake sms.' Fogmo also offers a similar service for e-mail.

With tools like this, you do not need to crack someone's password. You can just get them to give it to you – pretending to be a member of the royal family if necessary. You can send an e-mail purporting to be from a trusted colleague containing a link, and follow it up with an SMS urging the victim to act on it. You can also send a link – supposedly from a trusted contact – saying 'nice pic – take a look'. That is what happened one day to Chip. He received a text message seemingly from Pin, and when he clicked on the link, his phone seemed hard at work, but did not display any picture. When he asked her later that day, she was baffled, but both of them dismissed the episode as one of the strange quirks of modern technology. But the link to the 'picture' actually downloaded malware to Chip's phone, which not only enabled the remote diversion of his SMS messages, but also scooped up his contact list, enabling the attacker to attack all his friends and colleagues, using messages apparently sent from him.

On current trends, mobile phone companies are losing the battle against mobile malware. Those running the 'Android' operating system are particularly vulnerable, because anyone can produce software to run on these devices. Installing software on an Apple phone is much harder, because the company scrutinises 'apps' (special software for mobile devices) before they become available. The tools described above are trivial compared with those available to more devious attackers. In an attack discovered by the FireEye security firm in September 2014, 10,000 SMS messages were stolen from ninety-six devices – phones running the Android software – by malware called Korbanker.[1] Messages included the authentication codes discussed above. Malware known as AndroRAT can give an outsider complete control of a smartphone running Android software – and the user may never know about it until he finds his bank account empty and bailiffs coming to collect the bills run up in his name.

If the phone in your pocket can do you one kind of damage, the memory stick that you carry around does another. The hunt for convenience, which as we have seen above, usually trumps any considerations of security. In the early years of personal computing, persuading one machine to talk to another was hard: it involved installing special software (usually known as 'drivers') and often a series of complicated tweaks. Once a computer worked with one device – say, a new printer – it would often stop working with others.

The new era is often called 'plug and play' – modern computer users expect to be able to plug anything into their computer and for it to work immediately and smoothly. The USB standard is at the heart of this. It is designed to be easy and user-friendly. Computers are configured to accept USB devices, not reject them. They do not quibble when a USB device tries to do something unusual, because many devices do several things: for example, a camera or headphone set may also include a microphone. The computer will try to help that. Indeed, computers will try to accommodate as many USB devices as the user wants. USB (or Universal Serial Bus) is the standard plug-and-socket arrangement for all sorts of peripheral devices requiring low power. It is the way you connect a mouse and keyboard to your computer, but also many other devices. These range from the humdrum (readers for memory cards) to the exotic and amusing (fans, desktop toys, even small refrigerators, and devices to keep a coffee cup warm). Perhaps most dangerous of all, it is for many people the standard way of recharging their portable devices, such as music players and phones (or anyone else's who may ask). A real-world equivalent would (in the days when smoking was more common) be something like a cigarette lighter. Just like USB devices, these come in all shapes and sizes, from the fancy to the utilitarian. The technology varies a bit, from heirloom Zippos with flints and liquid to modern gas-filled ones. But they are (sentimental reasons aside) interchangeable. Nobody accepting a light from a stranger would worry about the risk of infection, or that it might blow up in your face. Many would behave in similar carefree style if someone asks to plug a phone into a computer to get a few minutes of electrical charge.

But as researchers from Security Research Labs (a German security firm) showed at the Black Hat conference in Las Vegas in 2014, the USB port is a gaping hole in computer security.[2] It means that the 'air-gap' – the physical disconnection of a sensitive machine from any outside system – is no longer much of a gap. That is not just the fault of USB devices: an advanced attacker can use any mobile phone, suitably doctored, to attack a computer which is not connected to the internet. But any stand-alone computer is likely to need some occasional connection to the outside world – for example, in updating its software, or giving it the data it needs to work with. That instantly creates room for attackers. If you know that someone regularly inserts a USB memory stick into a computer, then your target becomes not the computer, but the memory stick: can that be compromised? If you cannot reach the memory stick itself, can you at least reach another computer which it will be plugged into?

Savvy computer users may know that they should scan a USB memory stick before using it. But that is not enough. Anti-virus software can look for programs in a memory stick. But they cannot scan the 'firmware' (built-in proprietary software) that runs USB devices such as mice, web cameras, keyboards and so on. In their talk at Black Hat, the researchers showed how they could take control of a computer using a memory stick which appeared to be completely empty. Indeed it was empty – the flash memory part of it. The danger came from software planted in the chip which actually operates the device.

When the rogue USB changes its personality and takes on a malign form, the most that may happen is that a small window pops up briefly saying that a new device has been installed. Most users will regard that as part of the background confusion inherent in operating a computer.

Yet the new device can wreak havoc. Attackers will typically start by buying an off-the-shelf device and doctoring it with a malign program disguised as a software update. The booby-trapped device can then pretend to act as normal on one level, while wreaking havoc behind the scenes. A common form of attack is to bribe a cleaner or maintenance worker to see what sort of keyboard a potential victim is using. Then the attacker swaps the keyboard for another one, seemingly identical, but with the chip inside loaded with malware.

These attacks are common – the tactic of dropping USB sticks near the target building is thought to have been developed by Russian intelligence during an attack on NATO member states, involving the spread of malware called agent.btz. Swapping keyboards is a favourite tactic of Britain's GCHQ. America's NSA even intercepts computer equipment being ordered from the manufacturer in order to doctor it.

Attacks via USB are hard to contain. Any other USB stick put into an infected machine becomes infected – and can then transfer the malware to the next computer it touches. This has the advantage from the attacker's point of view that he can reach 'air-gapped' computers – those which are not connected to the internet.

An infected USB stick can hijack the computer's access to the network (impersonating a bit of equipment known as a 'network card'). It can change a computer's Domain Name Server (DNS) setting – in effect its address on the internet – to redirect legitimate traffic, or organise something harmful. It can redirect an online banking session, for example, so that a 'man in the middle' can gain the victim's banking details. It can help steal passwords, even if they are entered not from a physical keyboard, but from one displayed on your screen and activated by a mouse.

The USB device can also wait until it detects the computer is starting up, and then put a small virus on to the main machine which takes it over before the 'boot' sequence, when the computer's main programs start up. It can reprogram your computer so that it replaces the Basic Input/Output System or BIOS – the computer chip which controls the way your machine starts up.

Cleaning up a computer infected in this way is almost impossible. If you wipe the hard disk and reinstall the operating system (the main program, such as Microsoft Windows) which runs the machine, it will not help matters. The rogue device may still be connected. And even if it is not, it will have reprogrammed all the other peripheral devices – the keyboard, mouse, web camera, microphone, loudspeakers, headphones – or even USB components inside the computer. In short, the German researchers argue: 'once infected, computers and their USB peripherals can never be trusted again.'[3]

Taking precautions against this, even for those aware of the threat, is difficult. USB devices do not have unique serial numbers, so it is hard to check their authenticity against a central registry. The 'firmware' which runs the devices is proprietary, so it is hard for an ordinary computer to scan it to see if anything has changed or is missing. It would be possible (in theory) to apply tougher standards to USB devices in future, so that upgrades have to be cryptographically signed, making it hard for an attacker to use this means to infect them. But that would not help the fact that billions of USB devices are already in use, and likely to be used for decades to come. The only practical defence is to treat USB devices like keys: keeping a careful register of each device, who has access to it, who has signed it out, what they have done with and when they returned it. A security-conscious organisation may limit the number of computers that have a socket for USB devices. It may disable (where possible) the computers' ability to download and install automatic updates. It may prohibit the use of any other devices. When I gave a lecture at Britain's GCHQ, I had to hand over every electronic device, memory stick, card, chip and other material before I was allowed into the secure area.

Such precautions may be feasible in an organisation where security is the top priority, but they are unlikely to help the average user. We are like a world of chain-smokers, waking up to the idea that strangers' cigarette lighters can do huge damage, but unsure if we can even trust our own.

If the devices you have in your pocket are dangerous, what you have in the rest of your house is even more worrying. Dan Geer, one of the founding fathers of the internet, has highlighted concerns about the 'smart grid'. This is internet parlance for using computers to exchange data about electricity supply and demand. To be fair, the smart grid is a terrific idea – it could cut wasteful power consumption, reduce carbon emissions and greatly increase the power network's resilience to breakdowns and natural disasters. Devices on the smart grid do not dumbly switch on and off – they coordinate their consumption in order to be efficient: so an electric oven might tell a washing machine to wait until cooking is over, while a fridge would run its compressor only when the air conditioning is taking a rest, and a big pump in the sewerage system turns on when demand is light and electricity is cheap. Pin and Chip are already a small part of the smart grid. They have installed solar panels on their roof. The electricity feeds into the grid when the sun is shining, and makes them a little money. They have also programmed their hot water system to use cheap electricity, and they have connected their central heating thermostat to the internet, so that Chip, who works irregular hours, can turn it on before he arrives home. They have also installed a 'smart meter', at the electricity company's behest. This monitors their electricity consumption – and means that nobody needs to come and take a manual meter reading.

But the potential for sabotage and accident in the smart grid is huge. If a device can switch off another device to save power, it could also be programmed to do so maliciously. Food would rot in fridges; lifts and doors could stop working. Sewage pumps – which run intermittently and consume large amounts of power – could switch off, not to save the load on power stations, but in order to prompt a catastrophic public-health disaster.

The smart grid is a forerunner of a much bigger shift. The internet is moving away from being chiefly a way for people to communicate to being a network for machines to talk to other machines. The 'internet of things' marks a revolutionary change in the way computer networks enable modern life. The idea is simple and attractive: if computers organise the details of daily life, we can concentrate on things that we like. The Hakhetts are unlikely to buy a fridge that orders milk automatically, but they would be quite happy to have a thermostat that is turned on whenever Chip's car is approaching the house – it would be easier than trying to do it while driving. It is the same principle as one of the central advantages of the smart grid: the power network can tell electricity consumers to turn down their air conditioning or heating a notch during a power spike, saving the cost of running an expensive back-up power station.

The 'internet of things' is growing rapidly. With 1.9 billion gadgets online in mid-2014, it already comprises as many devices as there are old-style computers. By 2018, with a predicted nine billion, it will have more than computers, smartphones and tablet computers combined.[4] Uses for internet connections are mushrooming. In future, for example, light bulbs will not contain just a humble incandescent filament in a vacuum, but a complex array of light-emitting diodes (LEDs). In future they may be manufactured with sensors for smoke detection, carbon monoxide or earthquakes – plus an internet connection to help you manage your domestic power supply better. Already, internet-connected household devices have cut household waste and boosted recycling (by alerting people to the 'pay as you throw' tariffs) and cut water leaks (through hooking up pipes to sensors).

These countless small devices – at home in the fridge, car, fuse box or heating system, or in the networks that move power, water and sewage – form a dangerous monoculture. The complexity of the modern internet belies the lack of what in other walks of life would be called biodiversity. In nature, the wider the gene pool in a particular species the less it is likely to be victim of a disabling disease. But the way computers and networks have developed has more in common with industrial agriculture, where a single variant of a crop becomes prevalent and therefore vulnerable to a pest or blight.

Mr Geer argues 'as society becomes more technologic, even the mundane comes to depend on distant digital perfection'.[5] If devices don't seem to work smoothly and efficiently, we don't want them. But as with computers, behind the façade of convenience is an unpleasant mixture of careless design, corners cut and unforeseen problems.

Bruce Schneier, a security guru, argues that the inherent insecurity of computers, dating from the way they were developed in the 1990s, has abated somewhat because software manufacturers now repair and update their software.[6] But the new generation of devices are far more pervasive than computers. They are also inconspicuous (the Hakhetts would be baffled if you asked them to explain how the network connections of their central heating thermostat and electricity meter function). They are also not designed for human hands-on control. If your computer software is out of date, Microsoft or Apple can send you peremptory warning messages telling you to update it. But what about the small box in the corner, with its mystifying flickering lights, that does something clever with your power supply? Is it robustly designed and remotely accessible, so that the next nasty surprise – such as the Shellshock bug described earlier – can be fixed quickly, everywhere? Experience suggests not.

At the Black Hat security conference in Las Vegas in 2014 security experts produced a number of examples of attacks on the monoculture – devices which are hard to protect and easy to penetrate. Researchers from the firm Qualys, for example, showed how the scanners used by the American government to scan passengers at airport security controls could be attacked, thanks to a feature built in by the manufacturers to make maintenance easy.[7] This involved an 'embedded' (built-in) account with a default password which the owners of the machines cannot change. Some of these scanners are connected to the internet, meaning that an attacker could gain access to them remotely and, in theory, manipulate the results. That would be one way of helping a terrorist bring an explosive device on to an aircraft.

Also at Black Hat, researchers showed how they could turn a domestic thermostat into a spying device, given just fifteen seconds of access to it.[8] The device concerned is called a Nest. It learns your daily routine and creates a heating regime around it. It also allows you to control your home heating remotely – so that, for example, if you are working late (and live alone) you can save money on fuel. But it can be used for other purposes, too. It could be conscripted into a botnet – used as a robot slave in spam and other mass automated attacks. It could be used to capture the other traffic on a domestic network – helping to steal credentials for banking and other services. This would not require someone breaking into your home. The attacker would merely have to gain access to the devices at some point between their manufacture and installation. Given the speed with which they can be compromised – you just hold down the power button for ten seconds and then insert a USB stick containing the malevolent software – a well-organised attacker could compromise a whole consignment and then wait for the devices to report back to him once they were installed.

The 'internet of things' is already churning out problems before it has even begun to reach its full potential. According to the researchers who discovered the vulnerability in the thermostat, more than 750,000 spam and 'phishing' e-mails (those containing malware or links to toxic sites) have been sent out from seemingly innocent devices such as fridges and televisions. It has also aroused serious concerns about privacy. The first target of real-life hackers has been surveillance cameras. These include those used to deter intruders (which can also record the private activities of those legitimately in the house), and also those used to monitor babies. If these use wireless connections, they are vulnerable.

Marc and Lauren Gilbert, a couple in Houston, Texas, found a voyeur had hacked the baby monitor they used to keep an eye on their two-year-old daughter, and was using it to shout obscenities at her.[9] The man – unidentified – could be heard saying 'fucking moron', and 'wake up you little slut' (the child, who is deaf, was not disturbed). A presentation by Sergey Shekyan and Artem Harutyunyan, two security researchers, shows how a humble wireless camera can be attacked and reprogrammed, both to take part in malicious activities against other users and to infect the owner's computer.[10]

An even more troubling example came from a stunt by Jesus Molina, a security researcher staying in a hotel in the Chinese province of Shenzhen.[11] The hotel supplies every guest with an iPad (computer tablet) to be a 'digital butler', for ordering meals, controlling the room's window blinds, lighting and heating and so forth. But Mr Molina soon found he could do a lot more: with a little bit of fiddling he had access to these services in every room in the hotel (he restricted himself to turning on and off the 'Do not disturb' lights. Had he wished to, he could have enjoyed the same access from outside the hotel. And had he planted some malware on the network he could have done it from the other side of the world.

In February 2014 the US government's CERT (Computer Emergency Response Team) issued a formal warning to Belkin, manufacturer of one of the most popular ranges of home automation systems (it boasts 500,000 users in the United States alone).[12] Its products include a wi-fi-controlled power socket, which you can turn on and off remotely. The researcher Daniel Buentello started by hacking into a switch and making his brother's desk light turn on and off remotely, so fast that it created a strobe effect. That is an amusing prank – unless you suffer from epilepsy. It would be a lot less amusing to turn on all the electric heaters in a house, or the fire sprinklers.[13] (Belkin responded by saying it had already fixed the flaws, and that users should update the software on their devices). In September 2014, a big manufacturer of wireless thermostats, Heatmiser, advised its customers to disable the wi-fi capability (the main reason for buying them) when it turned out that an attacker could control them remotely simply by using the password '1234'.[14] A security researcher called Andrew Tierney, who discovered the problem, was able to find 7,000 vulnerable internet-connected thermostats using a simple internet search.[15]

As Mr Geer points out, the existing monoculture in the 'routers' (the small blinking boxes that run your wireless network) used in homes and small businesses is already a serious security threat – he likens it to a 'gasoline spill in an enclosed shopping mall'. Routers are the boxes which turn the internet connection that comes in via the phone company or the cable provider into a usable service for many computers (usually by wireless connection). The vast majority of internet users have no interaction with their routers. They may, if they are conscientious, install some limited password protection, which is roughly the equivalent of putting curtains on the windows in order that nosy passers-by do not look into your house from the street. Every few years, we may replace the router for a better one. But for the most part, these devices are the unsung ferrymen of our daily voyages into cyber-space.

Perhaps we should worry about them rather more. The routers are built with economy and low maintenance in mind. Nobody has full responsibility for their security. They use off-the-shelf software and the cheapest possible hardware. So long as it fulfils its main function, nobody minds much what else happens on a router. Mr Schneier notes: 'no one entity has any incentive, expertise, or even ability to patch the software once it's shipped. The chip manufacturer is busy shipping the next version . . . the ODM [original design manufacturer] is busy upgrading its product to work with this next chip. Maintaining the older chips and products just isn't a priority.'

As Mr Geer laments, most routers on offer are 'years out of date and there is NO upgrade path. These routers can be taken over remotely and . . . to do so requires low skill. That they have been taken over does not diminish their usefulness to their owner, nor is that takeover visible to their owner. The commandeered routers can be used immediately . . . or they can be staged as a weapon for tomorrow.' Routers were the subject of a hacking contest at the same Black Hat security conference in Las Vegas in 2014. The results were chilling. Five popular models were breached, with fifteen vulnerabilities discovered and exploited. Had the attackers been truly malicious, they could have employed the routers to attack people using them to connect to the internet, or hijacked them to spread spam and malware. Interestingly, some of the vulnerabilities in the routers were the result of neglect. As a journalist noted drily: 'only four of the reported vulnerabilities were completely new. The other ones had been discovered and patched in the past in other router models from the same manufacturers, but the vendors did not fix them in the routers selected for this competition.'[16]

Attackers have already noticed the potential of these simple, vital, outdated, ill-maintained, inconspicuous and ubiquitous machines. Mr Schneier highlights three recent examples. As early as 2008, a malicious program called DNSChanger was discovered to be attacking home routers as well as computers.[17] It would redirect the user's web traffic in order to allow its authors, a group of Estonian-based criminals called Rove Digital, to inject rogue advertising into the pages loaded (before it was shut down by a federal court order in America, this scam made the criminals $15 million).[18] In Poland, attackers hijacked computer users' routers in order to steal their banking details.[19] Users would think that they were logging in to their own banks, but in fact the criminals had produced phoney pages. The only difference would be that the web address did not start with the letters 'https' and a small padlock. In Brazil, attackers infected 4.5 million DSL routers to persuade users to download malware (disguised as legitimate security 'plugins') when they tried to reach well-known websites such as Google and Facebook. Fabio Assolini, a researcher for Kaspersky Lab, who discovered the scam, also managed to find an internet chat session where the attackers were boasting of the money they had made. One had spent \$50,000 on taking prostitutes to Rio.[20] Although the scam was uncovered, the owners of the routers were left with machines they could no longer access – the attackers had changed the passwords.

Another piece of malware that was discovered in 2013 targets routers (as well as cameras and similar devices). It was limited in its reach, working only with a particular kind of chip. The vulner-ability – in software written in the Linux open-source program-ming language – has been patched. But how many people have the inclination or knowledge to update Linux software running on the small box that controls their home wi-fi?[21]

An example of how such hijacked routers can be used in cyber-attacks is the 'Moon worm'.[22] This hops between routers made by Linksys, though for what purpose is unclear. Computer users who use routers for the wireless broadband in their homes or offices mostly do not bother to fiddle with the security settings. One of these allows the router to be managed remotely – a useful feature for someone trying to fix a problem without having to make a house call. But a criminal can also gain control of the router, and use it to direct users to a phoney internet banking site, where they may give up their login and passwords.[23] Or they can be used to run botnets and launch attacks. The owner of the network can install as much security software on his computers as he likes: it will make no difference. The adversary is not on the network, but outside it. It is rather as if you have a well-constructed front door, but a malignant demon on your porch invisibly searches you on entry and exit and is also able to send letters and make phone calls on your behalf.

Jacob Holcomb, a security researcher who pioneered research into the vulnerabilities of routers,[24] has now turned his attention to another dangerous monoculture: network-attached storage devices. These are unlikely to have crossed the path of most readers in their home computer use, but they are common in workplaces where they are used as a central memory bank for storing large amounts of information. This is a lot more convenient – and in theory safer – than storing important data on an individual user's computer. But Mr Holcomb has uncovered a series of dangerous vulnerabilities.[25] 'There wasn't one device that I literally couldn't take over,' Mr Holcomb said, after testing devices from ten manufacturers. The result of hijacking a storage device would be different from taking over a router. Routers control (and can compromise or hijack) the connection between a network and the internet. Storage devices hold data. So if the storage machine is compromised, that data can be copied, doctored or deleted irreversibly. One is the use of ransomware to encrypt files important to a business.[26] Another is the use of storage devices attached to other people's computers to generate $600,000 in digital currency[27] – this is a kind of cash which does not exist in physical form, but consists of solutions to cryptographic problems stored on a computer. It is 'mined' by getting computers to work out new problems, which requires huge and increasing amounts of processing power. In the early days of digital currencies, these calculations could be performed on an ordinary machine. Now they require much more powerful ones, meaning that thieves are trying to find spare capacity which can be hijacked in order to make money.

The attacks outlined above – on phones, USB ports and internet-connected devices – all exemplify the danger of what Mr Geer calls 'monoculture': a concept well known in biology, but of increasing importance in the security of our computers and networks.

8

The Danger of Monoculture

The internet is rife with monocultures – software or technology which is widely used for reasons of convenience or profit, but containing great dangers to the users once they draw the attention of attackers. This is a bit like having a world where every door in every building has the same kind of lock. Once you learn to pick that kind of lock, you can get in anywhere. The worst kind of monoculture is an invisible one. If you think that you have multiple versions of something important – several cars, several bank accounts, several phones – you can still be hit by an attack on the monoculture. Having several cars is no use if there is a petrol shortage (though a bicycle may be a boon). Multiple bank accounts are no use if a financial crisis shutters them all (but having some cash at home will save you). Multiple phones work only so long as the network does (but having an amateur radio licence may enable you to stay better informed during Armageddon).

One of the deepest internet thinkers, Dan Geer, has outlined the significance of this.[1] The internet was designed for resistance to random faults, not to targeted ones. In other words, he argues, it is immensely resilient to accidents, acts of incompetence, carelessness and technological breakdown. But the same qualities that protect it from random threats make it vulnerable to deliberate attacks.

That vulnerability has several roots. One is that the computers, networks and programs that we use are complicated, and cobbled together in ways that nobody can fully oversee. Yet the impossible complexity of the internet comes from the beguiling temptation of simplicity. For nervous, cash-strapped decision-makers it is better to have something that can be installed easily and works cheaply, but it is vulnerable to a small chance of catastrophe, than to have something inherently resilient, but which will be complicated and expensive to maintain. In short, nobody was ever fired for buying standard computers and running them with standard software – for example, a Dell machine running Microsoft software.

Yet, as in the real world, if everyone adopts a simple solution, then we create a dangerous monoculture. Nature likes diversity, because though it is less efficient in the short term it is much safer in the long run. We see this in agriculture, where ambitious farmers and crop companies fine-tune their seeds for maximum yield, which works perfectly in the short run, but proves disastrous when a predator appears. Such predators – whether they are insects, fungi or whatever – will munch their way through the monoculture until they run out of food, or until something in turn preys on them.

Microsoft Windows is perhaps the best-known monoculture: if you find a flaw in a version of Windows, you have access to any computer that runs it. The best example of this is the original Windows internet browser, Internet Explorer (IE). To be fair, IE was no worse than much other software around in the 1990s. But because it was so ubiquitous, it became a perfect target for attackers. They scrutinised IE for all sorts of flaws, and uncovered them fast. IE could be used to hijack the machine, to download malware, to export data and much else besides. Even when Microsoft starting updating IE to fix its flaws, sending out 'patches' to be installed on the vulnerable machines, the attackers were undeterred. For a start, not every computer user updates his software promptly, so plenty of old versions remain in the wild. And as fast as one flaw was patched, another could be found.

But as the security guru Mr Geer points out, the most dangerous monoculture now is no longer Microsoft Windows. One reason is that Microsoft has become a great deal better (although far from perfect) at repairing and updating its software. Another is that new dangers are mounting.

Heartbleed was seen as quite serious enough at the time – it involved 500,000 websites, including some of the most important on the internet. At issue was one of the commonest means of secure communication between computers, known as the Secure Socket Layer, or SSL. Broadly speaking, if you see the padlock at the start of an internet address, along with the letters 'https', then you are connected to another computer using SSL.* It is not necessary to understand the details of SSL (and of an extension called TSL), but it can easily be imagined as a tunnel created between two computers by mutual consent, through which messages can then pass securely and privately. Creating this involves a series of handshakes, where each of the two computers determines that the other one is to be trusted and sets up the encryption that allows the tunnel to function in a way that it will, supposedly, be impenetrable to outsiders.

Heartbleed is not malware – it was not created with malign intent. It is a mistake in a bit of software used to maintain the secure tunnel. At the start of a session, the two computers exchange digital handshakes, which, all being well, establish that the website is what it claims to be (and in some cases, that the customer is who he says he is, too). This relies on software called Open SSL which has a long and renowned history. It is not the result of a commercial enterprise – Open SSL was written by enthusiasts, part of a

---

* Technically minded readers will forgive a degree of oversimplification here. I am aware that https and SSL are not synonymous.

commendably public-spirited effort to write 'Open Source' software in which every detail is open to public scrutiny. This has some big advantages over products from companies such as Microsoft. One is that the resulting programs are free and cannot be monopolised. Why bother to use the expensive Microsoft Word program, for example, when you can use OpenOffice for nothing, which is almost as good?

Hierarchical private-sector companies such as Microsoft can find it difficult to manage the writing of big software projects: egos, budgets and rules get in the way of the best solution. An army of motivated volunteers can often do a better job: one that is faster and neater. Costs are defrayed by donations, or by consulting work for companies that want to use the software for other purposes. A whole world of programs exists based on such voluntary efforts, including the Firefox browser and the Linux operating system. These programs, like Open SSL, have regular updates, which many users will install automatically. But in 2011 a German computer programmer, Robin Seggelmann, then a PhD student at the University of Duisburg-Essen, accidentally introduced a flaw into Open SSL, with catastrophic consequences.

It worked like this. To keep the digital 'tunnel' open, regular test messages are exchanged. It would be insecure, and a waste of resources, to keep a connection open when it is not needed. Some computer users carefully exit their browser window when they have finished a secure connection. Others may not bother. This 'heartbeat' in Open SSL involves the user's computer sending a small question to the server, and checking to see that the right answer comes back. Assuming that the encryption is working and both ends are still connected, nothing changes. But the flaw in Open SSL meant that instead of the tiny answer coming back, the server could be tricked into giving a much larger dollop of data: whatever the last 500 characters were in the computer memory. It is rather as if as well as shaking hands with someone you were able to take whatever was uppermost in their pocket or handbag.

This could – potentially – include the crown jewels of any security system: the cryptographic keys used to decode messages sent by outsiders (for an explanation of the basic principles of encryption, see Appendix Three). If your computer has just been decoding some encrypted data (for example, because you have logged into your bank account) then it will have the key uppermost in its memory. The intruder, using Heartbleed, can simply walk off with it. It could also lead to the loss of 'cookies' – little lumps of data that identify a computer to a network, signifying that you have logged in recently with the right username and password. That would allow someone to impersonate your computer. Heartbleed could also allow an attacker to read e-mails, discover personal banking details or health records, launch sabotage attacks by scrambling data or sending false instructions, and many other kinds of mayhem.

The flaw in Open SSL was discovered by security researchers, purely by chance. It is not clear if anyone had found out about it earlier, or used it for nefarious purposes. The only confirmed reported use of it was in Canada, where 900 social security numbers were stolen from a government computer. But measuring the impact only by known breaches is misleading. That is one of the problems of cyber-attacks: they often leave no fingerprints, and it is hard to tell if data has been copied or misused. As soon as news broke of the flaw, big computer companies urged their customers to change their passwords. Tens of millions of computer users did so.

That reveals plenty that is wrong with security on the internet. Armed with the 'private key' an attacker can break the encryption on recorded internet traffic. In a well-run security system, using a technique called 'perfect forward secrecy' this risk can be mitigated:

each digital tunnel is created using a one-off set of passwords, so that its content remains scrambled even if an attacker has access to the private key of one party. But perfect forward secrecy is complicated to use and far too few people bother.

Heartbleed could have been a lot worse. It did not give attackers the right to give commands to the computers it affected, just to steal data from them. It did not steal passwords and other secret material directly from people who were using websites, only from organisations and companies running them. The haul was more random than targeted.

Yet both Heartbleed and Shellshock (which came later, and was even more serious) exemplify three grave and central flaws in the way our computers and networks work. One is complexity. As explained earlier, we depend on arrays of hardware and software which are so complicated that nobody can understand how it all works. This is aggravated over time. Even if a software developer has an idea of how his product works at the time he writes it, future generations of programmers will not. The mistake in Shellshock dates from 1992. That is not just a question of understanding spaghetti software, but getting to grips with twenty-year-old spaghetti.

A second is stinginess. The internet was designed and run by underpaid academics and amateurs. That approach remains at its heart. Nobody cares enough about security flaws to take full responsibility for fixing them. Both Heartbleed and Shellshock were mistakes in free software – written by enthusiasts and available to everyone. The people who maintain and develop these programs are underpaid volunteers. This approach is great for innovation, less so for security. It relies on the idea that the attention of many people will help plug gaps and iron out problems. But what in fact happens is that attention is drawn to the most interesting and glamorous issues, and not to the boring, complicated ones. It is true that Shellshock was discovered by a public-spirited researcher, Stéphane Chazelas, and the writers of 'open-source' free software scrambled to provide patches for the various programs affected. It is also true that those who make software for profit may be less willing to advertise the bugs they find. But none of these arguments are much comfort to those who are put at risk.

This brings us to the third and biggest point: irresponsibility. If I am the boss of an airline, my job (and perhaps my liberty) is at stake if the planes are carelessly flown and maintained. But where does the buck stop in the world of computers and networks? The supervisory bodies do not have the budget to make their recommendations happen. Commercial participants may be public spirited, but ultimately mind more about their profits than the safety of people who may be neither customers nor suppliers. Governments may wonder why they should spend that taxpayers' money on global security improvements.

In short, just as nobody ends up with the bill for fixing flaws on the internet, nobody is in charge. The non-profit bodies such as the two U.S.-based organisations, the Internet Corporation for Assigned Names and Numbers (ICANN), which maintains what is in effect the internet's addressing system, and the Internet Engineering Task Force (IETF), which makes sure that the technical standards remain up to date and universally workable, cannot force people to change their habits. Governments do not run the internet – and even in countries where they have a lot of clout they may not be interested in fixing problems quickly. It may be more attractive to exploit a vulnerability than to clean it up.

The lack of responsibility is particularly glaring in the world of security certificates, which underpin every transaction on the internet that we believe to be secure. Most people who use them have not the slightest idea about how they work, any more than they worry about the electronics inside their car. These connections were originally used mainly in shopping and business online, creating a safe way of making payments online. In essence, they allow someone visiting a site to be sure that what he sees on his screen is actually the destination he is looking for. The owner of the site buys a security certificate from a certificate authority who makes some checks to ensure that the site is genuine. Anyone visiting the site reads the certificate and can automatically verify it with the issuing authority. Assuming all is well the HTTPS prefix and a small padlock then appear in the address field of the browser, and the person visiting the site can safely assume that he has reached his destination, and that traffic between his computer and the website is properly encrypted.

But this system is full of holes. For site owners, installing and maintaining the certificates is a cumbersome and error-prone process. Worse, the authorities who issue these certificates have frequently slipped up. A particular scandal in 2011 involved the Dutch company DigiNotar, which allowed hackers, probably working on behalf of the Iranian government, to issue up to 500 fake certificates in its name.[2] The details are complicated, but the effect of the false certificates was catastrophic. Many public services in the Netherlands stopped functioning for a time, as the Dutch government said it was unable to guarantee the security of its own websites. DigiNotar's behaviour relating to the breach did not inspire confidence; nor did the Dutch government. Many outsiders found the explanations belated and incomplete. DigiNotar is now bankrupt.

This was bad enough for the seventeen million people who were told to return to using pen and paper for anything important. It was sad for the people who worked at DigiNotar, which almost immediately filed for voluntary bankruptcy. But it was worst of all for the many Iranians who had trusted Google's Gmail service for their private communications, including dissident and opposition activity. Up to 300,000 Gmail accounts were thought to be compromised.

A report by Trend Micro, a security firm, showed that the misuse of the security certificates had enabled a 'man-in-the-middle' attack which targeted Iranians trying to send encrypted messages. 'Their anti-censorship software should have protected them. In reality, however, a third party was able to spy on all of their encrypted messages.'[3] The reaction from opposition circles was despair. 'It's the greatest possible disaster for all Internet users, especially for Iranian users,' wrote a blogger.[4]

The mendacity and secrecy surrounding the breach at DigiNotar is typical of the way the computer security industry deals with bad news. The company (now indeed bankrupt) lied about the extent of the breach, and denied that the weaknesses which had been exploited by the attackers existed. The Dutch authorities also initially insisted that nothing was wrong with the country's e-government systems. And nobody has been willing to get to grips with the fundamental problem. Too many authorities issue security certificates. Systems of oversight or scrutiny are flawed. (A year earlier, one of the biggest security companies, Comodo, was involved in a similar incident when an Italian partner was attacked and certificates stolen.)

To see how weak the system is, recall the earlier comparison made with aviation. International standards for aeroplane safety, both human and mechanical, are rigid. Pilots must be properly trained. Strict rules govern airports – the necessary length of runway for different types of planes, capability in fog and at night and so forth. The reason is simple. Aviation is essential to modern life. The public has high expectations of safety. If anything goes wrong, it is carefully logged and examined. Manufacturers are expected to scrutinise their products for every possible defect that may have caused even a malfunction, let alone an accident. If something is wrong, all the planes are grounded until it is put right.

The internet is just as vital for modern civilised life. But nothing of the kind exists to keep it safe and reliable, or to examine mistakes and accidents when they occur. No international or national inspectorate examines security procedures at certificate issuers, for example, or how they screen their staff. Some certificate providers have close ties with their host country's intelligence services. Others may have been penetrated by organised crime, or by hacktivists.

Such problems in international cooperation and law enforcement are not unique. We are used to dealing with countries which have corrupt or politicised police forces, or shipping registers. We adjust our behaviour accordingly – a request for cooperation from a police force in Russia receives different treatment than from one in Switzerland. Some countries' driving licences are notoriously easy to acquire corruptly.

We are used to dealing with varying international standards of probity. If you fail to meet international aviation standards (of maintenance, noise, etc.) then you cannot land your airliner in any airport in the developed world. A smelly or dangerous merchant vessel is not allowed to dock in a civilised port. But on other issues we are more tolerant. If you arrive in Britain with any foreign driving licence, you can use it for twelve months – even if you bought it corruptly and never passed a test.[5] The risk of a bad foreign driver having a crash and hurting or killing someone is outweighed by the benefit (to tourism and the economy generally) of recognising all foreign driving licences. But the potential harm if a badly maintained foreign plane crashes at a big international airport, or if a rustbucket ship sinks in a vital navigation channel, is huge.

But what is the damage of a fake security certificate? This allows a hacker, a malicious foreign government, or a criminal, to impersonate a trusted website, typically in a 'man-in-the-middle' attack, where traffic going to and from a website is scrutinised by a third party. It is hard to imagine a more damaging flaw in the whole structure of the internet, or to find a real-world analogy.

A partial counterpart example would be a government that habitually issues false passports, or allows criminals to incorporate companies and open bank accounts. But even that is not really a complete equivalent. A false passport is damaging only if you suspend belief when you look at it. A company registered in a notorious legal black hole is unlikely to be able to do serious business. But a fake security certificate is both trusted and invisible. It is replicable hundreds of thousands of times. The entire internet is built on the idea that security certificates are trustworthy. But as the Electronic Frontier Foundation, a do-gooding outfit based in Washington, DC, notes, 'the security of HTTPS is only as strong as the practices of the least trustworthy/competent CA [Certificate Authority]'.[6] A new organisation called the Internet Security Research Group (ISRG), backed by mix of commercial and non-profit bodies including the EFF, Mozilla (which supports the Firefox browser) and Cisco (which makes networking equipment), aims to launch a new scheme offering free, scrutinised and constantly monitored security certificates in mid-2015.[7]

That may eventually change things for the better. But so far, even for (a highly atypical) suspicious and technically informed computer user, no practical way exists to check an individual certificate. Thousands of entities issue certificates (nobody keeps exact count, because some outfits pass on their rights to subsidiaries). Some have the authority to do this because they are part of some wider organisation, such as a university, or a national telecom company. The best check on their integrity is from browsers. Companies such as Google (which runs Chrome), Apple (Safari) and Microsoft (Internet Explorer) put a lot of effort into fine-tuning their software to make it recognise a flawed, out-of-date or dubious security certificate. Readers may have come across warnings from time to time, saying that a site they are trying to reach has an expired, mismatched or incomplete security certificate. That is better than nothing. But it is far from foolproof. One reason is that the government certification authorities in countries such as Turkey, the United Arab Emirates and other places have every reason to break the system. Remember that the security certificates enable internet users to create tunnels in which to exchange messages safely and privately. For an authoritarian government (or even an inquisitive one) having easy access to these tunnels is highly tempting. The best way is to do the 'man-in-the-middle' attack mentioned earlier. At each end of the tunnel, everything appears normal. But somewhere in between an intruder is monitoring and copying the traffic. Though the details of such attacks are complex, the principle is simple. And to launch them, the best means is to have access to the security certificate, and thus the computer handshakes that it generates.[8]

A second problem is carelessness. Many quite reputable sites fail to keep their security certificates up to date, or have sites with slightly different addresses from those given to the certificating authority (for example, the certificate may be for a site with the old-fashioned 'www' prefix to the address, whereas the server may allow visitors to use a simpler address, without the prefix).

Other certificate authorities delegate their authority. The parent certificate is trusted by browsers and their subordinate certificates follow in the slipstream, too. But we don't know how many such certificates are out there: there is no duty of public disclosure on the people who issue security certificates. If they receive a query from a computer asking if a certificate is valid or not, they will reply yes or no. But whether the certificate was indeed validly issued is another story. To make it even harder, any certificating authority can issue a certificate for any domain, anywhere in the world. So if, for example, I choose to try to defraud my employer by setting up a site called economist-subscriptions.com in order to steal subscribers' money, I can get a certificate from anywhere – for example, from an authority in a non-English-speaking country where my malign intent will not be spotted. Not only are certificates not properly checked, they are also issued with astonishing ease.[9]

A crime could look like this. I would steal a list of *Economist* subscribers (either by hacking into *The Economist*'s computer network, or by bribing or tricking an employee), and then send 'phishing' e-mails to hundreds of thousands of current and former customers, offering a convincing sounding special deal, available at this website. I would copy *The Economist*'s logo and wording verbatim. The only difference would be that the credit card details and payments would go to me. A big flaw in this scheme ought to be that the site would appear insecure. It would not get the little padlock and the 'https' prefix, which reassures customers that they are dealing with a reputable provider. But because of the flaws in the way that security certificates are issued, I would be able to buy that certificate quite legally.

In other words, a vulnerability at one point in the security system can become universal, not because of action by a wrongdoer, but just because of the way the system is designed. Imagine that a lock is designed carelessly, with a flaw: hit it hard with a hammer in just the right place and it springs open. Everyone who has installed that lock is vulnerable, though until the trick with the hammer becomes known it does not matter too much. Once it is known, the danger to personal security is huge and urgent.

My next example of the danger of monocultures comes from a part of computer technology even more ubiquitous than SSL – the 'Point of Sale' (PoS) terminals used to process payment card information. These payment cards have been vulnerable to fraud since they were invented. But in combination with the poorly designed and ill-guarded terminals that retailers use, the danger becomes much greater.[10]

Two recent attacks in Australia indicate the scale of the problem. A Romanian organised crime syndicate – which had never set foot in Australia – stole the details of 500,000 credit cards by hacking into PoS terminals in ninety-three small businesses. Those cards gave them access to more than £400 million (US$700 million). But the real value was in selling the details and creating fake cards. In all 30,000 were fraudulently used, netting the gangsters the equivalent of £16 million (US$28 million). The UPS Store – which sells shipping services, PO boxes and packing materials – admitted in August 2014 that attackers using malware called 'Backoff' – invisible to anti-virus software – had compromised terminals in fifty-one of its franchise outlets, starting in January. It admitted that it had found out about the attack only because it had been alerted by the government, and that it did not have enough information to be able to tell customers if their card details had been stolen.[11] An attack on Target, an American retailer, in December 2013, stole the details of forty million customers. The price range on the black market for the stolen cards and identities was between $18.00 and $35.70. Around two million were sold, meaning a profit to the attackers of around $54 million. The cost to banks of reissuing credit cards was $200 million. Target spent $100 million on new security measures (probably uselessly).[12] It faces lawsuits and its chief executive, Gregg Steinhafel, has resigned. In August 2014, news emerged of an attack – apparently by the same gang – on the Home Depot chain.[13]

Home Depot reported $7 million in costs for the first quarter of 2015. The retailer said information related to 56 million payment cards had been stolen. The company declines to say how much the breach cost but warned that it might have 'a material adverse effect on the company's financial results in fiscal 2015 and/or future periods'.[14] Target says the cyber-attack it suffered cost it $162m.

A recent report by a British body charged with improving security standards highlighted the many weaknesses in the system, ranging from tampering with the hardware, exploiting flaws in the software and intercepting the wireless transmission of the payment data.[15] The attacks range from the crudest (putting a fake device on top of the legitimate one) to operations which involve advanced hacking skills. But the modus operandi is the same – the automated collection of large amounts of valuable data which can then be traded on criminal markets of the kind discussed earlier in the book. Some of the tools require physical access to the terminals: criminals break into a store in order to do that, or hide in it overnight. Even while the business is open they can swap a doctored terminal for a real one (either finding an unattended till or by distracting an attendant). They can pose as technicians and swap the terminals in full view of the staff, or send new terminals to the store labelled with the manufacturer's address and a note to install them urgently because they contain better security software. The criminals particularly like terminals that are in continuous use and unattended – such as in car-park ticket machines. The harvest of stolen credentials is potentially high, and the risk of being caught when trying to doctor them is low.

The precautions needed to protect PoS terminals are alarmingly rudimentary. Retailers are advised to check the security stickers on the bottom of their terminals to see if they have been tampered with. They should check the cables (because devices to steal data can be concealed in a plug). They should look at ceiling tiles to see whether tiny cameras have been installed to watch customers insert their PINs. It is hard to see how an ordinary shopkeeper or petrol-station attendant is going to have the skills needed to see if subtle changes have been made to the PoS terminal. Yet these carelessly designed, easily doctored devices are the front line in the defence of our financial system from attackers. Evolution has helped us so well to cope with a life we have long abandoned. It has left us ill prepared for the world in which we now live.

9

Clearing the Jungle

We have a primitive ability to interpret our environment. A sharp stick is dangerous if jabbed in our eyes. A thick stick can be a truncheon. A cave may be a cosy shelter, or contain dangerous wild beasts. We cooperate because hunting and farming are easier that way. But we are selfish cheats when it comes to mating. These instincts have served us quite well in modern life, too. We know that guns and knives are dangerous, and that a clenched fist in a political context (among revolutionaries) is a friendly gesture, whereas in an argument it is a threatening one. We believe that we can recognise things and people.

That is the world that Chip and Pin Hakhett think they inhabit. But their instincts and reactions are dangerously out of date when it comes to technology. Miniaturisation and new battery technologies have made us utterly unable to distinguish threat from safety, either in our personal lives or professionally. Their favourite James Bond films exemplify the change. In *From Russia with Love*, 007 has a reel-to-reel tape-recorder concealed inside a camera. A recording device smaller than a cassette tape was a miracle of precision engineering in those days. A homing device in *Goldfinger* is hidden within the heel of Bond's shoe. A watch in *The Spy Who Loved Me* conceals a tiny teleprinter (a

device now all but forgotten: younger readers may try to imagine a slow low-quality printer attached to a telephone). But even
with a huge dose of Hollywood licence, the MI6 of the 1960s and
1970s could not produce anything of the kind that is now sold in
any electronics shop. Power sources were a particular weakness.
Batteries needed changing, which required elaborate disguises
and ruses. The KGB bugged the American Embassy in Moscow
by fitting devices into the steel girders that had been carelessly
bought from a Soviet source. The bugging devices were remotely
powered by microwaves blasted from nearby buildings – to the
point that the health of the diplomats and spies working there
was endangered.

Now inconspicuous surveillance is a lot easier. The aborted
Google Glass project gave a foretaste of the future. These devices,
made by the search engine company (but discontinued in January
2015), allowed the user to store and screen everything around
him, while displaying information on the screens of what look
like rather clunky spectacles. The concept will doubtless be taken
up by others. It promises to be fantastically useful – if you need
information, you would no longer need to find a computer and
a keyboard, but just to point your head in the right direction and
touch the side of the device, speak or wink. Surgeons in operating theatres, anyone trying to navigate an unfamiliar location,
or someone trying to match a name and a face would find it
invaluable.

But these gadgets also look pretty much like a regular pair of
spectacles, though containing, in effect, a concealed camera. Will
you notice if someone wearing an inconspicuous device visits your
offices and stands close to your desk? Can he record you typing
your password? Or see what is on your screen, or what papers you
have on your desktop. Supposing he can see your house keys – may
that be enough to print a copy on a 3D printer?

Mobile phones are getting smaller. The Boss X6 model is the smallest commercially available phone. Though doubtless designed purely for convenience, it is much favoured by prisoners. It can be smuggled inside the body (wrapped in Clingfilm or a plastic bag). It can charge from anything – a mains adapter, a computer, or solar panel, all of which may also be innocently used to charge a Kindle or other e-reader. Prisons are fighting a losing battle against the ban on inmates using mobile phones.

Move away from the general consumer-electronics market and the impact of miniaturisation becomes even more striking. Most portable electronic devices have a facility called Bluetooth, which allows data to be transferred smoothly between them – for example, to send a picture from a mobile phone to a laptop. But the Bluetooth software was not designed with security in mind. In theory, before another device gets access to your phone, computer or tablet, you have to accept it for 'pairing'. But hackers have ways round this requirement. An innocent-looking wristwatch, brooch, belt buckle or cufflink can easily contain a Bluetooth device which is probing the nearby environment to see if it can hack into another machine, either to plant data there or to steal something.

Miniature devices can be carried by one person and controlled by another. Imagine that I am trying to steal someone's password and login. I place my accomplice next to him on a plane or train, and wait until he opens his computer or smartphone. My friend's earring can be a camera – remotely controlled by me, or a microphone, or picking up the radiation from his screen and transferring it to my computer in a quite different location. Most computer users are pitifully unaware of how much their machine gives away in use. A keyboard sends acoustic and electromagnetic signals, as does the display. If it is connected to the internet (and even if it is not) the wireless connection can be intercepted or manipulated. A USB memory stick no longer looks like a memory stick. It can be the size of a thumbnail, and easily concealed in a piece of jewellery or other innocent item such as a button or spectacles.

This is not futuristic. Such devices are available right now on the internet, for modest amounts of money, such as cufflinks which are wi-fi-enabled and also contain two terabytes of storage.[1] Nor do these miniature devices need expert knowledge. If you can screw in a light bulb, you can plant a bug. Technology is far outstripping the ability of security procedures to cope. Standard practice in secure locations (such as embassies) used to be to ask visitors to put their mobile phones in a locker before entering the building. An X-ray machine could tell if anyone broke the rule – just as it might spot if someone was carrying a gun or a knife. Miniaturisation makes that far harder. We are not going to give body-cavity searches to everyone who visits an official building. Nor are we going to insist that all jewellery must be removed, along with belts, buckles and any clothes with buttons. In a really sophisticated set-up it may be possible to test if anything on the visitor's body is responding to electromagnetic radiation. But few premises will put up with the cost and inconvenience involved.

The next way in which evolution lets us down is in attribution. For most of human history, we have had a pretty good idea of who is attacking us. Surprise attacks are as old as human conflict itself, but they rarely happen without a second phase in which the other side becomes visible. We are deeply programmed by evolution to see patterns in events (sometimes spurious ones). But nothing has prepared us for the invisible, persistent attacker that we find online.

In the case of criminal cyber-attacks, we have at least some clues. If money has been stolen, it must end up somewhere. The process may be laborious, but the police have a chance of tracing the money – if it went to a bank account they can see who opened it and where the money was withdrawn or transferred to. But in other kinds of attacks, such as those involving sabotage or espionage, we may have no clue at all. Here the psychology of cybersecurity becomes closer to that of international espionage and special operations than to computer science.

One of the simplest and most effective tools in intelligence work is known as the 'false flag'. This was originally a naval term, dating from the days when a ship might carry out an action under another flag – enemy or neutral. In the days when flags were the only way of identifying a vessel at a distance this was a powerful tactic. But its more common use is in espionage parlance. During the Cold War, if the Soviet KGB wanted to recruit a patriotic, conservative official working in a Western country, it would have little success if it relied on trying to appeal to his sympathy with Communism. It might try coercion, flattery or bribery, but the best line of attack would be to pretend to be working for another country – such as South Africa. If the official in question was Jewish, the KGB could (and did) pretend to be working for Mossad, the Jewish state's intelligence service.

The 'false flag' approach has many advantages. It can be fine-tuned to fit exactly the targeted individual's known strengths and weaknesses. It is not hard to train and select an intelligence officer to pretend to be South African or Israeli – both countries have a wide range of people with immigrant backgrounds. The recruiters could appeal to the victim's gullibility, ego, greed and other weaknesses, but with the great advantage of purportedly coming from a country with which he was instinctively sympathetic.

False-flag operations on the internet are far easier. As we have seen, it is trivially easy to set up an e-mail address or a website pretending to be something that you are not. It is also easy to create an identity based on social media – Facebook, Twitter and the

like – where you can get real people to endorse you, even though
you do not exist (for example, put some photos of a pretty girl up,
create an enticing if sketchy persona and send friend requests to
young men).

Even more difficult than identifying the source of the attack
is identifying the real beneficiary. If you are a business hit by a
Distributed Denial of Service (DDoS) attack – swamping your
network so that customers cannot reach you and you cannot
process their orders – you have little chance of finding out who
the 'bot-herder' is who has organised the attack. And you have
even less chance of knowing why it is happening. Is it a business
rival? An organised crime gang? A prankster? Or maybe someone demonstrating their capabilities in order to impress a third
party?

So how should our thinking change? One of the biggest shifts
needed is to adopt the kind of ruses and precautions which are
part of the intelligence world. If you are responsible for a computer
network, for example, you should test it regularly both to see how
it can be breached, and what attackers will be able to do when they
are inside. Many companies now do this by hiring 'pen testers' –
professional hackers who for a fat fee will humiliate you by showing how useless your security precautions are. Richard Bejtlich of
FireEye tells a story of a client who asked him impatiently when
the firm was going to start work on this project. 'We're done,' said
Mr Bejtlich smoothly. 'Well, where's the report?' asked the client
crossly. 'On your computer screen,' replied Mr Bejtlich. Breaching
a network is easy – and once you are in, moving a file to a particular computer is hardly more difficult.

Testing a network is about more than technical wizardry. The
weakest link in any security system is human beings. They can be
gulled with 'social engineering' (confidence tricks) or misled by
conjuring (for example, when swapping one device for another).

Penetration testers may disguise themselves as maintenance workers or fire safety officers to gain access to the client's premises. They find out how credentials are issued and obtain them by trickery. One easy trick is to dial into an organisation and ask the switchboard to put you through to the reception desk. You then introduce yourself as a senior manager, and say that there is some kind of emergency and that a visitor will be arriving shortly to deal with it. He must be given a security pass and escorted to a destination – for example, the computer room. The reception dutifully follows the instruction – and the 'visitor' is able to get on with his task.

These are just the sorts of tricks that spies use. And organisations trying to defend themselves against attackers need to start thinking along the lines of a counter-intelligence officer. This involves thinking in detail about potential vulnerabilities and potential attackers, and working out ways of deterring and foiling them. Your intellectual property, your customers' financial and personal data, or your social network may be the attackers' main targets. You don't know until you start thinking about it. The crucial point is that you yourself may not be the real victim. You may be just the staging post for an attack on someone else.

Much of the discussion of security on the internet is far too narrow. Experts in computers tend not to be knowledgeable about the dark arts of intelligence. As a result, too much attention is paid to the technical side, adding ever-stronger layers of encryption, password protection and the like. These questions are intellectually interesting but ultimately irrelevant. If a serious adversary is determined to get hold of some digital data, it will most likely succeed, regardless of the level of encryption you use, and the precautions you think you are taking. If you want to be safe, do not keep the data in digital form. If you must rely on computers, all you can do is raise the cost to attackers by increasing the time and effort involved. But be aware that you are increasing your own level of inconvenience, too.

The best way of looking at this is by the Fort Knox analogy mentioned earlier. If your 'digital gold' is so well guarded that the only practical means of getting hold of it is kidnap, bribery or torture, then, for most people, the danger is reduced to a manageable level.

Once you assume that your network is likely to be breached, you need to think what happens next. This is called 'defence in depth': once on the network the attacker faces a series of obstacles of ever-increasing difficulty. The most important privileges such as 'root' – the ability to rewrite and overwrite rules – are strictly controlled. You should not be able to get those privileges simply from a keyboard, but only with a face-to-face meeting. They should be issued only briefly, and for a specific purpose. Technology offers other help, too: you can plant tiny 'beacons' in your sensitive files, which will alert you if they are removed outside the network. The more important the data, the harder it should be to get all of it in plain-text form. A well-run network does not rely on passwords alone, but on other forms of identification. If an important file is encrypted, the keys should not be stored on the network – they can be written on a piece of paper and kept in a safe.

You can create dummy files which will attract intruders, but not be of any use to them. This was the approach taken by Clifford Stoll in the Cuckoo's Egg attack. He created a file directory stuffed with interesting-looking but bogus documents. When the attacker followed up on the contents of the documents, he revealed his hand. Such files are called honeypots – a place on the network that will be instantly tempting to the attacker, but will also reveal his presence. A group of honeypots is called a honeynet. This sort of approach unsettles many of the sober types who run corporate security, for the same reasons that they feel uneasy about penetration testing. Deliberate deception is closer to the worlds of practical jokes, theatricals and espionage. But if it helps uncover an attacker, few are going to cast aspersions on the organisers.*

The security specialist Roger Grimes suggests sprinkling a little ingenuity and mischief over the network, too.[2] For example, the usual way to gain control of a device is to log in with the username 'admin' and a password. It is bad enough that most people do not bother to change the password. But why not change the user-name, too? Having a login called 'admin' is like having a large and conspicuous lock on your front door. Most attacks are automated. Having found a vulnerable device, the next stage is to search for the admin account. If it doesn't exist, the robot goes elsewhere. For that matter, why have a single account with access to the entire network? The people who run the network like the convenience of having instant access to everything. But this is a trade-off between productivity and security which nowadays helps attackers more than it benefits the victims. Once attackers get 'root' – the ability to issue instructions across the network – then they can do untold damage. Mr Grimes highlights a large American company (he does not name it, but says it is the only one in the Fortune 500 not to have been breached by attackers) which has restricted rights across the network on a case-by-case basis. Nobody – even at the highest

---

* A more technical, but also sensible idea is to shun the use of default ports. Most computer chips (put crudely) connect to the outside world through an array of different ports – rather like corridors leading to the outside world. Some of these connect to the internet, others to parts of the machine such as the monitor and keyboard. A common attack technique is a 'port scanner' which looks at a computer through the internet to see if ports are 'open' – in other words, if they will respond to an instruction. This is rather like an intruder trying all the doors and windows to see if they are locked, and how. But these scanners are usually set up to look at the ports in their usual configuration. If you change your default ports to something else, the attacking software will, most likely, simply not see it. This is rather like having a door disguised as a floor-to-ceiling bookshelf. It is still vulnerable to a burglar – but he has to find it first.

level – has automatic privileges. Any name being added to a group that does enjoy privileges triggers an e-mail to other members of that group, who then confirm the new member by phone or face-to-face contact.[3]

But perhaps the biggest way we need to change our thinking is how we treat anonymity and privacy. In the past, these went hand in hand. It is hard to be private in a village, and even harder to be anonymous. Simply by being a stranger one becomes conspicuous and identifiable. The growth of urbanisation made anonymity possible. When Chip or Pin Hakhett go to a big city, they expect to disappear among the crowds. Not only does nobody recognise them, but nobody knows what they are up to. This is not because they are wearing masks, but because the chances of being identified are so slim. The human brain simply cannot process all the images that the eye takes in. Some people may be lucky enough to have a very good memory for faces, and police and intelligence services employ a handful of people with preternatural abilities to identify suspects or targets in huge databases. But for the most part, we can be safe from discovery in a crowd. Why bother to put tinted windows on your car when one car is pretty much like another? That anonymity has also given us privacy. If you can put up with some inconvenience, you can pay for your transport and hotels in cash and leave your mobile phone at home. Your activities will be more or less untraceable, unless someone is actually willing to pay for detectives to follow you around.

In short, we have assumed that the greatest protector of privacy is not to be noticed, and that the best way to stay anonymous is to keep yourself to yourself. But these concepts are no longer two sides of the same coin. The reason is the snail's trail of digital information we leave in our daily lives. Even if our phone is not actually bugged, it is giving away details about us – for example, when it tries to connect with other people's wi-fi networks. The use of payment cards gives an almost complete record of both our spending habits and our whereabouts. Anyone with a camera can read the number plate on a car, and check it against publicly available databases. Any name can be checked for a credit reference. A photograph can be 'reverse-searched' on the internet – just paste it into the Google search bar and the search engine giant will tell you where else, if anywhere, it has appeared.

The technical term for this sort of information about our activities is meta-data. It is not a direct breach of our privacy, of the kind that occurs when someone eavesdrops on a phone call, bugs a room, or opens a letter. But the combination of many indirect breaches of privacy can be just as bad. The content of a message may be quite anodyne: if Chip sends an SMS at lunchtime saying 'here now' it is of no great significance. But if the meta-data shows he is texting from a hotel, not a restaurant, Pin may feel it has a rather more sinister implication.

Another form of meta-data is the digital fingerprint left by each computer. Most people assume that one computer is pretty much like another, and one web browser is pretty much like another. And so they are. But they also contain many minute differences. When you visit a website, it notices all sorts of things about you: the version of software you are using, the fonts, the location and so on. As the Electronic Frontier Foundation, an online-privacy campaign in Washington, DC, explains, your computer sends a string of seeming gibberish which can read like this

Mozilla/5.0 (Windows; U; Windows NT 5.1; en-GB; rv:1.8.1.6) Gecko/20070725 Firefox/2.0.0.6

This information helps the website display correctly. But it also narrows down the possibilities, perhaps to one. If you visit the EFF's Panopticlick website at panopticlick.eff.org you can do an interesting and rather chilling test. By analysing the data your computer sends, it can tell you how unique you are. My MacBook Air's particular combination of software, fonts and rules was the only one in more than four million tested. In other words, any website I visit would know that this particular computer, on this time zone and with this combination of software and hardware, was coming and going. It would not need to track me by trying to put 'cookies' (small bits of computer code which help websites track the people who are visiting them) on my computer.

This is a big change in computer security. Ten years ago, most computers were inherently anonymous, like faces in a crowd. If you wanted to identify a particular computer, you had to do something – either to get the user to provide some identifying information, or else to put some code on his computer. Now imagine that the person scanning the crowd has a fluke ability to recognise and remember faces. He may only see you once a year, but he will instantly recall the time and place where he saw you last, and what you were doing. That is what we have reached with browser fingerprinting. Every time you visit a website or a computer with a particular configuration, you leave digital fingerprints which can be linked to every previous foray you have made there.

The American journalist Julia Angwin has written a fascinating book, *Dragnet Nation*, on the difficulties of staying anonymous on the internet.[4] She rightly highlights the amount of data which our daily interactions leave behind. Google, Facebook, YouTube and other big internet companies, plus mobile-phone providers and credit card companies, know a huge amount about us: where we are, who we are with, what we are buying and selling, what our hobbies and interests are and so forth. She is shocked to find that Google, for example, knows every search she has ever made. Her shopping habits are analysed by computers, which then put advertisements tailored to her presumed needs on her computer screens. Some businesses even change their prices depending on the customer.

To thwart this, she tries creating an alternative identity (quite legally) in order to make purchases that will not be linked to her name. It doesn't work very well. Life is a great deal less convenient when you try to stay properly anonymous.

She finds this shocking. I don't. Commercial 'surveillance' (to use her pejorative term) is indeed a powerful business tool. Businesses like to know as much as possible about their customers. Some of them may be more intrusive than others. Data protection laws in the United States are flimsy in comparison with the European Union: individuals do not have a general right to know what information is held about them.

One of the big themes of Ms Angwin's book is that anyone using 'free' services such as those offered by Google (chiefly search and the Gmail e-mail service) or social-media services such as Facebook and Twitter should be clear that they are not the customer. They are the product. This is not necessarily a bad thing. The biggest companies in the world are investing enormous amounts in computers and software to make their users happy. The services work brilliantly. You can record a video on your phone and within a minute make it available to most of the people on the planet. You have access to treasure houses of information and cultural riches. You can set up a business, reach customers, conduct love affairs and stay in touch with your friends and family, all free of charge.

In return you let these companies sell access to your eyeballs. You may not think your humble attention span, and the spending power it determines, is valuable, but if it is sufficiently cheap to reach, then someone will be willing to pay for it.

But you do not have to be an entirely passive product. You can make some subtle tweaks to reduce the amount of data which is collected on you. Or you can make radical, inconvenient and costly changes in order to be a customer. It is up to you. Nobody is forced to use Google.

You have alternatives. You can use another search engine (I use duckduckgo, which is slower and less finely tuned, but does not store users' data). You can use a paid-for e-mail provider. You do not have to shop with Amazon. You can use different credit cards for different purposes. You do not have to give your home address and telephone number. If a company demands personal information, you do not have to do business with them. You can also install 'extensions' to your web browser that greatly increase your privacy and security. I am a big fan of Adblock, which simply prevents advertisements from loading (and speeds up web browsing as a result). I also use Ghostery, which tells you what 'cookies' are being planted on your computer. If you are really cautious you can also use Scriptsafe, which prevents websites running code automatically. I also use Calomel, which assesses the strength of security certificates on the sites I visit. Such tweaks can sometimes slow things down (you may have to give specific permission before a video will play, for example). But it puts you, the user, in control.

What Ms Angwin's book fails to appreciate is that the norms of life on the internet are evolving fast. The past ten years have been very bad for privacy, because people have been careless and ill-prepared. It has been very easy for unscrupulous companies to collect and sell data on people using their websites. Technology has outstripped even the ability of a technologically minded computer user to know what is going on. But these are not irreversible shifts. It is quite possible to trade a bit of convenience for a bit more privacy, and all the signs are that this is now happening.

Privacy does not come free. For example, some websites complain if people using them have installed Adblock because it removes a small slice of their revenue. A dating site called OK Cupid arranged for users with Adblock installed on their browsers to get a cross message asking them to pay $5 instead. That is inconvenient for both sides but you have a choice: either 'whitelist' the site concerned so that its advertisements are visible, or pay a subscription for the service you are using.⁵

The clear casualty in this is anonymity. The combination of large amounts of meta-data and data, plus computer-processing power, makes staying unnoticed much harder. Yet though the risks from misused computers and networks are worse than ever, the opportunities to stay private on the internet have also never been greater. If you are prepared to put up with a bit of inconvenience, you can send a highly encrypted e-mail, or a document, or chat online, in a way that is more secure than at any time in history. For people who care a lot about privacy, this is highly reassuring. For law-enforcement officials, this is troubling. They would like much better means for dealing with encrypted communications. They fear that the ability to stay private will be used by enemy spies, terrorists, criminals and perverts.

These complaints are something of a distraction and, in the case of the security services, largely bogus. Strong encryption is here to stay. There is no realistic way of regulating it. If your government really wants your data, it will find other ways of getting it. Privacy matters, but over time, and to a large extent, obsessive privacy becomes rather conspicuous. If there is one house in the street which has high walls, steel shutters on the windows, which never puts out any rubbish for collection and where cars arrive at high speed, with passengers hidden behind tinted windows, then the inhabitants are certainly private. But everyone else in the street will wonder what they are up to. If the house is sufficiently fortress-like, it may even attract the attention of the police.

Obsessive privacy online has a similar flaw. Though it is hard for the authorities to crack highly encrypted communications retro-spectively, it is much less hard to see who is using them. If someone is determinedly covering their tracks on the internet (for example, doing business in Bitcoin, and habitually using the slow but ultra-private Tor web browser), with no apparent need to do so, then outsiders may wonder why. If you are a law-enforcement officer pursuing, for example, a bunch of child pornographers, you may well concentrate on computers which send and receive large and heavily encrypted videos. If you are hunting money-launderers or arms dealers, their use of complicated digital-cash systems may offer you a lead (an interesting rumour is that the complexities of Bitcoin include a feature in which America's National Security Agency can track all users and transactions. That is probably false – but for most of the people who use the new crypto-currency there is no way of being certain).

This does not tip the balance conclusively in favour of the watchers over the hiders. Systematic use of heavy encryption is conspicuous. Occasional use is not. If you can conceal your encrypted data in a large file (such as in a video or a picture) you have a very good chance of staying undetected for the first few times you transfer it. There is enough random interaction on the internet to make it almost impossible for an individual burst of activity to be detected. The giveaway is a pattern. In short, we still have anonymity and privacy for one-off actions on the internet but the more we repeat them the more we lose – first our anonymity, and then, if law-enforcement officials become sufficiently interested, our privacy, too.

Computers have also helped us combine other bits of public information to draw powerful conclusions. Even if you do not know someone's name, if you know their sex, date of birth and part of their address you may be able to identify them. On their own, each of these bits of information does not narrow down a search. Combined, they are very powerful.[6] Similarly, once you know the kind of computer, the version of the software, the fonts it uses, the time zone and a few other details, you may well have narrowed down the search to the point where there is only one computer in the world with this exact combination. That does not necessarily mean that you know who is actually using the computer, but it certainly gives a useful basis for tracking its activity on your site.

In short, real anonymity on the internet – in the sense of being able to feel that you are just one person in a busy street – is shrinking. If someone with enough processing power and big enough databanks is interested in you, that person can work out who you are. Quasi-anonymity is still rife, in the sense that ordinary people cannot prove who they are when they want to. Nor can they find out definitively with whom they are dealing. But we do have a limited but important ability to be extremely private, which protects us from all but the most sophisticated and determined attacks. If a big government spy agency wants to know what you are doing on your computer, it will find out, devoting as much time and taxpayer cash as is necessary. Even then, your vulnerability starts only once someone is interested in you. Your defence is as strong as your own willpower. Unless, of course, you are relying on that weakest of links: a password.

10

Passwords Unscrambled

Keys and locks are comforting and familiar physical objects, but we all accept that they are only a small part of our security. Just as any password can be stolen, any key can be copied, and any lock can be picked. If you lock yourself out of your house, you call a locksmith, who may ask you to look away as he opens your front door with seemingly effortless ease. Expensive locks are harder to pick, but there is no such thing as an unpickable one. All the key does is push up some metal pins in a precise pattern, until they stop obstructing the turning of the lock's cylinder. The key is the easiest way to move the pins and turn the cylinder. But if you know what you are doing, you can use picks, or even improvise with innocent seeming and inconspicuous everyday objects.

In theory, that should worry people. Couldn't a criminal locksmith break into their house and steal their possessions? But few people lie awake at night worrying about that. They assume that lock-picking is a difficult skill and that most people who master it have better things to do with their time than burglary. This is a bit optimistic. Picking locks is not that difficult. It is easy to order a small metal device on the internet with which, given a few minutes and a bit of fiddling, anyone can open most cheap locks. At a pinch, one can often do the same thing with a bit of stiff wire and the metal clip from the cap of a pen. It is an amusing party trick and may be useful. But people who master the basics of lock-picking do not then go on to rob houses.

Vulnerability matters only if people are motivated to exploit it. Just because people can pick locks does not mean that they do. The risks and rewards involved, and our moral codes, deter most people from housebreaking. And for housebreakers, the end is more important than the means. If someone really wants to burgle you, he will not be deterred by the fact that you have a fancy lock on your door. He may instead try to get hold of your keys.

The context is crucial. If we lose a key, it can be copied or replaced. If you lose your keys along with something bearing your address, things become trickier. You worry that burglars may be heading to your home immediately. It is probably time for an emergency locksmith who will change your locks (or at least the cylinders in them), give you new keys – and present you with a fat bill. Similarly, if you lose a bit of paper with a password on it, it doesn't matter. Even if the paper has the login and the password, it won't matter, because a thief will have little idea which internet service they are used for. If it says 'bank' it matters rather more – the thief can try the top dozen British banks in a matter of minutes. If the paper says 'Amazon' or 'eBay' then losing it may matter a great deal.

Passwords are often likened to keys – but this is true only up to a point. Copying a key without having physical access to it is quite difficult – at least until recently (a photograph of a key, even from a distance, can be enough to print one on a 3D printer). If you lose a password, it is usually easy to replace it – just click on the 'lost password' button and you will be e-mailed another one, or a link where you can give a new one. A key can be copied, but it takes more time. You have to go to a locksmith, who will not know where you live and has usually no need to identify you. Some keys – maybe stamped 'do not duplicate' – are more tightly protected. You may need to produce some identification before a locksmith will agree to make a copy for you. A password, by contrast, can be copied instantly. Here is a super-strength password:

L1EHIJtwyljx1SIgBMunT1e9XpgRZoQfkbRmqszu1dKJUgQq-FAeax6bm5IGq

At first sight that seems far safer than a physical key. The number of possible combinations for this sixty-character password is 8.3 x 10^{81}, or more than the number of atoms in the observable universe (roughly 10^{80}). But that security is illusory.[1] For a start passwords can be cracked by other means than simply trying all the combinations (a so-called 'brute force' attack).* Moreover, unlike a physical key the line of text above can be copied any number of times, at no cost. It can be sent round the world instantly. Anyone with a copy of this book can copy it. Anyone with access to the computer on which I am writing this book can steal it. In short, gaining access to someone else's computer is far easier than most people realise.

An even bigger vulnerability than the password itself is the website where you use it. With a key, you have a good idea about the lock. It is theoretically possible that an ingenious burglar will X-ray your lock in order to make a copy of the key – but if he can do that, he can get into your house anyway. With a password, you (broadly speaking) entrust it to someone else every time you use it. Imagine if a copy of your house key, or at least clues to what it looks like, was stored in every shop you frequent. You hope they keep it safely. But you can't be sure.

---

* When LinkedIn's database of 6.5 million passwords was leaked in June 2012 Jeremi Gosney of Stricture Consulting Group, using easily obtainable legal tools, was able to break 1.3 million of them in thirty seconds, and over half in barely two hours. Within a day, he had broken four million.

Your identity credentials, such as passwords and logins may be carelessly stored at a site you visit. In theory, it should be encrypted ('hashed' in computer jargon) – so that if the attacker steals the data he has only a stream of gibberish, not the actual names and passwords. Furthermore, a well-run website should also ensure that user data is not just 'hashed' but 'salted' – meaning that the encryption is not just of the user's details but also of some randomly added extra data. That means that even if the website is breached, and its database of users downloaded, the attackers can neither turn the encrypted material into anything usable nor compare the encrypted versions of passwords with those on other databases. This should be standard practice, though many companies and organisations are shockingly lax.

Though hashing and salting sounds complicated, one way of visualising them is to think of an old-fashioned hotel where the keys (i.e. passwords) are kept at the reception.* Hotels, like websites, are busy places, with lots of people coming and going. You have to keep the room secure from intruders, while allowing access both to the guest and to the staff. You therefore have to create a security system in which you manage the guest's identity, his key (and copies of it) and access to the room. The danger is that someone steals the key and uses it to get into the room for malicious purposes.

The stupid way to manage this system would be to put all the guests' names up on an office wall with the key next to each one. That would mean that anyone who got past the reception desk would know who was staying where and could simply steal the desired key and loot the hotel room. That is the equivalent of storing credentials on your computer as an unencrypted file. Even a moderately talented attacker can get into your network and look for a document called 'customer passwords and logins', and copy it.

---

* In the real world, most keys are different. With computers, people often reuse their passwords, creating an extra layer of vulnerability.

It would be only marginally better if you have a semi-public list of which guest is staying in which room. For an intruder able to pick locks, that speeds things up a lot. Instead of having to pick locks at random in the hope of finding something lucrative, he can find out the names of rich guests and then go to their rooms and pick the locks. That is the equivalent of having an unencrypted document on your computer called 'customer logins'. That is better than having the passwords stored in plain text. But not much better. Once the attacker knows the login, all he has to do then is to guess the password – and, as we will see, most passwords are pretty easy to guess, or to find out by various mathematical and other tricks.

A more sensible system would be to allocate each key to a room number, but to keep a separate register which shows which guest is staying in which room. This is a mild form of encryption, which is in fact the standard practice in many hotels. If you snoop behind the reception desk, you may be able to see that room 319 is a suite on the third floor, and even to grab the key, but you do not know who is staying there.

A more secure system would be to encode the room number, for example by substituting a letter for a number. That is in effect a 'hash'. So room 319 would be CAI (using the childishly simple system where A is 1, C is 3 and so forth). If the intruder does not know the code, the value of his break-in is limited. He can see the keys but he does not know what the letters refer to. The intruder into a database can steal the data, but he cannot make sense of it unless he can crack the code.

If the attacker does crack the code, however, the hotel is vulnerable. He may steal the list of keys and get to work with a password-breaking program. In that case, he can find the key to every room.

So a well-run system will add another layer of security. Adding a random extra character somewhere in the code – 'salting' in computer parlance – would make it even harder. A thief who broke into the hotel reception would see a set of keys bearing only four-letter combinations – CAIX, or maybe XCAI. Without knowing that one character in the label should be ignored, his code-cracking abilities are useless.

Unfortunately, the procedures at websites which handle usernames and passwords have been shockingly lax. Readers may find it alarming to check their e-mail addresses on a website called haveibeenpwned.com ('pwned' is hacker jargon for 'breached' or 'taken over'). This looks at the thirty biggest public data breaches (where attackers have published the usernames and passwords which they have stolen). My own main e-mail address, edwardlucas@economist.com turns out to have been leaked, together with the passwords I used, in three big breaches.

The worst was at Adobe Acrobat – a company which makes software for reading and creating documents. In October 2013 attackers stole 153 million accounts, containing the internal ID, username, email, encrypted password and a password hint. This was a shocking breach for a company which hundreds of millions of people rely on (you do not need to be registered at Adobe to use its software simply to read its simple 'pdf' documents, but registration is necessary for other services, such as creating documents and – ironically – adding security features). I was also registered at Forbes, an American media company, which was attacked in February 2014 and lost more than a million user accounts. The attackers were thought to be the Syrian Electronic Army, a pro-regime group wanting revenge for *Forbes* magazine's robust foreign policy line.

Perhaps most embarrassing of all was the attack on Stratfor, a private-sector provider of what it calls 'intelligence'. Perhaps unwisely, Stratfor cultivated an air of mystery about its sources and operations, leading some to think it was a front for the CIA. In December 2011 a group of hackers called 'Anonymous' – who have a generally libertarian and anti-government position, but have also attacked groups such as the Scientology cult – breached Stratfor's security (which was allegedly substandard) and released hundreds of gigabytes of e-mail and tens of thousands of credit card details. These were purloined by the attackers and used to make donations and other payments. Luckily I had a complimentary media login to Stratfor but was not a paid subscriber. But the breach also revealed 860,000 user accounts complete with e-mail address, and hashed but unsalted passwords.

For users who use only one password per website, the damage done by such attacks is limited. But most users use the same simple passwords in many different locations – a recklessness which should attract the same censure as promiscuous condom-less sex. The reason is simple – passwords are hard to remember. But few people would accept a system in which a stay in one hotel meant that the same key could be used to open all future hotel rooms you stayed in. Nor would you accept a regime in which every time you used your credit card you handed over all the details necessary to make a payment from it.

The more information you steal about someone, the easier it is to impersonate them. Once you know someone's current and former addresses, the names and dates of birth of all their family members, where they went on holiday and what their favourite films, books and pets are, you can feed all those details into a readily available computer program and it will start guessing their passwords. Once you know some passwords, it is easy to start guessing others: people who are told to change their password every month tend to start off with Economist01 and then move to Economist02, Economist03, Economist04 and so forth.*

Sloppy encryption means that when an encrypted password has been cracked once, it is then vulnerable everywhere else – even

* This example is wholly fictional.

if used by different people. Any single word that appears in any dictionary is unsuitable as a password – even if it has been doctored with simple substitutions and additions.

So far banks and other institutions have responded to worries about security not through rethinking the whole idea of how they relate to their customers, but by setting more onerous rules about keys. Customers are often expected to have a memorable word, and a customer number, and PIN code, and to remember them correctly for every one of a dozen different companies, and also to change them regularly. This 'passworditis' is a recipe for disaster – we have created a system in which we expect people to use passwords which are hard for humans to remember, but which are easy for computers to guess. Indeed, it is high time that we stopped relying on passwords altogether – and the next chapter looks at ways in which this may eventually happen.

In the meantime, there are plenty of precautions that ordinary users can take to safeguard their credentials at least to some extent. For a start, it is important not to use the same password on several different accounts, or to 'daisy-chain' them, so that if an attacker gains one password (for example to your e-mail) he can then start resetting all your other passwords, too. So do not have the password reset for your Gmail account going to a Yahoo account and vice versa. It is better to set up a single e-mail account for password recovery, which you *do not use for anything else*. This minimises the likelihood of the fraudster knowing which account to hack, or being able to do so.

Next, you can use a password manager such as Lastpass. This creates a separate random password for each site you need – for example, one for e-mail, one for online banking, one for Skype, one for Facebook. These are stored in encrypted form on your browser (not on the Lastpass site). You protect these with a super-strong password or pass phrase. A phrase consisting of four or five random words is easy to remember and creates a password that will defeat any brute force attack.

But there is only so much an individual user can do. The most important contribution to password security comes not from the person the password belongs to, but from the person who asks for it. This is not just a matter of hashing and salting the passwords properly, but also of limiting the use to which a single factor of authentication can be put.

Many websites back up passwords by asking security questions (particularly if something important is being requested). These are typically asking for your date of birth, mother's maiden name, the name of your favourite sports team, or part of your home address. Such questions are worse than useless. They are easy for attackers to find – dates of birth, like social security numbers and home

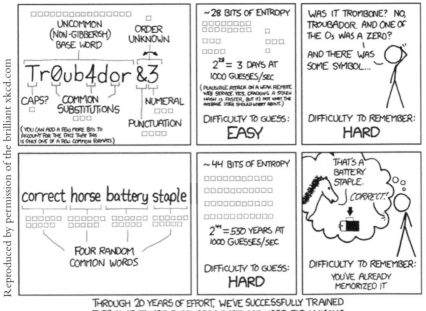

THROUGH 20 YEARS OF EFFORT, WE'VE SUCCESSFULLY TRAINED EVERYONE TO USE PASSWORDS THAT ARE HARD FOR HUMANS TO REMEMBER, BUT EASY FOR COMPUTERS TO GUESS.

addresses, are not private information. My own date of birth and mother's maiden name are both on my Wikipedia entry, and my home address is listed publicly because I am a company director – yet my bank persists in treating these as 'security questions'. Even questions such as 'name of first pet' or 'who was your favourite teacher' are vulnerable to a nosy outsider.

A much better kind of question is based on eliminating false information. Some British banks verify their debit cards in online transactions by offering a list of addresses and asking 'which of these have you *never* lived at?'. Sometimes only one of the addresses is bogus, sometimes more. It is very hard for an impersonator to deal with such a test. Asking people to state information may seem like a powerful tool. But negative information – asking people to contradict false statements – is more robust.

Tougher security can also involve seeing if the person sitting at the computer is also in possession of a physical object, such as a card or a dongle (like a key fob) with a computer chip on it, which produces a number you have to type in to the computer.

This already creates an extra layer of security. It is one thing to pinch a password. It is another to pick a pocket. But dongles suffer from a monoculture problem: if you can attack the organisation which issues them, you have a good chance of breaking the encryption on all of them. They generate a number depending on the exact time of day, using an algorithm and a random number which is 'seeded' in them at the time of manufacture. But if you can find out the random number and the algorithm, then you can find out the number they will generate at any given time. RSA Security, which issued the world's leading security dongle SecureID, had to replace forty million such tokens in 2011 after what it described as a highly sophisticated cyber-attack which led to security breaches at one of its most prized clients, the defence manufacturer Lockheed Martin.[2]

The same technology can be installed on a mobile phone. Google Authenticator, for example, is a clever bit of software which can be downloaded on to any smartphone. When I log in to Google from an unusual location, it asks me for a six-digit number that appears on my phone. Assuming Google looks after security better than RSA, only someone looking over my shoulder will know that (or perhaps an expert government security agency, in which case I have more problems to worry about than the security of my Google account). This sort of 'two-factor' authentication is far more secure than anything involving the sending of codes by text message. Though this creates a new level of difficulty for the attacker, it is not insurmountable. With the right malware (as explained in Chapter 7), you can intercept text messages and delete them remotely.

Next comes biometric recognition. This can involve fingerprints or scanning a retina, or analysing a heartbeat, breathing pattern, posture or gait. None of these is foolproof. It is possible to fool some fingerprint readers by using a gelatin-based sweet (candy), such as a jelly baby. If the device which takes the biometric data is poorly designed or administered, it may be possible to bypass it and inject the data directly: the computer thinks it is receiving a fingerprint, but in fact it is getting only the digital equivalent of the fingerprint, stolen on some previous occasion.

But such systems are increasingly well designed. They do not ask for the entire picture, but just an element of it. For example, the computer asks the reader if a finger has a particular whorl, and the reader replies either yes or no. The most sophisticated biometric security systems are also the least intrusive. They analyse the way you sit in the chair, what you look like, how you breathe and how you type. It may be that you have quite understandable reasons for not meeting the criteria – a pregnant woman who has cut her finger and is suffering from hay fever, for example. But in that case the other security questions can come into play, or a colleague can be asked to give extra verification.

The most sophisticated biometric techniques even safeguard against a so-called 'rubber hose attack' in which the victim is being forced by physical or other threats to break the rules on a computer. In highly secure environments, the computer will notice stress – either from heartbeat, breathing, or skin temperature – and flag up an alarm.

Another way of thinking is to expect some normal human prudence in the way we deal with friends, customers, suppliers and colleagues on the internet. The security specialist Roger Grimes has composed a useful list of what 'the real me would not do'. For example, he would not buy a product and have it shipped to another country; if he does order anything to be shipped anywhere but to his long-held home address, the company should call him – and not to a recently acquired phone number, but the one he has had for years. Once fraudsters gain access to one part of a person's identity, they then use that to change everything else, usually immediately, and then use those changes to start stealing. So Mr Grimes issues a general warning that 'I will never change my mailing address, phone number, and email address, then also transfer all my money to another bank within the same day, much less same web session.'

He also warns his bank that it should not empty his bank account or make foreign transfers without telephoning him – to his long-held phone number. His broker should note that he will never sell all his stocks and shares on a single day, at a loss, and transfer the money to a foreign bank. To anyone who deals with passwords, he says that he will not try to reset it without being able to verify plentiful information about the last transaction, such as the nature of the purchase, location and so forth. He tells his friends that he will never e-mail them saying that he is trapped and penniless in a foreign country. He will not e-mail them telling them to install cool new software, or ask for their passwords, or suggest strange financial deals, and so forth.

These suggestions sound sensible. But they all involve a big shift in the way that businesses deal with customers online. Firms have got used to running their authentication services as cheaply and automatically as possible. If the customer has the right login and password, you simply go ahead and do the transaction. Before criminals caught on to the opportunities this presented, such an approach made sense. The password was rather like the key for a safety-deposit box in a bank. If you have the key, you have access to the contents. So you had better guard the key carefully. Or – even better – keep your valuables elsewhere.

11

Identity Politics

Our thinking on identity has been muddled. We focus very hard on two rights: to be anonymous and to be private. Both of these are important (though, as shown earlier, being intensely private is so conspicuous that it can make anonymity difficult). We have focused much less on two other rights: to be able to identify yourself, and to know what data others are holding about you. Yet without these, our life online is fundamentally unbalanced.

In real life, we know that identification is a hassle, but we also believe it is a right. Countries which do not issue identity documents to some parts of the population are rightly castigated as human-rights abusers. Many Bedouin of Arab countries, Kurds in Syria, Muslim Rohingya in Burma and baby girls in some Islamic countries are not issued with identity documents. For illegal migrants in the United States, lack of proper documentation is a scourge, rendering them vulnerable to cheats and bullies.

For those of us in the enviable position of being able to identify ourselves in our daily lives, the thought of not being able to do so is irritating and frightening. We expect that when we produce a passport, driving licence or birth certificate we will be taken seriously, and that our decisions about our lives will be regarded as binding. It is true that most documents are voluntary. We do not need to take a driving test if we don't want to. We do not need to travel abroad. We do not need to have a bank account, or to own property. We may even (for example, if we are monks and nuns in a closed religious order) avoid paying any taxes. If we want, we can retreat from the modern world altogether. Yet, even then, we will have a vestigial identity. Everyone born in Britain must be registered by law, and has a birth certificate, and at the age of sixteen should get a National Insurance number (equivalent, roughly, to an American Social Security Number). You have to register on the electoral roll, even if you then choose not to vote. In some countries the law is tougher. Germany, like many continental countries, has an *Ausweispflicht*: any resident of Germany (citizen or not) is under a legal duty to identify himself to the state when asked. Residents must also register where they are living (*Meldepflicht*) and tell the authorities when they move out.

Cultures vary. But the key point is this. At a minimum, we do accept that our real-life identity should be independently verifiable by others: the mandatory birth certificate and some sort of tax or social-security identifier are not inherently oppressive. Once we venture on to the roads, we take it for granted that we have driving licences and that our cars have number plates. It is a striking chance aberration that the internet has grown up with anonymity as the default option. If thirty years ago policymakers had considered how best to use the explosive growth in computer capacity and connectedness, would they have agreed that the best way forward was that anyone – individual or organisation – could have in effect as many identities as they wanted, with no way for other people on the network reliably to verify and authenticate who they were dealing with? Perhaps. The original architects of the internet are delighted at the way it has developed but the anarchic freedoms it has brought have come at a cost – attackers flourish and we pay for it with our safety and freedom.

More importantly, we also expect that we should be able to identify ourselves when needed. We would be furious if when (say) we wanted to buy alcohol at a supermarket, the cashier would not accept our driving licence or passport as proof of age. We expect our documents to work not only when we cross borders, but on either side of them. In the past, we had special international driving licences; now we expect our national driving licence to be recognised wherever we go. We would fiercely resist any attempt to make us stateless, or undocumented – Bedouin in our own country.

Yet that is pretty much what we have on the internet. We are digital Bedouin, dependent on the trust and goodwill of others, and subject to whatever arbitrary rules and constraints they impose. There is no universally accepted form of identification, even for those who want it. When you are doing business with another individual online, you do not really know who you are dealing with. As we have seen, it is hard enough being sure that you are actually dealing with the right company (the SSL security certificates used to create a secure digital connection for online commerce are far less trustworthy than their ubiquity would suggest). When it comes to individuals connecting via e-mail, social media or other messaging, we are in the world of the Venetian masked ball.

Worse, we have to identify ourselves with others' rules, even if they are flimsy or intrusive. Why should you have to give a stranger your date of birth, mother's maiden name, home address, bank account details, credit card and much else besides? The abundant evidence of recent years is that third parties are not trustworthy when it comes to private data. Why should you have to think up a password and a login (with stupid, cumbersome rules about the number of characters, digits, capital letters, special characters, spaces and so on)? We also know that companies and governments are not particularly good at keeping passwords safe. If they let some attacker steal your login and password, you can be impersonated not only on that site, but perhaps on others, too. As explained in Chapter 10, passwords are becoming ludicrously insecure.

There are plenty of attempts to solve this problem. Many websites allow you to log in with your Google, Twitter or Facebook details. This has some advantages. It is usually seamless. It at least identifies you as being the same person who used those details in the past. For some things – for example, posting comments in online forums – that can be enough. Facebook has 1.3 billion monthly active users, Twitter 250 million. If you are willing to add a credit card to your social-media details, you have created a 'good-enough' way of buying things online. The company concerned will rely on your login to know it's you, and on your credit card company to provide the money. It may also use the details of your web browser (language settings and so forth) and cookies you have accepted on your computer as further identifiers, helping it to offer you things you are likely to buy (and charge prices that you are likely to pay).

That works well enough for small transactions. But it is not the basis for anything important. Anyone can set up a Twitter, Google or Facebook account – or several of them. The companies concerned do not make any effort to verify the information. You can buy a pre-paid debit card over the counter, and top it up with cash when it runs out. From the vendor's point of view, that may not matter. For individuals a slightly cumbersome but cheap and easy way of shopping on the internet is better than nothing, or something onerous and complicated.

But for society it does matter. Piecemeal patchwork identities are expensive. A study for the British government estimates that the cost of dealing with digital identities in the UK is over £3.3 billion – roughly half spent by organisations and the rest in the time that users waste. The haphazard system also makes life easy for attackers.

Once you steal Chip or Pin's Facebook identity, you can then raid the rest of their life. And it is also easy to impersonate people and organisations — a vital part of scams such as spear-phishing (toxic e-mails), or watering hole attacks (toxic websites). How is the individual supposed to know who he is really dealing with? And what about interactions on the internet that really matter, such as voting, dealing with government agencies, or signing documents?

One solution is ID cards issued by your own government, but in countries like Britain and America these are profoundly unpopular. People do not want the state to know what they are doing. The idea that your banking transactions, web-browsing, or e-mail should happen with government knowledge or involvement strikes most people as an intrusion into their privacy.

Another option is to use commercial ID. Companies commonly issue ID cards to their staff, for entry into and exit from buildings. These can also be used to access computers and networks. But using these cards (or other devices) outside work is rare. Companies do not want the hassle of providing ID verification to third parties, and employees will naturally be uneasy about the thought that their private lives become linked to their workplace. Even leaving privacy concerns aside, what happens if you change jobs? If you are using your company ID to send secure e-mail, to verify yourself during online banking transactions and to sign electronic documents then you have a big problem if you change employers. In the United States, employers are the main providers of health insurance. This hampers labour mobility — the ability of employees to move between jobs — in a phenomenon known as 'job lock'. Quitting an unsatisfactory job and searching for a new one makes sense when the cost is only a few weeks' wages. If it leaves your family without health insurance, it may be an intolerable risk.[1] Just as President Barack Obama's state-backed healthcare plan is beginning to deal with 'job lock', it would be a pity to replace it with a new drag on labour mobility, where employees fear that moving jobs will lead to cumbersome or risky changes in their online identity.

A better option is to use your existing banking or credit card identity. When shopping on the internet, you may well find that after you enter your payment details you are taken to a screen where your bank or credit card company asks you for more information, with security questions or an additional password. This certainly provides a higher level of reassurance to both sides engaged in that particular transaction. But it does not so far have much wider use. You cannot use your banking login to file your taxes online, for example.

Independent commercial and non-commercial providers of identity are trying to fill this gap. The miiCard, for example (pronounced 'my-card'), attempts to provide different levels of authentication depending on how much information you are willing to share. It can identify you by your computer, and the address from which you are sending and receiving data on the internet. It can verify your address against an electoral roll (if you are British) and also verify your banking details. It will provide you with an ID 'card' bearing a 2D barcode (like this).

Asked for your identity, you provide this, and the outfit seeking to verify you can then scan the card and check the details submitted with miiCard.

This has some advantages. But there are weaknesses, too. How can you be really sure that miiCard will keep your details safe? I signed up and noticed that I had to type in my full banking credentials – something which even my bank does not request (it asks for four random characters from the password, not the whole thing).* A vital principle of security is to give away as little data as possible in any interaction, so that if you are observed the damage

---

* Having completed registration, I immediately changed my banking password, wondering if I had been exceptionally foolish.

is limited. A sensible system for checking if someone is inside an age limit does not ask the person for his date of birth, and then check with a database to see if that matches. It asks a question on the lines of 'is this person over 65?' and receives a yes–no answer.

Another version is the French 'https card', which adopts a similar approach, with sixteen stages of verification, starting with the computer, then moving through a verified mobile phone number and e-mail, and going right up to biometric data (fingerprints or retina scans) and even, on request, DNA. Subscribers have to pay, quite substantially (€249, or £200 or $340 at the time of writing), for the highest level. The website might inspire more confidence if it did not refer to fees paid 'annualy' (sic) amid other oddities.

It is hard to see either of these catching on. Rather more promising is an attempt by the international association of mobile phone operators to use these devices as the basis for a secure digital identity. Mobile phones (known as cell phones in the USA and some other countries) are no longer exotic or expensive. They contain what are, in effect, powerful computers, they can browse the internet and they are inherently connected with authentication and payment systems. To direct a mobile phone call, the system needs to identify the devices at both ends. It must also work out who is going to pay. Moreover, many people now use their phones as mobile wallets. It is possible to pay for something by sending a text message, or using the phone to reach another payment system (such as PayPal), or simply by having the price of the goods or service added to the mobile phone bill. The phone can display a 2D barcode which the merchant can scan. The Apple pay system allows you to authorise a transaction with a fingerprint.

Even in the absence of a solid, ubiquitous digital identity, plenty of work has been done, however, on how to recognise those identities that do exist. A new effort launched in 2014 called OpenID Connect is particularly promising. It allows people running websites to get away from the dangerous and complicated business of storing other people's passwords. It allows users of those websites to use an existing ID, rather than having to create a new one. In effect, this does for internet use what recognition of passports does for international travel. Imagine that for each country you visited you had to get a particular travel document. You would need one kind of passport to go to Germany and another one to go to Japan. You had to put important personal information on the document, and it was no use for anything else. Worse, imagine that this document can be easily copied. Someone can quite easily replicate your passport and pretend to be you. If you want a passport that can't be replicated, it will be extremely complicated (imagine one made of paper that has to be folded in a particularly intricate form of origami before it is valid). That would be the counterpart of the hassle of creating and remembering a strong password.

The first stage towards a better system would be for countries to say that they recognised each other's travel documents. So if you have a passport that lets you go to Japan, you can also use it to go to Germany. This does not sort out the fundamental problem, which is that the passports are cumbersome, easily copied and contain too much personal information. But it would reduce the number you need. That is what has already developed with the use of Twitter and Facebook credentials to log into other places on the internet. Services such as OpenID Connect are the equivalent of a universal passport reader. If you turn up at a website with any of the credentials that its operators are prepared to accept, you are accepted. These operators may wish to have very strong identification, such as a government ID card, or something issued by a bank or credit card company. Or they may be happy simply with something that allows them to relate your activity on the site today with what you did yesterday and what you may do tomorrow.

All of this makes it easier to use whatever collection of electronic passports you may have. It does not solve the fundamental problem: that they are not that good.

But there is one country where this problem has already been solved: Estonia.[2] Unlike the citizens of any other country in the world, Estonians, through wise choices and good fortune, enjoy a combination of a secure, convenient digital identity, coupled with strong privacy protection and widespread public support.

The instant reaction of many people to the idea that a government-issued ID card could be the central feature of their life is horror. It immediately arouses nightmarish thoughts of Big Brother in outsiders' eyes. That the police could look at your medical records, and cross-reference them with your taxes, and also see your online banking, and details of every e-mail you send and receive, sounds like the worst kind of panopticon. But such thinking about security is flawed. Just as it is possible to identify yourself in the real world in lots of different locations using your passport, so, too, is it possible to use a secure digital ID in many different ways in the online world. If you use a passport to prove your identity at a bank, and then take it to a notary in order to show that you are indeed the person you claim to be when signing a document, and then take the same document to a register office in order to witness a wedding, and then use it to show that you are old enough to buy alcohol, and then use it to check in at an airport as you fly out of the country on a business trip, it does not necessarily hold that the passport office has details of every one of those actions. With a properly designed identity system, that can be true in online activity, too. You use your ID card to prove your identity to a bank, to sign or witness a document, to prove your age and to purchase an air ticket.

To be sure, a malevolent government wanting to control the lives of its citizens can use ID cards as part of that effort – but the bigger problem in such a country is not the document, but the nature of the government.

The Estonian system starts at birth. Secure digital ID is a birthright of every child born in Estonia. Even before a new-born baby has left the maternity hospital, it will be registered in the state health insurance system. The parents notify the tax authorities of the birth – online – and receive the maternity benefit (via an electronic bank transfer). The linchpin of the system is the digital ID card, issued to every resident of Estonia at the age of fifteen. You can use this card by putting it in a card reader. These are standard and inexpensive. Most Estonian computers have them fitted as a default feature. You can also buy a neat gadget which unfolds to become a card reader, and can be carried on a keyring. (The most modern variant of the scheme, as we shall see later, dispenses with the physical card altogether and uses the mobile phone instead.)

But an ID is useful only in so far as someone accepts it. The second big feature of the Estonian system is the 'X-road' – a network of networks in which all government agencies talk to each other – which provides what is in effect the operating system for the country.

This is not a 'Big Brother' system. A better way of looking at it is that the state gives you a passport which is so secure and versatile, and accepted so widely, that you do not need any other form of identification – no more logins, passwords, gizmos or text messages to unreliable mobile phones. The Estonian digital ID consists of a card and two codes. One is used for identification (answering the question: 'who is this person?') and the other for signing ('has this person agreed to this action?'). The card, for most Estonians, is a small piece of plastic. It bears a public cryptographic key, based on the person's name and date of birth, and a secret private key, encrypted on the card.

The card on its own is intrinsically not very useful to anyone other than its owner. If you lose it, you can get another one. So, too, if you lose or forget the two codes, for signing and identifying yourself: you can get a sealed, computer-generated envelope containing your new codes from a bank or government office.

The point about the Estonian ID card is that it eases and safeguards your ability to function in your interaction with government, with other people, and in business. You get up in the morning and use it to log into your bank account and pay your daily bills. Then you go to work – and use the card as a public transport ticket. At work you can send e-mails and documents signed with the card. You can send an encrypted document which only a specific recipient will be able to read. You can use it to log into to any website in Estonia that requires identification. You can collect an electronic prescription, or book a medical appointment. You can log into your university website and submit an essay or collect an assignment. You can pay your taxes (which in Estonia typically takes less than half an hour; refunds are processed in forty-eight hours or less). You can use it to vote. You can set up a company (in a few minutes). You can sign a legally binding contract, just as surely and irrevocably as if you had taken out a fountain pen and scribbled your signature in ink on paper. You can buy, sell, invest and travel without giving security a second thought.

In doing so, you do not give away personal information such as your mother's maiden name, your home address, or the name of your first pet. Nor are you asked to remember a whole series of passwords and logins. The beauty of the Estonian system is that the government gives you, as a resident of Estonia, a world-class digital identity. It uses the strongest available encryption – breaking it by brute force would require a super-computer running for years. Anybody can use it. You have to remember only your codes:

a four-digit one for identifying yourself and a five-digit one for signing documents. And that's it.

It is worth underlining that this happens with the state's coop-eration, but not with its knowledge. When an Estonian gets up in the morning and uses his ID card to access his online bank account, the government does not have access to the account. All that happens is that the bank's computer records a login attempt by someone using an encrypted combination of a particular key and a PIN code. The bank's computer then queries this combination – a very long number, in essence – with the central registry, which then responds that this combination of card and code is a valid identifier. Returning to the analogy of the universal passport, the central registry, in effect, simply agrees that the passport is valid and that the picture of the person presenting the passport accords with the picture in the passport.

In theory, if the person concerned was of great interest to the authorities, it would be possible for the Estonian police or security service, subject to the issuance of a warrant, to monitor meta-data around that person's activities through his use of his ID card: where he used it and for what purpose. But they could also be following him physically, tapping his phone, searching his house when he was away and intercepting his mail. In any advanced society, the police and other authorities will have the power to bug and snoop, usually with the authorisation of a judge or some other independent over-seer. But the state does not have the key for unlocking a citizen's encrypted documents.

The genius of the Estonian system is that it provides the minimum information to the government while providing the maximum convenience to the individual. The system is designed principally with convenience in mind. By law, no government agency is allowed to ask for data which are already held on the system. This is a huge difference from the typical citizen's experience when dealing with government in other countries, where the same information – address, date of birth, login, password, national insurance or health number – needs to be typed in at almost every instance.

Taavi Kotka, the head of Estonia's government digital services – the country's 'Chief Technology Officer' – says that people realise there is some trade-off between privacy and convenience. But they overwhelmingly prefer convenience. They also like the feeling of being part of an innovative experiment, which makes life in their country far easier and more convenient than in counterpart countries. 'We feel like test pilots, not laboratory rabbits,' says Mr Kotka.

It is worth noting that though Estonian ID cards are issued to every resident (rather like the birth certificates and national insurance numbers mentioned above), it is not mandatory to use them. If you want, you can go to a government office and fill everything in by hand (and using a quill pen and home-made ink if that is important to you). You can go to your bank and make transfers manually (or, indeed, you can refuse to have a bank account and keep your money in euros, or for that matter gold bars, cowrie shells and cattle). Nobody will stop you. You can send letters by post, sealed in sealing wax and using a cipher of your own design. Nobody will stop you from doing that either. But few if any choose to do so.

How has Estonia managed this when other countries have not? An easy but lazy answer is size. Estonia is small so it is easy to do things quickly. But a moment's reflection shows that this is not true. Small countries have higher costs proportionate to their population. They do not have the economies of scale which big countries enjoy. A rather more plausible reason may be that as a small country which re-emerged as an independent nation in 1991, after more than fifty years of foreign occupation, Estonians know they have to compete using their wits and flexibility. Estonians are technophiles.

They like to adopt new technology early and have an incentive to
do so.

But the biggest reason for the scheme's popularity is simply that
it works so well. It saves time and effort. In the time that they are
not queuing at the bank, or waiting at government offices, or visiting a notary to get documents and signatures copied and certified,
or waiting on the telephone for a helpline to answer, or trying
to remember their passwords and logins for innumerable different
websites, Estonians can get on with the things in their lives that
they actually like: singing, going to the sauna and enjoying the
countryside.

Strong and simple cryptographic signatures are one crucial
feature of the Estonian system. The other is the good design of the
X-road, the government computer network of networks. This has
three big features. One is that it allows every agency and department to communicate with any other. The second is that it allows
outside bodies – with the consent of the individual – to verify data.
So if you want to use your ID card to sign a letter – showing that it
is really you who sent it – or to encrypt it (so that only the person
for whom it is intended can read it) then you can use the services
of the state. This is rather like having a free state postal service. It
does not mean that the state reads your letters, but it guarantees to
get them to the right place. Another analogy would be a state-run
system of safe deposit boxes. If you want to make sure that your
material is safe, you can put it in a strongbox, owned by the state,
but to which only you and your trusted friends have the key.

The safety of the strongbox is important, too. Estonia's system
uses a top-of-the-range system. No encryption is perfect (not least
because it is vulnerable to 'rubber hose attacks', and end-point
vulnerabilities, as described above). But the Estonian system is
notably more secure than almost anything else used in daily life. If
you lose your card you can get another one. If you lose your card

and your PIN codes you have a problem, just as you do if you lose your wallet, passport, house keys and phone – but you can block your ID with a single phone call.

A further wrinkle in the system is that Estonia's data is all backed up abroad. Mr Kotka is developing a network of digital embassies – havens for the country's data so that even if the X-road inside Estonia is disabled (for example, by a swamping attack) or if the data is corrupted by attackers, the whole system can be restored from a valid database elsewhere. This is rather like the wise (but sadly rare) practice by which individuals regularly back up the contents of their computers to a safe, remote location.

The latest version of the scheme has an extra layer of convenience. It does not depend on a physical card. Instead it sits on the user's mobile phone, or to be exact on the SIM card, which identifies the phone to the network. The SIM card is, in effect, a powerful computer, with the ability to manage complicated encryption, and the mobile phone does not begin to use its full capabilities. The Estonian ID card software can be loaded on to the SIM card, so that instead of keeping his identity on a plastic card in his wallet, an Estonian can keep it on his phone. Just as with the plastic card, he uses two PIN codes, one to identify himself, the other to sign documents or make transactions.

These parts of the scheme offer added convenience. But the third really big feature revolves around an important principle: that Estonians own their own data. The information does not belong to the government. The individual has the right to decide what is done with it, and the right to see what has been done with it. Misuse of data by a public official is a serious criminal offence in Estonia. If you use your access to government databases to snoop on private individuals – celebrities, for example – you will be fired, prosecuted and may go to jail. Only with an explicit legal mandate (in effect a court order or search warrant) can the law-enforcement or security authorities look at data without the consent of the person involved. Even that is open to legal challenge, except in a small number of cases involving counter-espionage.

All this is in sharp contrast to the woeful state of government ID schemes in the rest of the advanced world. These are typically expensive, unpopular and inefficient.

It is therefore interesting that Estonia is making its scheme available to foreigners. A law that came into force in 2014 allowed non-resident foreigners to apply for an Estonian ID card. They will have to meet the same standards, including providing biometric data (retina scan and fingerprints) as well as other supporting documents such as a passport. This can be done either during a visit to Estonia, or – as from 2015 – at an Estonian consulate abroad. The cost is likely to be €50.

At first sight this seems a puzzling development. Why would foreigners want to have another country's ID? And what good would it do? If you live in London, or Berlin, or San Francisco, and you are not an Estonian, why would you want to have an Estonian ID? Moreover, why is it in Estonia's interest to make its treasured national ID card available to foreigners?

The last of these questions is the easiest to answer. Estonia needs friends. It is a small country with a population of just over one million, sitting next to Russia, a country of 143 million, which used to be its colonial master, and has also invaded and occupied it within living memory.[3] It has to cope with economic pressure, and a blizzard of Kremlin propaganda which depicts it as a fascist hellhole and a political and economic failure.

So signing up foreigners as what Mr Kotka calls 'satellite Estonians' makes a lot of sense. He aims to issue around ten million ID cards. Most of the new digital expats will be citizens of countries that already have visa-free access to Estonia, so it is likely that they will want to come and visit. For those that do need visas, an

Estonian ID card will mean that the authorities already have most of the information they need to decide whether to issue one.

Moreover, having an Estonian ID is likely to increase trade and investment. For a start, it becomes easy to set up a company in Estonia. This takes only a few minutes for an Estonian. Now foreigners will be able to do that, too. As Estonia is a member of the EU, a company registered there can compete anywhere within the single market. That means that an American, say, wanting to do business in the EU, could sign up for an Estonian ID (for example, at that country's consulate in New York), then set up a company and a bank account in Estonia, and start selling goods or services, without ever having to set foot in Estonia. He can register intellectual property, sign contracts with his digital signature and, when the time comes, pay his company's taxes online.

That will already be a big advantage for some people. But it is only the beginning. The Estonian ID card is not only useful in Estonia. Under EU rules, every state has to recognise every other state's digital ID. That means that whether you are doing business in France, Germany, Britain or Greece, you can use your Estonian ID to do anything online that you would otherwise use the national ID card for. In some of these countries, public take-up of digital IDs is low. But they can still be used.

It is not just dealing with government. Having a secure digital ID based on a smart card (or mobile phone) should also, eventually, allow satellite Estonians to do other things, such as open a bank account in any European country, and log into any website that operates a smart-card system. The Estonian ID card is designed to work with new standards such as OpenID Connect – the 'universal passport reader' mentioned above.

I am the first satellite Estonian. At a ceremony in Tallinn on 2 December 2014 I was given Estonian e-residency card No100001, with the personal code 36205030034. I have an e-mail address, edward.lucas@eesti.ee, from which I can send a signed e-mail. This is far more secure than my work e-mail or my private e-mail. These depend merely on the security of my password and my mobile phone and are vulnerable to snoopers, key-loggers and my carelessness. My Estonian e-mail works only if someone has used my card and my PIN.

Having checked my secure e-mail, the next thing I did with my card was to sign a document – for my travel expenses. I did this by typing in my second PIN into a small window on the screen of a laptop, and clicking OK. That was as legally binding as if I had signed a paper copy with my pen. My host logged into her bank account – using a digital ID – and sent the money instantly. The third thing I did was to send an encrypted document to my host, typing her personal code into the encryption box. Barring an attack by a sophisticated government intelligence agency, only she and I would have been able to read the message it contained (which was: 'Thanks').

To the technically savvy, much of this level of security is available already. You can download authentication and encryption software, and click on the 'sign' button that may be hidden somewhere in your e-mail options. But setting up this encryption is tricky. You have to create your public key (which is the equivalent of a lockable box which anyone can slam shut) and your private key (which opens it). I am more adept than the average user, but setting this up on my laptop took several evenings and a lot of frustration, and at the end of the day works less well than the service the Estonian state provides free of charge.

As well as signing e-mails, a secure digital ID also means you can encrypt your e-mail, so that only the person at the other end can read it. You will encode it using his public key. That is the equivalent of clicking the lock shut on a box he has provided you with. In order to decrypt it, he will have to use his card and PIN code, which are the equivalents of the keys that open the box.

The big question facing the scheme is whether people who are unwilling to take part in their government's ID schemes may be willing to sign up for the Estonian one. In the ten-plus years that it has been running, it has not suffered a data breach or serious breakdown. It is cheap. It clearly works. The people who run it are trustworthy, and have minimal interest in what a foreigner is up to. I have good reason not to trust the British government to be careful with my data. I will put up with quite a lot of inconvenience before I reluctantly trust someone whose integrity and competence have proven doubtful. I may be more willing to trust a disinterested third party whose record is flawless.

One way of looking at this is as a kind of credit card. Before American Express changed the world of international travel, going abroad meant carrying travellers cheques, bank drafts or cash, or sending (by telex) cumbersome and expensive requests for funds, to be paid out on presentation of a passport. I recall this system all too well when I was living behind the Iron Curtain, in Communist-era Czechoslovakia. Only one bank in the then West Germany, KKB, would pay out cash on a Visa card. As a result foreigners based in Prague would take it in turns to drive three hours to the undistinguished border town of Weiden, bearing a stack of friends' cards and PIN codes, in order to load up with cash and drive back again. That was cumbersome, but it was a great deal better than waiting for a wire transfer to arrive from the West.

Estonia's ID card, and the other rival schemes which will doubtless mushroom in the years ahead, will do for life on the internet what American Express did for international travel. Instead of a cumbersome and vulnerable system, you have a single piece of plastic and a signature (in the days of American Express, it was a handwritten one, now it is a PIN code). And just as American Express was originally designed for Americans, but was quickly adopted by other people, often with no connection at all to the United States, so the 'Estonian Express' card may become a global standard. As I finished this book, a team of experts from Singapore was visiting Tallinn. They are investigating the possibility of using the island state's reputation for excellent government to provide their national ID card to non-resident foreigners, too. Britain's government is pushing ahead with its own plan for identity based on third-party providers, called gov.uk verify. I was a guinea pig in that scheme, too. The process was speedy, linking together my details from the passport registry, driving licence agency and my credit reference. At the end I had a digital identity strong enough to do my tax return, though with no biometric verification and (as yet) no ability to sign or encrypt documents. It will be hard for the British scheme to match the power and simplicity of the Estonian one.

But even the widespread use of strong digital ID, if it ever comes, will not protect us from the biggest problem: our dependence on networks run badly by other people.

12

Turning the Tables

How do we get back the advantage in dealing with attacks on our computers and our networks? Elaborating on H. L. Mencken's aphorism, that every complex problem has a solution that is simple, clear and wrong, Dan Geer comes up with four rules that should be etched on the desk of everyone dealing with security of computers:

Most important ideas are unappealing.
Most appealing ideas are unimportant.
Not every problem has a good solution.
Every solution has side effects.

As public discontent and the costs of insecurity increase, there will be growing calls for simple and sweeping solutions, especially from those with a vested interest in selling something that will do just the trick. The public should mix its concern with scepticism.

For a start, the idea that software is 'unbreakable' is useless and dangerous. In theory, a piece of software can contain no flaws. But it runs on hardware which can contain flaws. It works in conjunction with other software which contains flaws, and it is operated by people who are vulnerable to social-engineering attacks (confidence tricks). Selling 'unbreakable' software is like selling a householder an 'unbreakable' lock. It arouses a false sense of security, and does not do the job it claims to do. Humility towards attackers is the first line of defence. Paranoia is the second.

A similar mistake is in assuming that complex cryptography works better than simpler kinds of encryption. This is part of a 'mine is bigger than yours' approach to security which may reflect the overwhelming male composition of the industry. It is true that a system based on very large prime numbers will take longer to crack than one based on shorter ones. But beyond a certain level, the length of the 'key' – the prime number in encryption – is irrelevant. Even quite a short key cannot be attacked with brute force – simply trying every possible combination of factors. If it is too long to crack with brute force, the attackers will simply resort to something else – perhaps the 'end-point vulnerability' attacks described earlier, where the attackers try to infect the machine in order to steal whatever is entered into the keyboard or shown on the screen. Long keys are also so cumbersome. Anyone who tried to secure a house by suggesting that the front door key should be so huge and heavy that only two men could carry it would be laughed to scorn. The same should apply to those who peddle super-strength encryption.

A similarly useless claim is that anti-virus software or firewalls offer reliable protection. It is true that an up-to-date anti-virus program helps security. It will warn you if you try to install already-known malware, and keep your computer free of the most common infections. But a highly sensitive anti-virus program will flag up far too many things as suspicious. A less sensitive one will let too many suspicious ones through.

Moreover, it cannot protect you against new threats. Attackers who are designing new malware start off by testing them against the main anti-virus programs. Those that foil detection are the ones that get deployed. There is also a trade-off between convenience and safety. Keeping track of new versions of malware is hard. Though the anti-virus companies can and do share information, it takes time for them to realise that a new bug is out in the wild, and to work out how to deal with it in a way that will not simply crash the computers and networks of those infected. Adaptive malware – which changes its behaviour according to its environment – is hard to spot. So are attacks that come via several different routes – a mobile phone, an open port and a watering hole attack all combined, for example. Vendors of anti-virus software do not offer guarantees. There is a reason for that.

Firewalls used to be the hottest topic in network security. These are supposed to block unauthorised traffic from entering or leaving the network. They do a good job, so long as the attackers are kind enough to make themselves known on entry and exit. But attackers are wily. They will find a way into the network that evades the firewall, and a way out that hops over or round it, too. Heartbleed is a good example. The best way to escape from a prison is in a prison guard's uniform. The best way to exfiltrate data from a network is to dress it up in a legitimate seeming guise. Blocking all access to a network may reduce vulnerability – but will also make it unusable. As explained above, the internet is inherently insecure. Building a big wall around bits of it doesn't change that.

In short, anti-virus software and firewalls are to computer security what the Maginot Line was to French defences against Nazi Germany: a magnificent defence against yesterday's threat, but not against tomorrow's. Another analogy would be wearing a condom. It may protect you against some sexually transmitted diseases – but it is not a licence for risk-free promiscuity. As Roger Grimes notes, if anti-virus programs and firewalls worked, everyone would be running them, and our problems would be over.

The problem of false alarms – known in geek-speak as 'false positives' – also plagues the programs that detect intrusions in networks. This is a marvellous idea (see below) in which any anomalous behaviour immediately triggers an alarm, and the lockdown of the computer concerned. But to be sufficiently sensitive to detect every instance of sinister anomalous behaviour, this software will also detect many other instances of innocent events. This does not make them useless, but it does mean that any claim of infallibility should be treated with extreme caution.

As Mr Grimes notes, the real solution to computer security problems is to look at what attackers are doing and try to stop them. As with most things in life, there are no big easy answers, only lots of difficult ones.[1] Most of the improvements which can be made come with trade-offs: we will pay in time, money or privacy if we want to be safer.

But some of those sacrifices are trivial for the benefits they will bring. The first step is to take the obvious precautions. This is the equivalent of locking doors and windows when we leave the house, and taking elementary hygiene precautions. Most criminals are stupid and opportunistic. They will go after easy targets rather than difficult ones. Britain's Centre for the Protection of National Infrastructure, or CPNI (a lightly camouflaged outstation of GCHQ), has produced ten simple recommendations which, if implemented, would deal with, it says, 80 per cent of the security breaches on the internet. The list should be as embedded in our culture as the Highway Code is in our driving habits. I highlight its main points in Appendix Three.[2]

The problem with lists such as these is that not everyone acts on them. So long as, say, only 90 per cent of computer users take the precautions recommended, the attackers – particularly if they are using automated attacks such as spam e-mails, or scanning the internet for important but lightly protected devices – will have plenty to work on. Also, they are aware of the advice being issued, and adapt their tactics in order to evade common precautions.

Public health, rather than locks and keys, offers some important ways of thinking about cyber-security. Norms of behaviour have transformed much of public health. It is bad manners to hawk or cough without a handkerchief. We wash our hands before eating or preparing food. We expect casual sexual partners to wear condoms. These are the equivalents of keeping your personal online life in good shape – practising proper password hygiene, checking web addresses carefully, not clicking on links and attachments from strangers, and installing patches and updates promptly, and using anti-virus software.

As Mr Geer notes, when you check into a hospital strict rules govern the handling of your data. You have high expectations of both privacy protection and consent. You will not be expected to accept treatment you disagree with. You will not have to give your entire medical history if you do not wish to. But if you show signs of infection of a nasty disease, a 'reportable condition' such as bubonic plague, typhus or Ebola, or if you have a mental illness that makes you a violent danger to yourself and others, your rights are severely constrained. Public health interests take precedence over your privacy and freedom. You can be incarcerated and forcibly medicated. The welfare of the community means that you cannot be let loose to roam the streets. This is not just true in Europe: every one of America's fifty states has a public health law defining such 'reportable conditions', and the steps that the authorities can take.

We do not regard that as particularly controversial. There may be debates on the margins (about the degree of mental illness that requires incarceration, for example) but even the most ardent libertarian would not expect to be allowed to deal random death sentences to other members of the public by infecting them with a lethal disease. It is worth applying that thinking to the internet. What would happen, for example, if we imposed a similar duty on the owners of severely infected computers? If you suffer from a nasty computer bug, should you have to notify it, in the same way as you have to notify a dangerous disease? What happens if you do not? You may be open to civil litigation from the victims of your infected computer. If you are a listed company, you should perhaps be under an obligation to report a serious cyber-attack to the public. After all, if an oil company drills a well and finds nothing (or something), it is expected to tell the public, because not to do so would create a time period in which insiders could buy or sell shares, based on information that other investors do not have. Is it inherently unreasonable to apply the same principle to a breach of internet security? Perhaps people who recklessly endanger the welfare of others, either by allowing their computers to be infected, or failing to deal with a problem promptly, should even face criminal charges, too.

The analogies go well beyond public health. Forty-eight American states make it a criminal offence to fail to report sexual abuse of children. Anti-bribery laws make it an offence to fail to report corruption; anti-cartel laws make it an offence to fail to report if your company is involved in restraint of trade. A general feature of the American criminal code makes it a crime to fail to report a felony of which you have knowledge. Already forty-six American states require mandatory reporting of data breaches. These are not quite the same as allowing an infected computer to continue to do its work – but the connection is clear.[3]

Working out what this means in practice involves tricky decisions. What happens if you discover that your computer has been hijacked and is being used in a botnet? You are perhaps sending spam e-mail as a result, or perhaps swamping some hapless website on the other side of the world. How promptly should you act? Is it worth making your computer-security people work night and day, over a weekend, or is the disinfection just a routine task, rather like removing rats from your basement? And if you do report it, what level of detail must you go into? Should you explain what made you notice that you were infected? And what about third parties? Suppose you notice that a customer is infected. Do you have to report him, jeopardising your commercial relationship? If you warn him and he does nothing, what do you do then? Are you happy if your provider of computer services – perhaps the internet service provider who keeps you online, or the company that manages the storage of your data on the internet 'cloud' – monitors (some would say snoops) on what you are doing, and reports that, with or without your knowledge? Suppose someone infects your website with a watering hole attack – one where an innocent looking graphic installs malware on the visitor's computer? You may be placed in the internet equivalent of quarantine, costing you sales, or damaging your reputation. Who is to decide if that isolation is proportionate to the danger of infection? You would not think it fair if you were incarcerated in a hospital because you had pneumonia. If you have pneumonic plague, it is another matter. A doctor can decide that, with appeal to more senior medical or judicial opinion if necessary. But who decides the severity of the infection of your computer?

America's Centres for Disease Control (CDC) have capabilities that are relevant in the world of defending our computers and networks against attackers. The first of these is that communicable diseases must be reported by law. The second is that the CDCs have the data and expertise to make sense of the reports. This is still largely lacking when it comes to malware. The taxonomy of viruses, bacteria and parasites is relatively straightforward. They can be examined under a microscope and their DNA can be isolated and sequenced.

Malware is much more difficult. Do you describe it by what it does, or how it works? Or by the presumed instigators? Or by the attack of which it forms part? All are possible. But in each case the category is fuzzy. A piece of malware that does one thing in one context may do another when deployed differently. The same fragments of code may be present in several different kinds of malware. In this sense the battle is much closer to that waged against the manufacturers of illegal pharmaceuticals, who tweak their products molecule by molecule to find something that has the desired narcotic or hallucinogenic effect, but is not prohibited by law.

We do not yet have a CDC for malware. In his report 'Surviving on a Diet of Poisoned Fruit' the American security expert Richard Danzig suggests using the model already extant in aviation, where aircrew are encouraged to report near-misses.[4] Individually, airlines do not like reporting their mistakes: it erodes public confidence in their brands. But collectively they all benefit from a culture which identifies safety threats before they cause a crash.

The public health model of thinking about computer security has its limits. There is no equivalent of a doctor in the world of infected computers. A serious disease outbreak will bring attention from a team of professionals who have many decades of training between them. We have – at least in the rich world – a whole series of procedures, institutions and resources which we can deploy. Computer security is necessarily a matter for amateurs. People who own or use a computer may have no training or experience whatsoever. But they may be confronted with malware produced by the most expert and malicious attackers in the world. Disease outbreaks happen in countries: if necessary, as with the Ebola outbreak in West Africa in 2014, the authorities can screen travellers or even seal borders. Perhaps most significantly, disease is the outcome of random behaviour in a predictable environment. Outside the real threat of biological warfare, we are not dealing with sentient opponents: drug-resistant bacteria may emerge as a result of evolution, but nobody is actively trying to breed them. In the world of computers and networks, the attackers are human – and highly motivated.

In the real world we have social norms which help us balance deviancy, privacy and autonomy. But in the digital world we are still groping for them. If we saw an intruder in our own garden, we would call the police. If we see a stranger in our neighbour's yard, we have to ask ourselves if this is just a houseguest or a robber. We have all sorts of mental habits to help us decide, based on past experience. Have there been break-ins recently in the street? What does he look like? We can approach the stranger verbally and assess his response. The decisions are not always simple. We would not accept as a general rule that the right response is always to retreat into our own private space and ignore everything that happens in our neighbourhood. Screams, breaking glass and shots being fired will move even the most disengaged neighbour to take notice: after all, he might be next.

So beyond a social code that expects proper personal computer hygiene and vigilance, we need some norms that apply to institutions. Customer and shareholder pressure may help that. But it would be even better if the sanctions for institutional carelessness were tougher. Perhaps those who recklessly endanger the welfare of others, either by allowing their computers to be infected, or failing to deal with a problem promptly, should face even criminal charges, too. It is a criminal offence to drive an unroadworthy car, or fly an unairworthy plane. Why in principle should it be different to allow a computer to endanger other people?

Paul Venezia, a writer on security, hit the nail on the head in an article in 2011 in which he argued that badly written code should be a felony.[5] Criminal responsibility may be the best answer in cases of reckless carelessness, but in fact even applying civil liability would have a good effect. If you build a bridge you do not ask everyone who crosses it to sign a disclaimer saying that if it falls down they waive their rights to sue you. But that is exactly what you do when you click 'agree' on the lengthy, incomprehensible and usually unread list of terms and conditions that accompany everything we do on the public internet.

Mr Venezia wrote:

> The company and employees directly responsible for constructing code so poorly that it stores plain-text passwords of millions of users and can apparently be compromised at will should, at the very least, be fined a vast amount, with some portion of that money going to each possibly affected user and the rest used to assist in addressing identity theft problems that will inevitably appear following a breach. If I had my way, there would also be mandatory loss of employment and possible jail time involved for those whose unspeakably poor decisions led to this event.

After all, if someone writing a program turned out to have deliberately created a flaw in order to steal passwords, he would expect to be fired at a minimum, and possibly prosecuted. If the loss of innocent people's information – perhaps in a life-ruining way – is merely an accident, is it really right that the world of computer experts simply shrugs its shoulders and says nothing can be done?

Businesses display a wide range of behaviour on their customers' privacy, just as they do on other things. Some will be scrupulous and ethical in the hope of building valued long-term trust. Others will gouge, wriggle and cheat in the hope of making a fast buck. Within the law, that is their right. The authorities can play a role in encouraging public-spirited behaviour, but the three big constraints are criminal sanctions, civil litigation and preservation of reputation.

Each of these is evolving. They deserve to be dealt with separately and carefully, not lost in a sea of panicky outrage.

But that is not nearly enough. As this book has shown, there are fundamental problems in the way the internet is constructed, and in the way we use it. Better passwords, more scrutiny of e-mails, more cautious behaviour with links and attachments, more professional network design, running up-to-date software with anti-virus programs installed is all the equivalent of keeping doors and windows locked and not leaving valuables in plain sight in an empty car.

Slightly more sophisticated attackers still have plenty of weapons in their armoury, and will deploy them against harder but more lucrative targets. To see this, it is useful if we think ourselves into the attackers' shoes. What are we trying to protect and against whom? This is a harder question than many companies realise. As shown earlier, you may be important to an attacker not because of who you are, but because of whom you know, or whom you do business with. Your thinking about the threat needs to include your customers, your suppliers and your social life. You may think you are a humble supplier of a boring and unimportant product. But if your customers trust you, they will open your e-mails without thinking. If you send a regular weekly e-mail – perhaps with an attachment called 'invoice' or 'report', you are a tempting gateway into their network. The ability to send a single, authentic seeming e-mail from your account, with an attachment that contains malware (or even an ingredient that can later be combined into malware), will be a huge advantage to an attacker.

Dan Geer, one of the fathers of the modern internet, floated a new 'Ten Commandments' at the Black Hat conference in 2014, in a talk called 'Cybersecurity as Realpolitik'.[6] It bears reading in full, but perhaps the most important point he made was that 'power exists to be used'. A besetting conviction of many of those involved in the internet is that the exercise of power is inherently suspicious, and that the internet is a politics-free zone where solutions can be based on elegant combinations of hardware and software, to everyone's benefit. This is a fantasy. Perfect safety and perfect order are impossible. In the search for the least bad solution, users of computers and networks must realise that the anarchic, trusting and idealistic values of the early internet are not enough for something that has become the world's central nervous system. If you have power and do not use it, someone else will.

But accompanying a clear-eyed view of power should be a sense of humility. As Mr Geer noted, this does not mean timidity, but the willingness to accept that facts have proved you wrong.

Another big shift is in the liability of the businesses which make their profits from providing computer services to the public. The first category is those who run the physical infrastructure – the cables and routers – of the internet. A fierce, complicated and self-interested debate has been raging for years on the issue of 'net neutrality'. In a nutshell the issue is whether the internet should be like a simple postal service, in which every package, regardless of what is in it, pays the same and is treated the same. Internet providers have a paradoxical attitude to this. They strongly oppose the idea that they should have to police their customers, and even more that they should be liable for the use of their networks by criminals. But they also yearn to be able to favour some kinds of traffic – such as that involving their own customers. Those who pay more would get super-fast premium service. Others would take their chance.

Mr Geer suggests an ingenious solution to this. The companies that run the internet should have to choose. Either they can become common carriers, like the postal service or the railway, where they are immune from liability for what they carry, but must treat all customers equally. Or they can offer tailored service and charge what they like – but in that case they must police the traffic.

A second liability question involves software providers. As noted above, software is written to be cheap and adequate and still function. But the definition of 'still function' is changing. What was tolerable when the internet was used mainly by academics for research collaboration, or by hobbyists and computer enthusiasts, is not tolerable when it is vital to modern life. In the pages above I have suggested the analogy of transport: trains do crash, but we expect the railway operators to write their timetables and install equipment to ensure that they do not. When something does go wrong, it is carefully investigated to make sure it does not happen again. Carelessness when other people have trusted you with their lives means lawsuits, firings, bankruptcy or even jail.

It is tempting to think one can attack the problem through the criminal justice system. The problem here is so huge that it deserves a book all on its own. The sort of people who work as police and prosecutors are not, on the whole, computer experts. Their idea of criminals is chiefly people who use violence against the innocent, steal things from shops, or who sell illegal drugs. White-collar crime – even involving the most reprehensible breaches of trust towards colleagues, customers or shareholders – is scarcely prosecuted in Western countries outside the United States. Yet breakthroughs are occurring. The FBI has made inroads into seemingly untouchable groups by using old-fashioned American policing methods: running agents inside criminal organisations, recruiting informers and then making arrests and driving hard plea bargains. In 2012 the Bureau broke the Anonymous group of hackers and activists, which had carried out high-profile attacks on Stratfor, the Texas-based private intelligence company, and others, by recruiting as an informant 'Sabu' (whose real name was Hector

Xavier Monsegur) who was a leader of Lulzsec, a splinter group.[7] Although Monsegur had carried out 250 attacks, at an estimated cost to the victims of $50 million, he did not serve the twenty-six-year sentence which could have been imposed: instead he walked free from the courtroom after being praised by the judge for his 'extraordinary cooperation' with the FBI, which led to numerous attacks on various targets being thwarted and to six other members of the group being convicted and jailed.[8]

But so long as criminals can retreat to lawless jurisdictions, or enjoy tacit or even explicit support from countries such as China and Russia, motiving defenders is going to be a better bet than deterring attackers. Mr Geer uses an earlier technology for his discussion of liability, quoting from the Code of Hammurabi, from 1750 BC: 'If a builder builds a house for someone, and does not construct it properly, and the house which he built falls in and kills its owner, then the builder shall be put to death.' Software is the only product where customers sign away all their rights to complain, no matter how disastrously it fails (though Mr Geer suggests religion could also fit in that category). A new liability regime could work like this: the liability is limited to a refund if the software is written and labelled in a way that allows users to see how it works (by supplying the 'source code') and to disable any feature they choose. This would be rather like a restaurant meal – but with the advantage that the users could decide which bits they want to eat and which they do not trust. If you don't like garlic butter on your steak, you ask the waiter not to bring it.

This sounds simple, though it will be highly disruptive for software providers in the short term. They will claim that this is the end of the era of cheap, easily available software. They will be right. But it will also be the end of an era in which you eat food stuffed with secret ingredients, with no recourse if they make you ill. The software companies' business model, in most cases, rests on keeping their code secret, rather as Coca-Cola guards the mixture of herbs and spices that makes its sweetened fizzy water so lucrative.

Fourth on Mr Geer's list is retaliation. This is one of the thorniest issues in policy. What rights do you as a private individual or company have against someone who attacks your computer or network? The laws governing physical self-defence are of limited use. You are unlikely to know for certain who your attacker is. And if you hit back, you may do damage to other people. Imagine, for example, that your business is being crippled by a botnet which is running a DDoS (swamping) attack, as explained at the start of Chapter 4. Suppose you find the 'command-and-control' computer which is running the botnet. In theory, you could sue, or call the police. But that is unlikely to work. The computer may have been hijacked. So you would have to sue the unwitting owner of the computer for not safeguarding it properly, and he in turn could try to sue the hijacker. Good luck with that if the computer is in China or Russia.

Now imagine that you have some kind of software missile – something that you can send to the offending computer which will disable or damage it. It would be tempting to fire it. After all, in most legal systems householders have the right to use some degree of force against robbers.

It is tempting to argue that anyone who is so careless as to let their computer be hijacked deserves their punishment. But the problem is collateral damage. Suppose that the botnet is run from a hijacked computer which also runs a hospital. If you disable it, you are putting all the patients at risk. The hijacker has in effect made them the human shields for his crime.

For an individual it is hard to imagine a legal or moral framework in which retaliation would be permissible. But for governments it is another matter. Military and intelligence agencies have two advantages. They are more likely to be able to target their retaliation accurately. And they are better equipped to mitigate the collateral damage, for example by forewarning the owners of the hijacked computers. Mr Geer foresees more cooperation between governments and businesses, particularly on the most damaging malware such as Gameover Zeus, the pernicious ransomware discussed in Chapter 4.

Another huge problem is 'embedded systems' – computer code that runs on devices that are largely invisible to the average user. As discussed above, the 'internet of things' is growing rapidly, and is full of devices that have been designed and marketed on the basis of convenience rather than security. Routers are a particularly dangerous monoculture, reliant on cheap, vulnerable software and chips. It would be possible to design malicious code which would hijack them in huge numbers, or sabotage them irreversibly. Even if customers were willing to pay more for dependable routers, and learn the habits and skills necessary to keep them safe and up to date, we would still be vulnerable to the many tens of millions of old ones already in use.

No solution is perfect. If these devices can be managed remotely, they are vulnerable to mass hijack. If they cannot be managed remotely, then it is hard to protect them against other attacks – such as the one demonstrated against the Nest thermostat, which required the attacker to have access to it for only fifteen seconds. Mr Geer suggests that manufacturers should, as a rule, install code that is 'mortal' – i.e. that will stop working after a certain period of time – unless the device can be managed remotely.

Many people assume – wrongly – that problems in life require individual monetary incentive for their solution and computer security is no different. Just as the early hackers were motivated mostly by the desire to display prowess, rather than to cause damage, make a political point, extort money, or serve the interests of a government, finding flaws in software was also a sign of technical wizardry rather than a career. That has slowly changed. You can now earn large amounts of money – known as 'bounty' – by pointing out to software manufacturers things they have got wrong. That has increased incentives – but it does not necessarily make us safer, because the market is so secret: the price of vulnerabilities is not set publicly and the same flaw can be sold many times over – first to companies trying to defend their networks, and then to adversaries wanting to attack them. There is no after-sales service for zero-days: if the hole turns out to be plugged when you want to use it, that is bad luck. And if plugging the hole only leaves you vulnerable to an attack using a different technique, that is your bad luck, too.

In short, companies may be overpaying or underpaying for what they buy. That is chiefly a problem for their shareholders. The wider worry for society is that we do not know how many vulnerabilities there are. As Bruce Schneier, the security expert mentioned in an earlier chapter, argued in a magazine article in May 2014, we do not know if the population is 'dense or sparse'.[9] If there are rather few vulnerabilities, it makes sense for governments to try to buy them and publish them. If there are plenty, that is waste of time. You are not making life safer for the public, because the attackers will simply find more. Instead – at least for governments that want to wage war or espionage on the internet – it makes more sense to buy them and use or stockpile them.

Mr Geer suggests that the American government enters the market for previously unknown vulnerabilities – the so-called 'zero-day exploits' – and buys the lot, overpaying if necessary, publishing all of them. This would have several beneficial effects. The bounty would enlarge the numbers of those trying to find the vulnerabilities. Their publication would devalue the price of those already discovered. Criminals and hostile governments would be less willing to pay big bucks for an exploit if they were worried that in days, weeks or months it might be found, published and fixed.

That approach would work beautifully if the number of vulnerabilities is indeed sparse. But supposing they are dense? That would create a large industry, and cost the taxpayer a packet, but it would not actually make us safer. Mr Geer believes that vulnerabilities are scarce enough for this to work – particularly if the search for them can be automated. Perhaps the only way to find out who is right is to test his theory. It would certainly be cheaper than the huge sums spent on bogus security software and lost to criminals.

The more we worry about security online, the more we are moving – even as amateurs – into the world of intelligence, with its bluffs, disguises, dupes, bugs, fall-backs, stunts, counter-surveillance routines and elaborate concerns about trust and integrity. The internet has killed distance – you can be stalked by someone on the other side of the world. Your 'digital exhaust' – the trail of information you and your devices leave behind you, deliberately or accidentally – gives a rich and unique seam of data for other people to mine. Moreover, the watchers can compare your data with other people's, on a scale quite impossible only a few years ago. Even slightly anomalous behaviour is now far more conspicuous. As Mr Geer notes, 'privacy used to be proportional to that which it is impossible to observe or that which can be observed but not identified'. But those denominators have shrunk.

One solution to that is tighter rules on the way personal data is handled. This is not useless: it constrains the law-abiding who might be tempted to be nosy or careless. But it does nothing to stop those who feel either contempt for the law (such as criminals) or exempt from it (intelligence and security agencies). Another solution is much stronger encryption and the use of multiple identities: what

Mr Geer calls 'the effective capacity to misrepresent yourself'. This is the approach that Ms Angwin, the privacy conscious journalist, took, creating a separate persona named after Ida Tarbell, a notable journalist of the interwar era (she used this identity to obtain a different credit card and to make restaurant reservations). This mirrors the established practice in the world of intelligence agencies of creating 'legends' – cover identities for intelligence officers. Paradoxically, though it has never been easier to create a fake identity (simply opening a Facebook, LinkedIn and Gmail account in the same name), it has never been harder to create a reliable one that will stand sustained scrutiny.

America's FCCX standard is trying to mimic the Estonian system described in the previous chapter, creating an 'Identity Ecosystem' in which every individual, organisation, computer and network can be authenticated. The choice is a hard one. People may like to pay in a weak currency, but they almost always prefer to be paid in a strong one. We want the right to identify ourselves unambiguously when we so choose, and also want to be able to identify those we are doing business with. But we also want the right to be ambiguous when we choose. That requires other people to be willing to accept our own weak, ambiguous identities, even though we would not be prepared to accept them ourselves if used by others.

Here I disagree with Mr Geer. I think that digital life will evolve, just as it has in the real world. If you want to eat in a restaurant you have several choices. You can turn up and pay cash. You can book by phone and leave a false name, meaning that if you do not turn up you have incurred no cost except to your conscience. You can book in a false name and leave a false phone number. That risks cancellation – if the restaurant phones to check the reservation and can't reach you. Or you can give a false name and your own phone number. That way you can confirm the reservation, but if you then do not show up, and are too lazy to cancel, you will have to lie if the restaurant calls to complain. Or the restaurant may take your credit card, and charge you if you do not turn up. You can give them a fake credit card number (which is verging on criminality) or you can if you really want to take the trouble to set up a special credit card account simply for making restaurant bookings.

In each of these cases you are trading off convenience, security and anonymity. If you leave no trace at all, you risk not getting the restaurant meal you want. If you meet the strictest standards, then you will have to turn up or else pay the restaurant for a meal you haven't eaten. Or you can choose not to go to a restaurant at all.

My guess is that the same will happen on the internet. If you run a restaurant you can have an online booking system where you require customers to identify themselves with their government-issued digital ID, and to pay a non-refundable deposit on their bill. That will make perfect sense if you are an upmarket restaurant in hot demand. It would be stupid if you are a cheap and cheerful joint. Restaurants that make too many demands on their customers will go out of business. Customers who guard their privacy above all may end up going hungry.

To be sure, most of Mr Geer's suggestions are beset with diffi-culties. One would be to stop innovation until we are certain that the new systems we are introducing are properly secure. This worked with Microsoft, which stopped rushing buggy versions of Windows to market, and instead took a lot of time and effort to make sure that the new releases were properly checked. That was a good business decision in the long run. The company used to be a laughing stock among cyber-security experts. Now it attracts grudging respect.

So waiting has a lot to recommend it. Rather than race into creating irreversible dependence on machines and systems which we cannot understand, and which were not built with safety in mind, we could just hold back until standards rise. Just as we would not want to fly on an experimental plane, why should we entrust our safety and happiness to what is in effect an experimental computer network?

In other walks of life, we do accept intense scrutiny as the price of safety. New aeroplanes go through a detailed process of certification, as do new medicines. Could that work on the internet? In theory, we should be even more eager to accept delay, inconvenience and cost, because cyber-attacks come from sentient opponents. We may worry about the long-term effect of cosmic rays on cockpit electronics, or new antibiotic-resistant bacteria, but we know that our adversaries for the most part are the laws of nature, not malefactors. What makes attacks on computers so dangerous is that real people are behind them, who put great effort and ingenuity into finding the weak points in our system.

Such caution is understandable from a technical point of view, but hard from a political one. The convenience of the internet so far has hugely outweighed concerns about safety, creating a juggernaut of expectation and habit which will be hard to halt. Moreover, greater use of the internet offers not just more consumer satisfaction and lower costs but also benefits in, for example, lower energy consumption. Those eager to save money, and the planet, by installing smart grids in order to consume less power will not be receptive to putting progress on hold.

Other options would be to rewrite the rules of the internet to make remote attacks impossible. We could insist on a much higher standard of proof before one device or program accepts the authenticity of another. This is known as 'language theoretic security', or LANGSEC.[10] As Mr Geer notes, this would require a rewrite of the foundations of the internet, but at the same time deal with its most fundamental weakness: the assumption of good faith and benevolence, on the basis of ad hoc connections. Another would be to improve the pace of evolution, so that we, the prey, improve our defences faster than our attackers.

This might seem difficult: it would require a central remote management machine, so that, for example, every flaw can be spotted and fixed on every machine that it could potentially affect. For many devices, this is impossible. We are deploying gadgets and machines which have no ability to be maintained or updated remotely. It is as if a kind of light bulb was found to be a fire hazard, capable of wreaking devastation on a whole neighbourhood. But the only way to change them is to knock on every door, inspect every room and replace them one by one. When it comes to the internet of things, that is going to be difficult. Some devices will be hard to find, others will be inaccessible. To illustrate the difficulty, try turning off every single device in your home, so that the electricity meter no longer moves. Getting power consumption down to a trickle is easy enough. But finding every single device is surprisingly hard. You turn off the lights, the heating, the kitchen appliances, the home entertainment, you go round every socket unplugging and switching off – but still a tiny trickle of power remains (when I tried this the elusive device was the control panel of the burglar alarm). In the electronic age it will be far harder. Houses will be built with devices that keep them warm, safe and efficient. The householder will have no more idea where they are than he does of how many computer chips are in his car.

This sets up a race against time which is skewed in favour of malefactors. Mr Geer notes worriedly, 'the longer-lived the devices really are, the surer it will be that they will be hijacked within their lifetime'. He compares the unthinking installation of networked devices to the tendency to leave toxic waste or space debris for future generations to deal with, or to inflation – a 'continuous quiet theft' for which no lawmaker needs to vote.

Conclusion

Digital technology exposes every area of our lives to attacks, and renders outdated our assumptions about safety, which are based on our own and other people's ability to do physical damage. We have been slow to realise this. The Munich Security Conference – the most important get-together of its kind – had its first panel on cyber-security only in 2011. We are still worrying too little about the threats to the networks and computers on which our infrastructure, financial system and public services depend. Nor have we grasped the extraordinary new criminal mercantilism being practised by China, in which the theft of intellectual property from foreign competitors is part of state-owned enterprises' research and development strategy.

At a time when we should have been vigilant about these pressing threats, the revelations of Edward Snowden, the fugitive former contractor for the NSA, have corroded trust between the Western democracies (particularly between Europe and America) and also within them: in the fears now harboured by citizens about their authorities. Those fears have also set back the chances of improvements in areas such as medicine (where the intensive study of big anonymised data sets is now hampered by fears about privacy). From having a naïve and ill-formed view of online privacy, we have moved to a paranoid, but still uninformed, view.

The result is not more freedom but less. The 'revelations' of NSA and GCHQ capabilities – which in truth affect only a tiny minority of citizens, and have been exercised under democratic political direction and in accordance with the law – strengthen authoritarian regimes who want to argue that the West's talk of legality and rules is hypocrisy. The struggle for a free, law-based international order is being waged on a new front: over our computers and networks. And we are losing.

The biggest looming defeat is the breakdown of the internet. For all its shortcomings in the realm of security, our online world has some commendable features. It is universal, open and borderless. A poor-world farmer going online for a few pennies on a shared smartphone has the same rights to send and receive information as the president of the United States or a Wall Street plutocrat. National jurisdiction applies lightly, if at all. That is changing – a term which some call 'Balkanisation' but for which Estonia's president Toomas Hendrik Ilves has coined the better, and less pejorative, 'Westphalianisation', referring to the principles of the Treaty of Westphalia in 1648, in which European countries agreed not to interfere in each other's affairs, but to allow each ruler to treat his subjects as he wished.[1]

Exaggerated fears about American 'control' of the internet are stoking demands for it to be run by national governments, or through the International Telecommunications Union, part of the United Nations. That would give authoritarian governments a chokehold over the internet's development, squeezing out the other 'stakeholders' such as the engineers who administer the technical standards and the non-governmental outfits and individuals who work on other issues.

National control over the internet will not just stop the free flow of information. It will mean that it becomes harder to store data in another country. It could lead to a ban on the use of foreign-made software and hardware. It will make the information-technology industry, which is responsible for the biggest increase in human happiness and creativity since the invention of electricity, look like the defence industry: politicised, murky and expensive.

The gulf between those who understand computers and those who understand the way a modern society works is deep. Policymakers still struggle to understand the way that digital technology changes the framework for their decisions. Many people who work on the technological side are either overly blithe about the capabilities they are developing, or overly suspicious about the way governments may use them.

Restoring confidence will be hard. When people and countries are scared they make bad decisions. And the world of computers and networks is getting more frightening, not less. This book has highlighted three big points which may help us avert the gloomy prospects of a broken internet and rampant crime.

The first is that complacent, careless and amateurish behaviour on the internet is as out of place as it is in transport or health. If you do not take the elementary precautions (outlined in Appendix Three) needed to avoid toxic links and e-mails, and to secure your computer from the most basic threats, you are a menace not just to yourself, but to others. The second is that we need to be more cautious about all our behaviour with services that purport to be 'free'. When you pay for something, you have a justified expectation of integrity and competence. When you are selling yourself – in the form of your attention, your privacy, or your friends, your rights are a lot less. Third, strong digital identities are friends, not foes. You may have good reasons to be anonymous on the internet, just as you may wish to attend a masked ball. But you will benefit more from the right to identify yourself to others, and to establish their credentials before you deal with them.

Appendix One

Who Runs the Internet?

Because the internet does not fit neatly into national jurisdictions, the rules that govern it are much fuzzier. It has no single governing body. Rules and standards are set by a loose collection of non-profit outfits, who reach decisions by consensus and have only limited powers of enforcement. Amid the alphabet soup are: the Internet Society, which anyone can join (membership is free), is mainly a talking shop and do-gooder organisation. The Internet Engineering Task Force (IETF) coordinates work on technical standards, trying to make sure that the internet works on a day-to-day basis. The Internet Corporation for Assigned Names and Numbers (ICANN) is another non-profit body which maintains the system of addresses – making sure that, for example, edwardlucas.com takes you to my site. ICANN is where controversy meets computer science. The United States tried to stop it creating a new .xxx suffix for use by the sex industry. Victims of terrorist attacks sued it because they wanted to seize the suffixes .ir (Iran) .sy (Syria) and .KP (North Korea).[1] ICANN has few friends. It is seen as secretive, dominated by Western, male engineering types, and prone to security lapses. One of these, in late 2014, may have allowed hackers access to the directory name servers which send traffic round the internet.[2] ICANN is struggling to keep control of the ability to run the internet addressing system, which has long relied on a contract from the US government (a relic from the internet's roots in defence research and American universities). This contract runs out in late 2015 and the American administration, mindful of worries about surveillance and spying, is keen to pass it to a neutral body to forestall calls from China and other authoritarian countries to put the internet under formal international control.

The Elements of Cryptography

Cryptography serves two functions on the internet. It encodes messages to make them private, and it identifies the sender. The maths behind this is sound. A sufficiently strong dose of encryption makes a code theoretically uncrackable, and identity unchallengeable.

This may sound intimidating, but the fundamental principle is extremely simple. If you multiply something by a big number, you get a bigger number. But a person who sees that bigger number can't easily find out the smaller numbers. As every child knows, multiplication is easier than division. Creating a large number by multiplying smaller ones is easy. Breaking a large number down into small ones by division is much harder. Take, for example, the following simple sum:

2 x 3 x 4 x 5 x 6 x 7 x 8 x 9 = 362880

Even with elementary maths you can work out in your head that 362880 is divisible by 10. With a bit of effort you can work out it must also be divisible by two and three. With a pencil and paper you can then work out the other factors. Now imagine you are given the number 362,881. As it happens, that number is 19 x 71 x 269. These three 'prime factors' are not divisible by anything else. But finding them out is hard: most people could not do that in their head. Then imagine that the number is 1,299,827. That is a prime number – it is divisible only by itself and one. But you would need a calculator and quite a few minutes to find that out. When you get to 982,451,653 (which just happens to be the fifty millionth prime number), you will need a serious computer.

This helps create codes. Imagine that I want to encrypt my own office phone number: 75761180. So I multiply it by my 'key': say the prime number 269. The result is 20379757420. I can do that quite easily with a calculator, or even with pen and paper. Now imagine that you are trying to crack the code. You know that there is an eight-digit phone number hidden inside there. But how do you find it? Perhaps with a calculator you could work that out in ten or fifteen minutes. But now imagine that the 'key' with which I am multiplying my phone number is not 269, but 982,451,653. That would be a daunting task for anyone except a mathematician.

This idea of the 'one-way function' – where the creation of the code is easy, but the breaking of it is hard – is the foundation of modern cryptography. Time was when only governments could do this efficiently. Finding and multiplying really large numbers required powerful computers. Now you can do it on a mobile phone. You can generate a 'key' simply by moving your mouse around for a few seconds – the random movement of the cursor on your screen creates what is in effect a very large number. Such 'keys' do not need to be prime numbers – just very big ones. You can then use them to encrypt an e-mail, or a document, or a phone call, and only some-one who also has the same key can understand it.

A particularly ingenious twist to this is that you can have a public key, with which anyone can send you an encrypted message, while you keep the private key needed to decrypt it. This may sound paradoxical, but it is no more difficult to understand than a letter-box (anyone can put letters in, but only the owner can retrieve them), or a door with a latch, which can be locked by anyone, but which only key holders can unlock.

There are three main ways of attacking encryption. One is known as 'brute force'. Given a sufficiently powerful computer and enough time, any code can be broken. The time taken may be longer than the life of the universe, and the computer required might consume all the energy on the planet, but it is still theoretically possible. More to the point, new advances in computing mean that what once seemed an insurmountable challenge may now be feasible. Today's computers can crack codes that only a couple of decades ago were thought to be effectively unbreakable.

The race is unequal, though. The gap between the computing power available to people wanting to encrypt messages, and those wanting to decrypt them, is shrinking. Cracking a code requires a computer many times more powerful than the one used to encrypt it. Even a government intelligence agency cannot crack every code it needs to by using brute force. In particular, they cannot crack codes if they were not able to interfere with you or your computer at the time you created them.

A good example of this emerged in 2014 in Germany, where the authorities arrested an official whom they believed was spying for the United States. He had been communicating with his case officers, the Germans believed, by visiting a website which gave details about the weather in New York. Concealed in one of the videos on the site was sophisticated encryption software which allowed him to upload data from his computer and receive instructions. But the contents of suspect's computer, when the German counter-intelligence service seized it, turned out to be encrypted. The suspect refused to give them the password, and they were unable – even with all the resources of German electronic intelligence – to break the encryption.

Had they known in advance that they would need the contents of the laptop, they could have used the second big vulnerability in encryption: trickery. If you can read over somebody's shoulder, it does not matter if they receive messages secretly. The most powerful tools for intercepting communications rely not on breaking encryption, but on reading the message either before it is encoded, or after it is decoded. These are known in computer jargon as 'end-point vulnerabilities'. They can in some circumstances involve literally putting a camera in a position where it can read a computer screen. Modern spy cameras need only a pinhole and are effectively invisible. Computer screens also give off radiation, so a carefully placed bug can pick up this electronic signal and transmit to the snooper.

Keyboards are another line of attack. They offer plenty of scope for snoopers. Each key on the board makes a slightly different sound, so a sensitive microphone can tell what is being typed. The keyboard gives off electro-magnetic radiation when you type on it. These are signals, which can be picked up by the right kind of bug – or even a mobile phone sitting near the keyboard.

The subtlest attacks at the end-points involve planting snooping software on the actual computer. A 'key-logger' will record everything that is typed on the keyboard, encrypt it and send it all but invisibly to the customer (this does not need to involve an internet connection: the data can be brought out of an air-gapped network via USB stick or some other physical means). Key-loggers are a particularly powerful form of attack. It doesn't matter how long and strong your password is, if it is copied whenever you use it. To foil key-logging software, some programs ask users to type in their password not from a physical keyboard, but by moving a mouse around letters displayed on the screen. That feels a lot more secure. But it isn't. Attackers often use a 'screen-grabber', too. This makes regular copies of whatever is on your screen and sends them off. Key-loggers and screen-grabbers are designed to be invisible. They use tiny amounts of computing power, so you will not notice anything amiss. They hide in parts of your computer which are not easily searched. It is hard to be sure if you have removed them – they may leave a tiny chink in the computer's security to enable later reinfection, even after you have scrubbed your computer's insides clean.

Such snooping programs are childishly easy to install. The easiest way is to get the victim to install them himself, through the usual means of a toxic e-mail or website. But it is also possible to install them physically – typically by putting a memory stick into the victim's computer and turning it on. Any casual visitor to the office can do this if a computer is unguarded. A cleaner or maintenance worker can be bribed to do it, too. Unless your computer is in a locked box and switched off, it is vulnerable.

Trickery can also involve simple human weakness. If someone phones you claiming to be from your company's IT services department, and asks you to install an urgent security update, why would you not follow the instructions given? You obligingly go to a website with a name like security-update.net, which looks entirely convincing, and click on the button named 'update'. Your computer buzzes and wheezes briefly, and you click 'yes' in answer to questions asking if you want to download and install software. A few minutes later you are done, and the friendly colleague from IT thanks you for your help. In fact, you have just downloaded malware which turns your computer into a bugging device, rendering all your security software and encryption useless. This kind of trickery is called 'social engineering' in computer parlance. It can be used to deliver all kinds of other malware, too, but because it is quite time-consuming for the attacker, and needs to be done well if it is to work, it tends to be used against particularly valuable targets.

The third way to deal with powerful encryption is the 'rubber hose attack'. This relies on attacking people, not computers. It can mean the actual use of physical force (beating someone with a rubber hose) or it can involve blackmail or other forms of psychological pressure. The best encryption in the world cannot make up for human weakness.

These three weaknesses are serious. But they all involve a lot of time and effort by the attacker. If a crime gang, a government intelligence agency, or a group of politically motivated computer experts ('hacktivists') are really determined to attack your computer and read your encrypted messages, they will find a way. But before they do that, they have to do a lot of work.

Advice from GCHQ

Britain's security and intelligence services have an excellent reputation, not least thanks to the books of John le Carré and the films of Ian Fleming's James Bond. If MI6 (as the Secret Intelligence Service is colloquially known) were to give British citizens 'life-hacks' (advice) based on its expertise in spycraft – a mixture of smooth talking and unarmed combat, say – people would sit up and listen. It is odd, therefore, that the Centre for the Protection of National Infrastructure (CPNI) has had less attention than it deserves for its advice on securing computers and networks.

It might help if it used plain English, so here is a translation, aimed at conscientious but non-technical users such as the Hakhetts. First, work out who is in charge of your computer and networks, and what the risks are. What information are you actually trying to protect? Who might be trying to steal it? Who is going to make the rules about securing your computers and networks, and how are those rules going to be communicated? When you start and finish projects, how will you make sure that questions of computer security are looked at properly? This pompously named 'Information Risk Management Regime' is the foundation for the other steps.

Second, make rules about the computers and other devices inside your organisation. Who is allowed to connect to your network, for how long and with what permission? Test your network regularly to see how long it actually takes to detect a new device which has been connected to it. What are the rules for keeping software up to date? What happens to people who break those rules? Who can install new software on computers in your organisation? What kind of records do you keep of these things, and who has access to them? This is known as having a 'secure configuration'.

Third, what are you doing to keep your network secure? Do you have firewalls in place to prevent someone attacking you over the internet? What happens if someone breaches those firewalls? Keep records of everything that happens on your network, so if you are breached, you can see who has been where, and what they have done. Test your network security by commissioning people to attack it, using a mixture of computer skills and confidence tricks.

Fourth, what are your rules about who can do what? (In computer jargon these are known as 'user privileges'.) Make sure that people do not have more rights than they need. If someone has special rights, do they need to have them all the time, or just for particular tasks? Perhaps nobody should have the right to do absolutely everything on your network. Make sure that big decisions – such as issuing new credentials – involve not just people clicking boxes on screens, but also talking to each other. Keep an eye on who does what with their rights and privileges. Review them regularly.

Fifth, make sure that everyone is properly trained. What happens with new staff members, temporary workers, interns and other outsiders who use your network? What rights do they have? Make sure that when they leave the organisation, their credentials expire promptly.

Sixth, have a plan for when things go wrong. Make sure that the person in charge is senior enough to make the right decisions. Work through eventualities in advance. Simply 'pulling the plug' on your organisation's network may be the wrong response to a breach. If the attacker's aim is to disrupt you, then he has succeeded.

Seventh, be ready for malware. What are your rules on e-mails that contain links and attachments? How can people quickly check if they are safe? The more important the computer, the harder it should be to infect it. Make sure the balance between safety and convenience is thought through for every bit of your organisation.

Eighth, what is your policy on gadgets and storage devices that can be plugged into computers on your network, such as USB sticks? Do you have more USB ports than you need? (It may be that not every computer needs them.) Does every computer need to have the capability to burn data on to a CD? Make sure that every computer that can accept a USB stick also has up-to-date software to scan it for malware. Make sure that people know the risks they are running when they plug anything from outside into the network.

Ninth, what is your policy on monitoring traffic in and out of the network? Are your staff aware of the privacy implications? What are you looking out for? Make sure that alarms are triggered if anything unusual happens (such as data leaving an office computer outside normal working hours).

Tenth, what are your rules about people working from home or from outside the office? Make sure you know what devices are being used, and where the data are stored.

None of this sounds particularly dramatic. But combined, such measures will deal with many of the everyday threats to our computers and networks – and most of the problems outlined in this book. That would allow us to concentrate on the really dangerous threats – to which we still lack answers.

Notes

PREFACE

1 'Charlie Chaplin made Hitler cry' https://medium.com/war-is-boring/charlie-chaplin-made-hitler-cry-17f8c7d611f9

2 'Internet Usage Statistics' http://www.internetworldstats.com/stats.htm and 'Key ICT indicators for Developed and Developing Countries' International Telecommunications Union, Geneva, Switzerland https://www.itu.int/en/ITU-D/Statistics/Documents/statistics/2014/ITU_Key_2005–2014_ICT_data.xls

3 The Radicati Group, E-mail Market Report http://www.radicati.com/wp/wp-content/uploads/2014/10/Email-Market-2014–2018-Executive-Summary.pdf

4 The annual total for physical mail was just under 340 billion items in 2013. 'Development of Postal Services 2013', Universal Postal Union, Berne, Switzerland. http://www.upu.int/fileadmin/documentsFiles/resources/postalStatistics/developmentOfPostalServicesIn2013En.pptx

5 'What do 12 Terabytes of information look like?', Alex Santoso Tuesday, Neatorama, 8 July 2008. http://www.neatorama.com/2008/07/08/terabyte/

6 'First of the Leaks', by Risk Based Security of Richmond, Virginia. https://www.riskbasedsecurity.com/2014/12/a-breakdown-and-analysis-of-the-december-2014-sony-hack/

7 'New Clues In Sony Hack Point To Insiders, Away from DPRK' Security Ledger, 28 December 2014. https://securityledger.com/2014/12/new-clues-in-sony-hack-point-to-insiders-away-from-dprk/

INTRODUCTION

1   Jonathan Hall, 'Shellshock: The Ninja Turtles Aren't The Only Ones Who Felt The Hurt', Future South Technologies. http://www.futuresouth.us/wordpress/wp-content/uploads/2014/10/Shellshock.pdf

2   George Tenet, 'Information Security Risks, Opportunities, and the Bottom Line' (Sam Nunn Nations Bank Policy Forum, Atlanta, 6 April 1998). https://www.cia.gov/news-information/speeches-testimony/1998/dcI_speech_040698.html. Quoted in Richard Danzig, 'Surviving on a Diet of Poisoned Fruit: Reducing the National Security Risks of America's Cyber Dependencies', CNAS, July 2014. http://www.cnas.org/sites/default/files/publications-pdf/CNAS_PoisonedFruit_Danzig_0.pdf

3   Kurt Stamberger of Norse speaking on CBS News, 23 December 2014. http://www.cbsnews.com/news/did-the-fbi-get-it-wrong-on-north-korea/

4   This became public in an unprecedented report by Mandiant, a security company. Dan Mcwhorter, 'Mandiant Exposes APT1 – One of China's Cyber Espionage Units', 18 February 2013. https://www.mandiant.com/blog/mandiant-exposes-apt1-chinas-cyber-espionage-units-releases-3000-indicators/

5   Ben Lovejoy, 'After the celebrity hacks, the vulnerability that still exists and what needs to be done', 9to5mac.com, 3 September 2014. http://9to5mac.com/2014/09/03/opinion-after-the-celebrity-hacks-the-vulnerability-that-still-exists-and-what-needs-to-be-done/

6   Naoki Hiroshima, 'How I Lost My $50,000 Twitter Username', Medium, 29 January 2014. https://medium.com/@N/how-i-lost-my-50–000-twitter-username-24eb09e026dd

7   Warwick Ashford 'Sony data breach: 100m reasons to beef up security', 3 May 2011 http://www.computerweekly.com/news/1280097348/Sony-data-breach-100m-reasons-to-beef-up-security

8   Details are hazy, and the company which disclosed the attack attracted some criticism for charging a fee to those who wanted to see if their identity was one of those compromised. The firm's announcement is here http://www.holdsecurity.com/news/cybervor-breach/Graham Clulely, 'CyberVor hacking gang steals 1.2 billion usernames and passwords', 6 August 2014. http://www.welivesecurity.com/2014/08/06/cybervor-hacking-gang/ For a slightly friendlier take, see Brian Krebs, 'Q&A on the Reported Theft of 1.2B Email Accounts', 14 August 2014. https://krebsonsecurity.com/2014/08/qa-on-the-reported-theft-of-1–2b-email-accounts/ Statistics on such breaches are based on known incidents, so are bound to be

understatements. But the recorded figure is rising sharply, nearly doubling since 2011. According to Symantec, a security firm, eight of the breaches in 2013 exposed more than ten million identities each. I am indebted to this summary 'The Best of the 2014 Information Security Threat Reports' by Kelly White of dieselcafe.com, available at https://docs.google.com/file/d/0B_GoF8uQ95lGWnFKWHBsdmlnTVk/edit@k3strel

9 'Who's selling credit cards from Target', 13 December 2013. https://krebsonsecurity.com/2013/12/whos-selling-credit cards-from-target/

10 Brian Krebs, 'Home Depot Hit By Same Malware as Target', 9 September 2014. https://krebsonsecurity.com/2014/09/home-depot-hit-by-same-malware-as-target/

11 Jonathan Bishop, 'The effect of de-individuation of the Internet Troller on Criminal Procedure implementation: An interview with a Hater', *International Journal of Cyber Criminology*, Vol. 7, Issue 1, January–June 2013. http://www.cybercrimejournal.com/Bishop2013janijcc.pdf

12 Danzig, 'Poisoned Fruit'.

13 'Cyber security: first mover disadvantage', Lex, *Financial Times*, 12 September 2014. http://www.ft.com/cms/s/3/803ea71e-3948–11e4-9cce-00144feabdco.html

14 'Net Losses: Estimating the Global Cost of Cybercrime', by Mcafee, the Center for Strategic and International Studies (CSIS) and Intel, Washington, DC, 2014. http://www.mcafee.com/ca/resources/reports/rp-economic-impact-cybercrime2.pdf

15 'The Cost of Cybercrime' UK Cabinet Office, London 2011. https://www.gov.uk/government/uploads/system/uploads/attachment_data/file/60943/the-cost-of-cyber-crime-full-report.pdf

16 I am indebted to my colleague Martin Giles, whose special report on cyber-security for *The Economist* is an admirably researched and argued study of the subject, and includes many of the points made in this book. It is available here: http://www.economist.com/news/special-report/21606416-companies-markets-and-countries-are-increasingly-under-attack-cyber-criminals

17 Lee Matthews, 'Excess of stolen identities leads to massive price cuts, US ID costs just $25', geek.com, 21 November 2014. http://www.geek.com/news/excess-of-stolen-identities-leads-to-massive-price-cuts-us-id-costs-just-25–1577923/

18 Khristen Foss, 'Hackers Arrested In Biggest Bank Robbery In World History', Ananova, 4 March 2014. http://www.ananova.com/hackers-arrested-in-biggest-bank-robbery-in-world-history/

19 United States District Court, Eastern District of New York, indictment CR13–0259 http://online.wsj.com/public/resources/documents/
hackindict0509.pdf
20 'Cybersecurity as Realpolitik', Black Hat keynote speech, 6 August 2014.
http://geer.tinho.net/geer.blackhat.6viii14.txt

1 MEET THE HAKHETTS

1 No resemblance to anyone or any business with these or similar names in
real life, living or dead, is intended.
2 I deal at length with this subject in my book *Deception: Spies, Lies and How
Russia Dupes the West* (Bloomsbury, 2010).
3 'Nortel hit by suspected Chinese cyber-attacks for a decade', CBC News,
14 February 2012. http://www.cbc.ca/news/business/nortel-collapse-linked-
to-chinese-hackers-1.1260591

2 THE UNRELIABILITY OF COMPUTERS

1 Gregory Gromov, 'Roads and Crossroads of the Internet History',
self-published. http://www.netvalley.com/cgi-bin/intval/net_history.
pl?chapter=1
2 Quinn Norton, 'Everything is broken', 20 May 2014. https://medium.com/
message/81e5f33a24e1
3 Dave Lee, 'Shellshock: "Deadly serious" new vulnerability found', Technology reporter, BBC News, 25 September 2014. http://www.bbc.co.uk/news/
technology-29361794
4 Michael Lin and Larry Seltzer, 'The Shellshock FAQ: Here's what you need
to know', Zero Day, 1 October 2014. http://www.zdnet.com/article/the-
shellshock-faq-heres-what-you-need-to-know/
5 Michael Mimoso, Shellshock Worm Exploiting Unpatched QNAP NAS
Devices, ThreatPost, 15 December 2014. https://threatpost.com/shellshock-
worm-exploiting-unpatched-qnap-nas-devices/109870
6 Steve McConnell, *Code Complete*, 2nd edn (Redmond, WA: Microsoft Press, 2004). http://testa.roberta.free.fr/My%20Books/Computer%20
programming/Java/Code%20Complete%20%20Second%20Edition%20
By%20Steve%20Mcconnell%20(Microsoft%20Press%202004).pdf, quoted in
Robert Danzig, 'Surviving on a Diet of Poisoned Fruit', CNAS, July 2014.
http://www.cnas.org/sites/default/files/publications-pdf/CNAS_Poisoned
Fruit_Danzig_0.pdf

7   http://en.wikipedia.org/wiki/Spaghetti_code
8   The software had a latent defect rate of just 0.11 errors per 1,000 lines of code. http://history.nasa.gov/sts1/pages/computer.html. See also Edward Joyce, 'Is Error-Free Software Achievable?', *Datamation*, 15 February 1989, pp. 53–6; B. G. Kolkhorst and A. J. Macina, 'Developing Error-Free Software', *IEEE AES Magazine* (November 1988), pp. 25–31; and A. J. Macina, 'Independent Verification and Validation Testing of the Space Shuttle Primary Flight Software System' (Houston, Texas: IBM, 28 April 1980).
9   Ron Pollett and Dorian Pyle, 'What happens when chip-design complexity outpaces development productivity?', McKinsey on Semiconductors, Autumn 2013. http://www.mckinsey.com/~/media/McKinsey/dotcom/client_service/Semiconductors/Issue%203%20Autumn%202013/PDFs/4_ChipDesign.ashx
10 'GM recalls 220,000 cars over brake defect', BBC News, 21 September 2014. http://www.bbc.com/news/business-29304282 and 'General Motors recalling 7.6 million vehicles from 1997–2014 model years'. Click on Detroit (anonymous) 6 August 2014. http://www.clickondetroit.com/consumer/automotive/general-motors-recalling-76-million-vehicles-from-19972014-model-years/26729110
11 James Topham and Alwyn Scott, 'U.S., others ground Boeing Dreamliner indefinitely', Reuters, 16 January 2013. http://www.reuters.com/article/2013/01/17/us-boeing-dreamliner-idUSBRE90F1N820130117
12 Demonstrated at https://www.youtube.com/watch?v=3WPMq8owYFY
13 Dan Tynan, 'The 25 Worst Tech Products of All Time', *PCWorld*, 26 May 2006. http://www.pcworld.com/article/125772/worst_products_ever.html?page=3

3 IDENTITY AND ITS ENEMIES

1   At the time of writing (January 2015) a copy of this was available at http://speedydeletion.wikia.com/wiki/Blackett_Janeiro
2   Chris [surname not given], 'How to Manipulate Google Suggest', 21 March 2011. http://www.reseo.com/blog/how-to-manipulate-googles-suggested-search
3   Leandra Ramm and Lisa Della Rocca, *Stalking a Diva* (Black Diamond Books, 2012).
4   see http://bits.blogs.nytimes.com/2014/05/29/cyberespionage-attacks-tied-to-hackers-in-iran/?_php=true&_type=blogs&_r=0 and http://www.isightpartners.com/2014/05/newscaster-iranian-threat-inside-social-media/
5   Kim Willsher, 'France's burqa ban upheld by human rights court', *Guardian*, 1 July 2014. http://www.theguardian.com/world/2014/jul/01/france-burqa-ban-upheld-human-rights-court

6 The only minor constraint is the requirement on anyone launching a website to register its address. Someone, somewhere in the world will need to host this site on a computer – known as a server. And for the computers that route traffic on the internet to be able to find the site, it must have a usable address. In theory, that should leave some traces of who is behind a website. But the system makes anonymity easy. A service such as whois.net may give the name, home address and phone number of the real person behind the site. But only if they are willing. Anyone wishing to conceal their identity can give fictitious details, or use a third-party nominee. I have spent a lot of time investigating sites which I suspected were linked to Russian espionage and information-warfare, such as the now defunct axisglobe.com and icdiss.org. Invariably, the details provided proved fictitious or so incomplete as to be useless. I investigated the ICDISS here. 'Covering Tracks', 3 August 2006. http://www.economist.com/node/7258534. For Axis Globe see also my book *Deception*, pp. 106–11.

4 COLLATERAL DAMAGE

1 Brian Krebs runs the excellent blog krebsonsecurity.com. The graphic is available at https://krebsonsecurity.com/2012/10/the-scrap-value-of-a-hacked-pc-revisited/

2 For a useful overview, read the testimony of Leslie Caldwell, assistant attorney general, criminal division of the US Department of Justice to the Senate judiciary sub-committee on crime and terrorism, 15 July 2014. http://www.judiciary.senate.gov/imo/media/doc/07–15–14CaldwellTestimony.pdf

3 Published in *The Apple Tree* (Gollancz, 1952).

4 The company's farewell message is at http://www.codespaces.com/ The attack is described at http://www.welivesecurity.com/2014/06/21/internet-firm-ddos-extortion-attack/

5 The Evernote attack is well described by the excellent Graham Clulely on his blog 'Evernote? Ever not! Cloud service brought down by denial-of-service attack', 11 June 2014. http://grahamcluley.com/2014/06/evernote-attack/

6 'Computer says no', *The Economist*, 22 June 2013. http://www.economist.com/news/international/21579816-denial-service-attacks-over-internet-are-growing-easier-and-more-powerful-their

7 From the outside, it was hard to see what the fuss was about. The statue – on a busy road intersection near a bus stop – was attracting unwelcome attention from extremist groups. Russian nationalists regarded it as a sacred symbol of the 'liberation' of Estonia from Nazi rule. Many Estonians saw it

as an affront and an eyesore: for them Hitler's defeat marked the end of one torment but the beginning of another at Stalin's hands. Estonian far-right groups threatened to take matters into their own hands. But the government's decision to shift the statue to the peaceful surroundings of a military cemetery where other countries' war dead are also honoured turned a minor public order problem into a national security emergency.

The Kremlin propaganda machine denounced the statue's hurried removal as a blasphemous assault on the sacrifice of past generations. Riots ensued in Tallinn. But it was the disruption to computer networks that was far more significant.

Arbor Networks, a security firm, counted 'at least 128 separate attacks on nine different websites in the country, including 35 attacks against the Estonian police, another 35 attacks against the Ministry of Finance and 36 against the Estonian parliament, Prime Minister as well as other general government web properties.' Thanks to good intelligence work, Estonians (and NATO) have concluded that the attacks were the work of pro-Kremlin activists sponsored by the Russian authorities. Sergei Markov, a notable propagandist for the regime, even admitted (or boasted) that the attacks were 'carried out by my assistant'. But the first clues for that came from snooping on online chat-rooms, where the people concerned were engaged in careless boasting about their misdeeds. They did not come from any clues left on the internet. Dan Holden, 'Estonia Six Years Later', 16 May 2013. https://www.arbornetworks.com/asert/2013/05/estonia-six-years-later/ For a presentation by Gadi Evron, watch this presentation from the Defcon conference. https://www.youtube.com/watch?v=YNt1LRCkamY

8 '8 Signs Your PC Might Be A Zombie', Zonealarm, 28 May 2014. http://www.zonealarm.com/blog/2014/05/8-signs-your-pc-might-be-a-zombie/

9 Kane Fulton, 'Microsoft and FBI team up to take down GameOver Zeus botnet'. Techradar Pro, 3 June 2014. www.techradar.com/us/news/internet/web/microsoft-and-fbi-team-up-to-take-down-gameover-zeus-botnet-1251609

10 'Microsoft helps FBI in GameOver Zeus botnet cleanup', 2 June 2014. http://blogs.microsoft.com/blog/2014/06/02/microsoft-helps-fbi-in-gameover-zeus-botnet-cleanup/

11 Documents available at http://www.justice.gov/opa/gameover-zeus.html

12 'Botnet Enlists Firefox Users to Hack Web Sites', 13 December 2013. https://krebsonsecurity.com/2013/12/botnet-enlists-firefox-users-to-hack-web-sites/

13 Ernie Smith, 'Ad Association Takes On Click Fraud With New Coalition', 16 July 2014. http://associationsnow.com/2014/07/ad-association-takes-click-fraud-new-coalition/

14 Brian Krebs, 'Service Drains Competitors' Online Ad Budget', Krebs on Security, 25 July 2014. https://krebsonsecurity.com/2014/07/service-drains-competitors-online-ad-budget/

15 Dancho Danchev, 'New service converts malware-infected hosts into anonymization proxies', Webroot Threat Blog, 2 March 2012. http://www.webroot.com/blog/2012/03/02/new-service-converts-malware-infected-hosts-into-anonymization-proxies/

16 Nicole Kobie, 'StubHub fraud: how hackers stole $1m using tickets', *PCPro*, 24 July 2014. http://www.pcpro.co.uk/news/389965/stubhub-fraud-how-hackers-stole-1m-using-tickets

17 Elizabeth Clarke, 'Hackers Sell Health Insurance Credentials, Bank Accounts, SSNs and Counterfeit Documents, for over $1,000 Per Dossier', 15 July 2013, Dell Secureworks. http://www.secureworks.com/resources/blog/general-hackers-sell-health-insurance-credentials-bank-accounts-ssns-and-counter-feit-documents/#sthash.6NgMEfy8.dpuf   http://www.secureworks.com/resources/blog/general-hackers-sell-health-insurance-credentials-bank-ac-counts-ssns-and-counterfeit-documents/

18 Jérôme Segura, 'Hiding in plain sight: a story about a sneaky banking Trojan', Malwarebytes Unpacked, 17 February 2014. https://blog.malwarebytes.org/security-threat/2014/02/hiding-in-plain-sight-a-story-about-a-sneaky-banking-trojan/

19 For a detailed explanation of how these scams work, http://krebsonsecurity.com/2014/09/whos-behind-the-bogus-49-95-charges/

20 Keith Moor, 'Australian Federal Police foil Russian crime gang's $570m cyber theft bid as nation loses $4.6 billion-a-year to computer crime', *Herald Sun*, 23 July 2014. http://www.heraldsun.com.au/news/law-order/australian-federal-police-foil-russian-crime-gangs-570m-cyber-theft-bid-as-nation-loses-46-billionayear-to-computer-crime/story-fni0ffnk-1226999310954?nk=010e299055b71f00a3a7c2ead3d99663

21 Mike Sutton, 'How Prolific Thieves Sell Stolen Goods', *Internet Journal of Criminology*, 2008. https://www.academia.edu/attachments/3445129/download_file?s=regpath

22 'HSI investigation leads to 5 arrests, indictments in identity-theft ring' Department of Homeland Security, 9 October 2014. https://www.ice.gov/news/releases/hsi-investigation-leads-5-arrests-indictments-identity-theft-ring

23 Jeremy Kirk, 'Banks shouldn't use text messages for two-factor authentication', *PCWorld*, 12 December 2013. http://www.pcworld.com/article/2079620/banks-shouldnt-rely-on-mobile-sms-passcodes-security-firm-says.html

24 Brian Krebs, 'Turning Hot Credit Cards into Hot Stuff', Krebs on Security, 11 October 2014. http://krebsonsecurity.com/2011/10/turning-hot-credit-cards-into-hot-stuff/

25 This article includes a video showing how a fake anti-virus program tries to install itself on your computer. Dan Goodin, 'What a fake antivirus attack on a trusted website looks like', Ars Technica, 2 February 2014. http://arstechnica.com/security/2014/02/what-a-fake-antivirus-attack-on-a-trusted-website-looks-like/

26 Caldwell testimony, p. 6.

27 Keith Jarvis, 'CryptoLocker Ransomware', Dell SecureWorks CounterThreat Unit Threat Intelligence, 18 December 2013. http://www.secureworks.com/cyber-threat-intelligence/threats/cryptolocker-ransomware/ http://www.geek.com/news/cryptolocker-malware-masterminds-make-around-30-million-in-ransom-in-100-days-1580168/ and Lee Mathews, 'Cryptolocker malware masterminds make around $30 million in ransom in 100 days', geek.com, 19 December 2013.

28 Graham Cluley, 'How to recover files from a CryptoLocker attack – for free!', 6 August 2014. http://grahamcluley.com/2014/08/fix-cryptolocker-files-free/ The decryption service is available at decryptcryptolocker.com/

29 Naoki Hiroshima, 'How I Lost My $50,000 Twitter Username', Medium, 29 January 2014. https://medium.com/@N/how-i-lost-my-50–000-twitter-username-24eb09e026dd

30 Mat Honan, 'How Apple and Amazon Security Flaws Led to My Epic Hacking', *Wired*, 6 August 2012. http://www.wired.com/2012/08/apple-amazon-mat-honan-hacking/ He eventually got most of the data back, paying a specialist firm $1,690 (around £1,000) to work on his laptop. http://www.wired.com/2012/08/mat-honan-data-recovery/all

5 THE GEOPOLITICS OF THE INTERNET

1 Clifford Stoll, *The Cuckoo's Egg: Tracking a Spy Through the Maze of Computer Espionage* (Doubleday, 1989). Clifford Stoll, 'Stalking The Wily Hacker', *Communication of the ACM*, Vol. 31. No. 5, May 1988. http://pdf.textfiles.com/academics/wilyhacker.pdf For an explanation of how a penguin-keeper at a zoo came up with the title for the books, see 'Cuckoo's Egg', Booknotes, 3 December 1989. http://www.booknotes.org/Watch/10122–1/Clifford+Stoll.aspx

2 For a detailed account of Chinese espionage, see 'Crouching Tiger, Hidden Dragon, Stolen Data' (Context Information Security, 2012). http://www.contextis.com/documents/8/Crouching_tiger_hidden_dragon.pdf

3 Richard Nieva, 'Big banks stage mega-cyberattack drill', @CNNTech, 18 July 2013. http://money.cnn.com/2013/07/18/technology/security/bank-cyberattack/

4 'Waking Shark II Desktop Cyber Exercise: Report to participants', November. http://www.bankofengland.co.uk/financialstability/fsc/Documents/wakingshark2report.pdf

5 'Department of Defense Fiscal year 2015 budget request, program acquisition cost by weapons system', March 2014. http://comptroller.defense.gov/Portals/45/documents/defbudget/fy2015/fy2015_Weapons.pdf#page=65

6 'Dragonfly: Cyberespionage Attacks Against Energy Suppliers' Symantec Security Response White Paper, 17 July 2014. http://www.symantec.com/content/en/us/enterprise/media/security_response/whitepapers/Dragonfly_Threat_Against_Western_Energy_Suppliers.pdf

7 'Uroburos: Highly complex espionage software with Russian roots', G Data SecurityLabs, February 2014. https://public.gdatasoftware.com/Web/Content/INT/Blog/2014/02_2014/documents/GData_Uroburos_RedPaper_EN_v1.pdf

8 'Kaspersky Lab Identifies Operation "Red October," an Advanced Cyber-Espionage Campaign Targeting Diplomatic and Government Institutions Worldwide', 14 January 2013. http://www.kaspersky.com/about/news/virus/2013/Kaspersky_Lab_Identifies_Operation_Red_October_an_Advanced_Cyber_Espionage_Campaign_Targeting_Diplomatic_and_Government_Institutions_Worldwide and http://securelist.com/analysis/publications/36740/red-october-diplomatic-cyber-attacks-investigation/

9 'Internet Explorer Zero-Day Used in Watering Hole Attack', 31 December 2012. http://www.symantec.com/connect/blogs/internet-explorer-zero-day-used-watering-hole-attack-qa

10 Kim Zetter, 'The Evidence That North Korea Hacked Sony Is Flimsy', Wired, 17 December 2014. http://www.wired.com/2014/12/evidence-of-north-korea-hack-is-thin/

11 'Foreign Spies stealing US economic secrets in Cyberspace: Report to Congress on Foreign Economic Collection and Industrial Espionage, 2009–2011'. http://www.ncix.gov/publications/reports/fecie_all/Foreign_Economic_Collection_2011.pdf

12 Dan Mcwhorter, 'Mandiant Exposes APT1 – One of China's Cyber Espionage Units', 18 February 2013. https://www.mandiant.com/blog/mandiant-exposes-apt1-chinas-cyber-espionage-units-releases-3000-indicators/

13 I wrote about this in my e-book The Snowden Operation (Amazon Kindle Singles, 2014).

14 Shane Harris, 'Inside the FBI's Fight Against Chinese Cyber-Espionage', *Foreign Policy*, 27 May 2014. http://www.foreignpolicy.com/articles/2014/05/27/exclusive_inside_the_fbi_s_fight_against_chinese_cyber_espionage

15 James Woolsey, 'Why We Spy on Our Allies', *Wall Street Journal*, 17 March 2000. http://online.wsj.com/article/SB95326824311657269.html

16 French electronic intelligence is formidable and operates with what some might think rather scanty oversight. http://www.nytimes.com/2013/12/15/world/europe/france-broadens-its-surveillance-power.html and http://www.nytimes.com/2013/07/05/world/europe/france-too-is-collecting-data-newspaper-reveals.html

6 SPIES V. WARRIORS

1 Richard Danzig, 'Surviving on a Diet of Poisoned Fruit: Reducing the National Security Risks of America's Cyber Dependencies', CNAS, July 2014. http://www.cnas.org/sites/default/files/publications-pdf/CNAS_PoisonedFruit_Danzig_0.pdf

2 David Sanger, 'Obama Order Sped Up Wave of Cyberattacks Against Iran', *New York Times*, 1 June 2012. Marc Ambinder, 'Did America's Cyber Attack on Iran Make Us More Vulnerable?', *The Atlantic*, 5 June 2012. http://www.theatlantic.com/national/archive/2012/06/did-americas-cyber-attack-on-iran-make-us-more-vulnerable/258120/. Steve Coll, 'The Rewards (and Risks) of Cyber War', *The New Yorker*, 7 June 2012. http://www.newyorker.com/online/blogs/comment/2012/06/the-rewards-and-risks-of-cyberwar.html. David Sanger, *Confront and Conceal: Obama's Secret Wars and Surprising Use of American Power* (Crown, June 2012), ISBN 978–0307718020.

3 Pete Yost, 'Report: Retired general target of leaks probe', Associated Press, 28 June 2013. http://bigstory.ap.org/article/reports-retired-general-target-leaks-probe

4 Speaking on a PBS program on the subject http://www.pbs.org/wnet/need-to-know/security/video-cracking-the-code-defending-against-the-superweapons-of-the-21st-century-cyberwar/9456/ (four minutes from start).

5 Marc Ambinder, 'Did America's Cyber Attack on Iran Make Us More Vulnerable?', *Atlantic Monthly*, 5 June 2012. http://www.theatlantic.com/national/archive/2012/06/did-americas-cyber-attack-on-iran-make-us-more-vulnerable/258120/ The misunderstandings about the Enigma machine contained in the short reference made in the article are too numerous, and too depressing, to go into here.

6 Ellen Nakashima, 'U.S., Israel developed Flame computer virus to slow Iranian nuclear efforts, officials say', *Washington Post*, 19 June 2012. http://www.washingtonpost.com/world/national-security/us-israel-developed-computer-virus-to-slow-iranian-nuclear-efforts-officials-say/2012/06/19/gJQA6xBPoV_story.html

7 David Shamah, 'Stuxnet, gone rogue, hit Russian nuke plant, space station', *Times of Israel*, 11 November 2013. http://www.timesofisrael.com/stuxnet-gone-rogue-hit-russian-nuke-plant-space-station/

8 Ellen Nakashima, Greg Miller and Julie Tate, 'U.S., Israel developed Flame computer virus to slow Iranian nuclear efforts, officials say', *Washington Post*, 19 June 2012. http://www.washingtonpost.com/world/national-security/us-israel-developed-computer-virus-to-slow-iranian-nuclear-efforts-officials-say/2012/06/19/gJQA6xBPoV_story.html

9 Jānis Bērziņš, 'Russia's new generation warfare in Ukraine: Implications for Latvian defence policy', National Defence Academy of Latvia, Centre for Security and Strategic Research. April 2014. http://www.naa.mil.lv/~/media/NAA/AZPC/Publikacijas/PP%2002–2014.ashx

10 Michael Schmitt (ed.), *Tallinn Manual on the International Law Applicable to Cyber Warfare* (Cambridge University Press, 2013). An electronic version of the Tallinn Manual is available here http://nuclearenergy.ir/wp-content/uploads/2013/11/tallinn_manual.pdf

11 Martin Libicki, 'Cyberwar Fears Pose Dangers of Unnecessary Escalation', Rand Review Summer 2013. http://www.rand.org/pubs/periodicals/rand-review/issues/2013/summer/cyberwar-fears-pose-dangers-of-unnecessary-escalation.html

12 John Kennedy, 'When Woman is Boss', interview *Colliers Magazine*, 26 January 1926. http://www.tfcbooks.com/tesla/1926-01-30.htm

7 THE SPY IN YOUR POCKET

1 Hitesh Dharmdasani, 'We Steal SMS: An insight into Android.KorBanker Operations', FireEye, 3 September 2014. http://www.fireeye.com/blog/technical/2014/09/we-steal-sms-an-insight-into-android-korbanker-operations.html

2 See srlabs.de/badusb and (for slides) Karsten Nohl, Sascha Krißler and Jakob Lell, 'BadUSB – On accessories that turn evil'. https://srlabs.de/blog/wp-content/uploads/2014/07/SRLabs-BadUSB-BlackHat-v1.pdf

3 See Nohl, Krißler and Lell, op. cit.

4 Emily Adler, 'The "Internet Of Things" Will Be Bigger Than The Smartphone, Tablet, And PC Markets Combined', *Business Insider*, 21 July 2014.

http://www.businessinsider.com/growth-in-the-internet-of-things-market-2–2014–2

5 Dan Geer, 'We Are All Intelligence Officers Now', 28 February 2014. http://geer.tinho.net/geer.rsa.28ii14.txt

6 Bruce Schneier, 'The Internet of Things Is Wildly Insecure – And Often Unpatchable', *Wired*, 6 January 2014. https://www.schneier.com/essays/archives/2014/01/the_internet_of_thin.html

7 Fahmida Rashid, 'Airport Scanners Have Account Backdoors, Default Passwords', *PCMag*, 10 August 2014. http://securitywatch.pcmag.com/travel/326265-airport-scanners-have-account-backdoors-default-passwords

8 Grant Hernandez, Orlando Arias, Daniel Buentello and Yier Jin, 'Smart Nest Thermostat – A Smart Spy in Your Home'. https://www.blackhat.com/docs/us-14/materials/us-14-Jin-Smart-Nest-Thermostat-A-Smart-Spy-In-Your-Home.pdf

9 Alana Abramson, 'Baby Monitor Hacking Alarms Houston Parents', 13 August 2013. http://abcnews.go.com/blogs/headlines/2013/08/baby-monitor-hacking-alarms-houston-parents/

10 'To Watch or be Watched'. http://conference.hitb.org/hitbsecconf2013ams/materials/D2T1%20-%20Sergey%20Shekyan%20and%20Artem%20Harutyunyan%20-%20Turning%20Your%20Surveillance%20Camera%20Against%20You.pdf

11 Kim Zetter, 'Here's How Easy It Could Be for Hackers to Control Your Hotel Room', 17 July 2014. http://www.wired.com/2014/07/hacking-hotel-room-controls/

12 For the CERT advisory, http://www.kb.cert.org/vuls/id/656302. The story was covered here: Ms Smith (pseudonym), '500,000M users could be hacked; CERT issues advisory', Network World, 14 February 2014. www.networkworld.com/community/blog/half-million-belkin-wemo-users-could-be-hacked-cert-issues-advisory for the IOActive report on the vulnerability, see http://www.ioactive.com/pdfs/IOActive_Belkin-advisory-lite.pdf. For its part, Belkin issued this statement http://www.belkin.com/us/pressreleases/8800681821244/

13 'Weaponising your Coffee Pot' http://danielbuentello.blogspot.com/2013/07/toorcon-seattle-2013-weaponizing-your.html

14 John Leyden, 'Heatmiser digital thermostat users: For pity's sake, DON'T SWITCH ON the WI-FI!', *The Register*, 24 September 2014. http://www.theregister.co.uk/2014/09/24/heatmiser_digital_thermostat_insecure/

15 'Heatmiser WiFi thermostat vulnerabilities'. http://cybergibbons.com/security-2/heatmiser-wifi-thermostat-vulnerabilities/

16 Lucian Constantin, 'Fifteen new vulnerabilities reported during router hacking contest', IDG News Service, 12 August 2014. http://www.cio. com/article/2464301/fifteen-new-vulnerabilities-reported-during-router-hacking-contest.html?linkId=9235577

17 Elinor Mills, 'New DNSChanger Trojan variant targets routers', 17 June 2008. http://www.cnet.com/news/new-dnschanger-trojan-variant-targets-routers/

18 Tim Conneally, 'Estonian company Rove Digital taken down in massive clickjacking fraud sting', Betanews, 10 November 2011. http://betanews. com/2011/11/10/estonian-company-rove-digital-taken-down-in-massive-clickjacking-fraud-sting/ An FBI paper on DNSchanger attacks can be found here http://www.fbi.gov/news/stories/2011/november/malware_110911/ DNS-changer-malware.pdf

19 'Large-scale DNS redirection on home routers for financial theft' http:// www.cert.pl//news/8019/langswitch_lang/en

20 Graham Cluley. 'How millions of DSL modems were hacked in Brazil, to pay for Rio prostitutes', Naked Security, 1 October 2012. http://nakedsecurity. sophos.com/2012/10/01/hacked-routers-brazil-vb2012/ and Fabio Assolini, 'The Tale of One Thousand and One DSL Modems', Securelist, 1 October 2012. http://securelist.com/blog/research/57776/the-tale-of-one-thousand-and-one-dsl-modems/

21 Elinor Mills, 'New DNSChanger Trojan variant targets routers', CNET, 17 June 2008. http://www.cnet.com/ule/news/new-dnschanger-trojan-variant-targets-routers/, and Dan Goodin, 'New Linux worm targets routers, cameras, "Internet of things" devices', Ars Technica, 27 November 2013. http://arstechnica.com/security/2013/11/new-linux-worm-targets-routers-cameras-internet-of-things-devices/

22 Lucian Constantin, 'There's now an exploit for "TheMoon" worm targeting Linksys routers', Computerworld, 17 February 2014. http://www.computer-world.com/s/article/9246392/There_s_now_an_exploit_for_TheMoon_worm_targeting_Linksys_routers

23 Lucian Constantin, 'Cybercriminals compromise home routers to attack online banking users', Computerworld, 7 February 2014. http://www. pcworld.com/article/2095860/cybercriminals-compromise-home-routers-to-attack-online-banking-users.html

24 'SOHO Network Equipment . . . and the implications of a rich service set', Independent Security Evaluators, 26 July 2013. https://securityevaluators. com/knowledge/case_studies/routers/soho_techreport.pdf

25 Lucian Constantin, 'NAS boxes more vulnerable than routers, researcher finds', PC World, 7 August 2014. http://www.pcworld.com/article/2462600/

networkattached-storage-devices-more-vulnerable-than-routers-researcher-finds.html

26 John Dunn, 'Synology users told to update DiskStation NAS drives after "SynoLocker" ransom attack', Techworld, 5 August 2014. http://news.techworld.com/security/3534684/synology-users-told-to-update-diskstation-nas-drives-after-synolocker-ransom-attack/

27 Pat Litke, 'Hacker Hijacks Synology NAS Boxes for Dogecoin Mining Operation, Reaping Half Million Dollars in Two Months', Dell Secureworks, 13 June 2014. http://www.secureworks.com/resources/blog/hacker-hijacks-synology-nas-boxes-for-dogecoin-mining-operation-reaping-half-million-dollars-in-two-months/

8 THE DANGER OF MONOCULTURE

1 Dan Geer, 'Heartbleed as Metaphor', Lawfare blog, 21 April 2014. http://www.lawfareblog.com/2014/04/heartbleed-as-metaphor/ See also his speech at the NSA: 'APT in a World of Rising Interdependence', 26 March 2014. http://geer.tinho.net/geer.nsa.26iii14.txt

2 For details, see Robert Charette, 'DigiNotar Certificate Authority Breach Crashes e-Government in the Netherlands', IEEE Spectrum, 9 September 2011. http://spectrum.ieee.org/riskfactor/telecom/security/diginotar-certificate-authority-breach-crashes-egovernment-in-the-netherlandsand for the government-sponsored report into the breach 'Black TulipReport of the investigation into the DigiNotar Certificate Authority breach' by Hans Hoogstraaten (team leader), 13 August, 2012. http://www.rijksoverheid.nl/bestanden/documenten-en-publicaties/rapporten/2012/08/13/black-tulip-update/black-tulip-update.pdf

3 Feike Hacquebord, 'DigiNotar: Iranians – The Real Target' Trend Labs security intelligence blog, 5 September 2011. http://blog.trendmicro.com/trendlabs-security-intelligence/diginotar-iranians-the-real-target/

4 Anonymous, 'DigiNotar Debacle and Internet Security', 'News About Iran', 6 September 2011. https://iransnews.wordpress.com/2011/09/06/diginotar-debacle-and-internet-security/

5 The rules are here https://www.gov.uk/driving-nongb-licence/y/a-visitor-to-great-britain/any-other-country

6 https://www.eff.org/observatory

7 Chris Brook, 'EFF, others, plan to make encrypting the web easier in 2015', 18 November 2014. https://threatpost.com/eff-others-plan-to-make-encrypting-the-web-easier-in-2015/109451

8 For details of such 'man-in-the-middle' attacks and their use by authoritarian governments, see http://papers.ssrn.com/sol3/papers.cfm?abstract_id=1591033

9 For more details, see http://www.freedom-to-tinker.com/blog/felten/web-certification-fail-bad-assumptions-lead-bad-technology

10 Lillian Ablon, Martin Libicki and Andrea Golay, 'Markets for Cybercrime Tools and Stolen Data: Hackers' Bazaar', Rand Corporation National Security Research Division, 2014. https://www.rand.org/content/dam/rand/pubs/research_reports/RR600/RR610./RAND_RR610.pdf

11 Data Security Incident Information (undated). http://www.theupsstore.com/security/Pages/default.aspx

12 Brian Krebs, 'What Target and Co aren't telling you: your credit card data is still out there', *Guardian*, 6 May 2014. http://www.theguardian.com/commentisfree/2014/may/06/target-creditcard-data-hackers-retail-industry

13 John Leyden, 'Target, Home Depot and UPS attacks: Dude, you need to rethink point-of-sale security', 12 November 2014. http://www.theregister.co.uk/2014/11/12/pos_malware_attacks_should_prompt_security_rethink_report/ For a longer report, see Marion Marschalek, Paul Kimayong and Fengmin Gong Cyphort, 'POS Malware Revisited – Look What We Found Inside Your Cashdesk', November 2014. http://www.cyphort.com/wp-content/uploads/2014/11/POS-Malware-Report-WEB.pdf

14 'Home Depot still paying for data breach', *The Hill*, https://thehill.com/policy/cybersecurity/242510-home-depot-still-paying-for-data-breach

15 'Skimming Prevention: Best Practices for Merchants', Payment Card Industry Security Standards Council, September 2014. https://www.pcisecuritystandards.org/documents/Skimming%20Prevention%20BP%20for%20Merchants%20Sept2014.pdf

9 CLEARING THE JUNGLE

1 http://www.firebox.com/product/5012/WiFi-USB-Flash-Drive-Cufflinks?aff=512&awc=550_1399733081_E281a2d9a694ef07b097545d76713999

2 '10 crazy IT security tricks that actually work' Infoworld Security Central, 9 July 2012. http://www.infoworld.com/d/security/10-crazy-it-security-tricks-actually-work-196864

3 Roger Grimes, 'The One Company that wasn't Hacked', Infoworld, 29 May 2012. http://www.infoworld.com/d/security/the-one-company-wasnt-hacked-194184?page=0,0

4 Julia Angwin, *Dragnet Nation: A Quest for Privacy, Security, and Freedom in a World of Relentless Surveillance* (Times Books, 2014).

5 For a discussion of this, see Ken Fisher, 'Why Ad Blocking is devastating to the sites you love', Ars Technica, 6 March 2010. http://arstechnica.com/business/2010/03/why-ad-blocking-is-devastating-to-the-sites-you-love/

6 For a detailed explanation, see https://www.eff.org/deeplinks/2010/01/primer-information-theory-and-privacy

10 PASSWORDS UNSCRAMBLED

1 Dan Goodin, 'Why passwords have never been weaker—and crackers have never been stronger: Thanks to real-world data, the keys to your digital kingdom are under assault', Ars Technica, 21 August 2012. http://arstechnica.com/security/2012/08/passwords-under-assault/

2 Peter Bright, 'RSA finally comes clean: SecurID is compromised', Ars Technica, 7 June 2011. http://arstechnica.com/security/2011/06/rsa-finally-comes-clean-securid-is-compromised/

11 IDENTITY POLITICS

1 Jonathan Gruber, 'Health Insurance and the Labor Market, in A. J. Kuyler and Joseph P. Newhouse (eds), *Handbook of Health Economics*, Vol. I (Amsterdam: Elsevier Science, 2000), pp. 654–5.

2 For a detailed account of Estonia's e-services, I recommend: eServices in Estonia: a success story: A Secure Identity Alliance Visit Report, June 2014. http://secureidentityalliance.org/index.php/blog/item/16-eservices-in-estonia-a-success-story-a-secure-identity-alliance-visit-report

3 I deal with Estonian history at length in two previous books, *The New Cold War* and *Deception*.

12 TURNING THE TABLES

1 Mr Grimes lists some snake oil services here. Roger Grimes, 'Security-vendor snake oil: 7 promises that don't deliver', Infoworld Security Central, 12 May 2014. http://www.infoworld.com/d/security/security-vendor-snake-oil-7-promises-dont-deliver-242138?page=0,0

2 A wide range of sensible advice is available at https://www.cpni.gov.uk/advice/cyber/

3 Dan Geer, 'We Are All Intelligence Officers Now', 28 February 2014. http://geer.tinho.net/geer.rsa.28ii14.txt

4 Richard Danzig, 'Surviving on a Diet of Poisoned Fruit: Reducing the National Security Risks of America's Cyber Dependencies', CNAS,

July 2014. http://www.cnas.org/sites/default/files/publications-pdf/CNAS_
PoisonedFruit_Danzig_0.pdf

5 Paul Venezia, 'It's time to make poor coding a felony', Infoworld, 11 July
   2011. http://www.infoworld.com/d/data-center/it-might-be-time-make-
   poor-coding-felony-417

6 Dan Geer, 'Cybersecurity as Realpolitik', 6 August 2014. http://geer.tinho.
   net/geer.blackhat.6viii14.txt

7 Mark Mazzetti, 'FBI informant is tied to cyber-attacks abroad', New York
   Times, 23 April 2014. http://www.nytimes.com/2014/04/24/world/fbi-
   informant-is-tied-to-cyberattacks-abroad.html?_r=0

8 Ed Pilkington, 'LulzSec hacker "Sabu" released after "extraordinary" FBI
   cooperation', Guardian, 27 May 2014. http://www.theguardian.com/
   technology/2014/may/27/hacker-sabu-walks-free-sentenced-time-served

9 'Should U.S. Hackers Fix Cybersecurity Holes or Exploit Them?',
   Atlantic Monthly, 19 May 2014. http://www.theatlantic.com/technology/
   archive/2014/05/should-hackers-fix-cybersecurity-holes-or-exploit-
   them/371197/?single_page=true

10 For more details of LANGSEC please see http://spw14.langsec.org/ and
   http://langsec.org/

CONCLUSION

1 I am indebted to Mr Ilves for many of the other thoughts in this conclusion. His speech to the 2014 CyCon (cyber-security conference) organised by the NATO Cooperative Cyberdefence Centre of Excellence can be
   found here, http://www.president.ee/en/official-duties/speeches/10270-
   president-toomas-hendrik-ilvess-opening-speech-at-cycon-in-tallinn-on-
   june-4–2014/

APPENDIX ONE: WHO RUNS THE INTERNET?

1 Paul Rosenzweig, 'The Fight to Seize Iran's Domain Name Continues',
   30 July 2014. https://www.lawfareblog.com/2014/07/true-lawfare-the-
   fight-to-seize-irans-domain-name-continues/

2 Kieren McCarthy, 'ICANN Hacked: Intruders poke around global
   DNS innards', The Register, 17 December 2014. http://www.theregister.
   co.uk/2014/12/17/icann_hacked_admin_access_to_zone_files/

Bibliography

Two blogs are invaluable: krebsonsecurity.com is by Brian Krebs, the foremost American expert in cyber-crime. The other is lawfare.org, sponsored by the Brookings Institution and edited by Benjamin Wittes. I commend the websites listed in the footnotes, and particular that of Dan Geer: geer. tinho.net

The annual reports by security firms contain a wealth of data about attacks. I particularly recommend those by FireEye (which has taken over Mandiant).

FICTION

Doctorow, Cory, *Little Brother*, Harper Voyager, 2008
Gibson, William, *Neuromancer*, Harper Voyager, 1995

GENERAL

Anderson, Ross, *Security Economics: A Personal Perspective*, University of Cambridge Computer Laboratory, 2012
Brangetto, P., Maybaum, M., and Stinissen, J. (eds), *6th International Conference on Cyber Conflict*, NATO CCD COE Publications, 2014
Cornish, Paul, Livingstone, David, Clement, Dave, and Yorke, Clare, *Cyber Security and the UK's Critical National Infrastructure*, Chatham House, 2011
Podins, K., Stinissen, J., and Maybaum, M. (eds), *5th International Conference on Cyber Conflict*, NATO CCD COE, 2013
Tendulkar, Rohini, *Cyber-crime, securities markets and systemic risk*, OICU-IOSCO, 2013

STATE CYBER-ATTACKS AND CYBER-WARFARE

APT1: Exposing One of China's Cyber Espionage Units, Mandiant, 2013

Atlantic Council of Canada, *NATO Going Forward: Boots on the Ground to Wireless Warfare*, The Atlantic Council of Canada, 2013

Brenner, Susan W., *Cyberthreats: The Emerging Fault Lines of the Nation State*, Oxford University Press, 2009

Clarke, Richard A., and Knake, Robert K., *Cyber War: The Next Threat to National Security and What to Do About It*, HarperCollins, 2010

Deibert, Ronald J., *Black Code: Inside the Battle for Cyberspace*, McClelland & Stewart, 2013

Hagestad II, William T., *21st Century Chinese Cyberwarfare*, IT Governance Publishing, 2012

Harris, Shane, *@war: The Rise of Cyber Warfare*, Headline, 2013

Healey, Jason, *A Fierce Domain: Conflict in Cyberspace 1986 to 2012*, Cyber Conflict Studies Association, 2013

Rid, Thomas, *Cyber War Will Not Take Place*, C. Hurst & Co. Publishers Ltd, 2013

Sanger, David, *Confront and Conceal: Obama's Secret Wars and Surprising Use of American Power*, Broadway Books, 2013

Schmitt, Michael N. (ed.), *Tallinn Manual on the International Law Applicable to Cyber Warfare*, Cambridge University Press 2013

Singer, P. W., *Wired for War: The Robotics Revolution and Conflict in the 21st Century*, Penguin Books, 2009

—, and Friedman, Allan, *Cybersecurity and Cyberwar: What Everyone Needs to Know*, Oxford University Press, 2014

Stoll, Clifford, *The Cuckoo's Egg: Tracking a Spy Through the Maze of Computer Espionage*, Doubleday, 1989

Zetter, Kim, *Countdown to Zero Day: Stuxnet and the Launch of the World's First Digital Weapon*, Crown Business, 2014

PRACTICAL PRECAUTIONS

Anderson, Ross, *Security Engineering: A Guide to Building Dependable Distributed Systems*, John Wiley & Sons, 2008

Baker, Stewart, *Skating on Stilts: Why We Aren't Stopping Tomorrow's Terrorism*, Hoover Institution Press, 2010

Bejtlich, Richard, *The Practice of Network Security Monitoring*, William Pollock, 2013

Engebretson, Patrick, and Broad, James, *The Basics of Hacking and Penetration Testing: Ethical Hacking and Penetration Testing Made Easy*, Syngress, 2011

Schneier, Bruce, *Carry On: Sound Advice from Schneier on Security*, John Wiley &
Sons, 2014

SURVEILLANCE AND PRIVACY

Angwin, Julia, *Dragnet Nation: A Quest for Privacy, Security, and Freedom in a World
of Relentless Surveillance*, Times Books, 2014
Greenberg, Andy, *This Machine Kills Secrets: Julian Assange, the Cypherpunks, and
Their Fight to Empower Whistleblowers*, Penguin Books, 2012
Greenwald, Glenn, *No Place to Hide: Edward Snowden, the NSA and the Surveillance
State*, Penguin Books, 2014
Harding, Luke, *The Snowden Files: The Inside Story of the World's Most Wanted Man*
Guardian Books, 2014
Schneier, Bruce, *Liars and Outliers: Enabling the Trust That Society Needs to Thrive*,
John Wiley & Sons, 2012

SOCIETY AND THE INTERNET

Goldsmith, Jack, and Wu, Tim, *Who Controls the Internet? Illusions of a Borderless
World*, Oxford University Press, 2006
Hammersly, Ben, *Now for Then: How To Face The Digital Future Without Fear*,
Hodder & Stoughton, 2012
Lanier, Jaron, *Who Owns The Future?*, Allen Lane, 2013
Mayer-Schonberger, Viktor, and Cukier, Kenneth, *Big Data: A Revolution That
Will Transform How We Live, Work and Think*, John Murray, 2013
McChesney, Robert W., *Digital Disconnect: How Capitalism Is Turning the Internet
Against Democracy*, The New Press, 2013
Morozov, Evgeny, *The Net Delusion: How Not to Liberate the World*, Penguin
Books, 2012
—, *To Save Everything Click Here*, Allen Lane, 2013
Raymond, Mark, and Smith, Gordon (eds), *Organised Chaos: Reimagining the
Internet*, CIGI, 2014
Wu, Tim, *The Master Switch: the Rise and Fall of Information Empires*, Atlantic
Books, 2012

CRIME

Anderson, Nate, *The Internet Police*, W. W. Norton & Company, 2013
Bartlett, Jamie, *The Dark Net: Inside the Digital Underworld*, William Heinemann,
2014

Coleman, Gabriella, *Hacker, Hoaxer, Whistleblower, Spy: The Many Faces of Anonymous*, Verso Books, 2014

Glenny, Misha, *Dark Market: Cyberthieves, Cybercops and You*, Bodley Head, 2013

Krebs, Brian, *Spam Nation: The Inside Story of Organized Cybercrime: From Global Epidemic to Your Front Door*, Sourcebooks, 2014

Libicki, Martin C., Senty, David, and Pollak, Julia, *Hackers Wanted: An Examination of the Cybersecurity Labor Market*, Rand Corporation, 2014

Mitnick, Kevin, and Simon, William L., *Ghost in the Wires*, Back Bay, 2012

Acknowledgements

I am grateful to Richard Bejtlich and Jen Weedon of FireEye (now Mandiant), Jason Healey of the Atlantic Council, Benjamin Wittes of Brookings (and the Lawfare blog), and Brian Krebs. Many Estonians helped with this book, including Luukas Ilves and his father. The organisers of the Tallinn Cyberconference and the staff of the NATO Centre of Excellence there have helped me greatly, as has Heli Tiirmaa-Klaar. In London Keir Giles shared his knowledge of Russian thinking on cyber-warfare. I am also grateful to Thomas Rid, David Clemente and Ross Anderson. All the mistakes are mine.

My family, particularly my wife Cristina, put up with the absence and absent-mindedness that this book entailed. They also stimulated my thoughts and helped with my research. I am grateful to my sons for their observations about real-life cyber-security and social media, and especially to Johnny for his work on the bibliography. My father John Lucas was a pioneer in the use of personal computers at Oxford in the 1980s and I am grateful for his critiques of weak security in banking and financial services. In the 1970s my mother Morar let me learn to type on her manual typewriter. But my first encounter with a digital device was when my aunt Sarah showed me a gadget called a pocket electronic calculator, in around 1971. This book is dedicated to her, and all to those who continue to be open-minded about new technology.

Index

A Note on the Author

Edward Lucas is a senior editor at the *Economist*. He has been covering Eastern Europe since 1986, with postings in Berlin, Moscow, Prague, Vienna, and the Baltic states. His expertise includes energy, cyber-security, espionage, Russian foreign and security policy and the politics and economics of Eastern Europe. He is a regular contributor to the BBC's *Today* and *Newsnight* programmes, and to NPR, CNN and Sky News. He is the author of *The New Cold War*, which is regularly updated and has been published in more than fifteen languages. He is married to the columnist Cristina Odone and lives in London.

@edwardlucas

A Note on the Type

The text of this book is set in Bembo, which was first used in 1495 by the Venetian printer Aldus Manutius for Cardinal Bembo's *De Aetna*. The original types were cut for Manutius by Francesco Griffo. Bembo was one of the types used by Claude Garamond (1480–1561) as a model for his Romain de l'Université, and so it was a forerunner of what became the standard European type for the following two centuries. Its modern form follows the original types and was designed for Monotype in 1929.